MW01672648

FINC 600
Student Notebook
University of St. Thomas
Financial Management: Theory and Practice

Eleventh Edition

Brigham - Ehrhardt

THOMSON
SOUTH-WESTERN

Australia · Canada · Mexico · Singapore · Spain · United Kingdom · United States

THOMSON
SOUTH-WESTERN

FINC 600
Brigham - Ehrhardt

Custom Editor:
Dan Suckert

Project Development Editor:
Lea Riddle

Marketing Coordinator:
Sara Mercurio

Production/Manufacturing Supervisor:
Donna M. Brown

Project Coordinator:
Rebecca Walker

Pre-Media Services Supervisor:
Dan Plofchan

Rights and Permissions Specialist:
Kalina Hintz

Senior Prepress Specialist:
Kim Fry

Cover Design:
Krista Pierson

Printer:
RRD

Printed in the United States of America
1 2 3 4 5 6 7 8 9 08 07 06

For more information, please contact Thomson Custom Solutions, 5191 Natorp Boulevard, Mason, OH 45040.
Or you can visit our Internet site at www.thomsoncustom.com

FINC 600 / Brigham - Ehrhardt – Eleventh Edition
p. 470
ISBN 0-324-33605-5

Custom Contents

1 - 1

CHAPTER 1
Overview of Financial Management and the Financial Environment

- Financial management
  - Forms of business organization
  - Objective of the firm: Maximize wealth
  - Determinants of stock pricing
- The financial environment
  - Financial instruments, markets and institutions
  - Interest rates and yield curves

1 - 2

Why is corporate finance important to all managers?

- Corporate finance provides the skills managers need to:
  - Identify and select the corporate strategies and individual projects that add value to their firm.
  - Forecast the funding requirements of their company, and devise strategies for acquiring those funds.

1 - 3

What are some forms of business organization a company might have as it evolves from a start-up to a major corporation?

- Sole proprietorship
- Partnership
- Corporation

1 - 4

Starting as a Sole Proprietorship

- Advantages:
  - Ease of formation
  - Subject to few regulations
  - No corporate income taxes
- Disadvantages:
  - Limited life
  - Unlimited liability
  - Difficult to raise capital to support growth

1 - 5

Starting as or Growing into a Partnership

- A partnership has roughly the same advantages and disadvantages as a sole proprietorship.

1 - 6

Becoming a Corporation

- A corporation is a legal entity separate from its owners and managers.
- File papers of incorporation with state.
  - Charter
  - Bylaws

1 - 7

Advantages and Disadvantages of a Corporation

- **Advantages:**
  - **Unlimited life**
  - **Easy transfer of ownership**
  - **Limited liability**
  - **Ease of raising capital**
- **Disadvantages:**
  - **Double taxation**
  - **Cost of set-up and report filing**

1 - 8

Becoming a Public Corporation and Growing Afterwards

- **Initial Public Offering (IPO) of Stock**
  - **Raises cash**
  - **Allows founders and pre-IPO investors to "harvest" some of their wealth**
- **Subsequent issues of debt and equity**
- **Agency problem: managers may act in their own interests and not on behalf of owners (stockholders)**

1 - 9

What should management's primary objective be?

- **The primary objective should be shareholder wealth maximization, which translates to maximizing stock price.**
  - **Should firms behave ethically? YES!**
  - **Do firms have any responsibilities to society at large? YES! Shareholders are also members of society.**

Corporation a part of
Society & community
by giving back
Hiring people from area

1 - 10

Is maximizing stock price good for society, employees, and customers?

- Employment growth is higher in firms that try to maximize stock price. On average, employment goes up in:
  - firms that make managers into owners (such as LBO firms)
  - firms that were owned by the government but that have been sold to private investors

1 - 11

- Consumer welfare is higher in capitalist free market economies than in communist or socialist economies.
- *Fortune* lists the most admired firms. In addition to high stock returns, these firms have:
  - high quality from customers' view
  - employees who like working there

1 - 12

What three aspects of cash flows affect an investment's value?

- Amount of expected cash flows (bigger is better)
- Timing of the cash flow stream (sooner is better)
- Risk of the cash flows (less risk is better)

1 - 13

What are "free cash flows (FCF)"

- Free cash flows are the cash flows that are:
  - Available (or free) for distribution
  - To all investors (stockholders and creditors)
  - After paying current expenses, taxes, and making the investments necessary for growth.

1 - 14

Determinants of Free Cash Flows

- Sales revenues
  - Current level
  - Short-term growth rate in sales
  - Long-term sustainable growth rate in sales
- Operating costs (raw materials, labor, etc.) and taxes
- Required investments in operations (buildings, machines, inventory, etc.)

1 - 15

What is the weighted average cost of capital (WACC)?

- The weighted average cost of capital (WACC) is the average rate of return required by all of the company's investors (stockholders and creditors)

1 - 16

What factors affect the weighted average cost of capital?

- Capital structure (the firm's relative amounts of debt and equity)
- Interest rates
- Risk of the firm
- Stock market investors' overall attitude toward risk

High rates - firms will most likely use equity
Low - incur the debt

1 - 17

What determines a firm's value?

- A firm's value is the sum of all the future expected free cash flows when converted into today's dollars:

$$\text{Value} = \frac{FCF_1}{(1+WACC)^1} + \frac{FCF_2}{(1+WACC)^2} + \dots \frac{FCF_\infty}{(1+WACC)^\infty}$$

showed & will need to use this formula

1 - 18

What are financial assets?

- A financial asset is a contract that entitles the owner to some type of payoff.
  - Debt
  - Equity
  - Derivatives
- In general, each financial asset involves two parties, a provider of cash (i.e., capital) and a user of cash.

1 - 19

What are some financial instruments?

Instrument	Rate (April 2003)
U.S. T-bills	1.14%
Banker's acceptances	1.22
Commercial paper	1.21
Negotiable CDs	1.24
Eurodollar deposits	1.23
Commercial loans	Tied to prime (4.25%) or LIBOR (1.29%)

(More . .)

1 - 20

Financial Instruments (Continued)

Instrument	Rate (April 2003)
U.S. T-notes and T-bonds	5.04%
Mortgages	5.57
Municipal bonds	4.84
Corporate (AAA) bonds	5.91
Preferred stocks	6 to 9%
Common stocks (expected)	9 to 15%

1 - 21

Who are the providers (savers) and users (borrowers) of capital?

- Households: Net savers
- Non-financial corporations: Net users (borrowers)
- Governments: Net borrowers
- Financial corporations: Slightly net borrowers, but almost breakeven

1 - 22

What are three ways that capital is transferred between savers and borrowers?

- Direct transfer (e.g., corporation issues commercial paper to insurance company)
- Through an investment banking house (e.g., IPO, seasoned equity offering, or debt placement)
- Through a financial intermediary (e.g., individual deposits money in bank, bank makes commercial loan to a company)

1 - 23

What are some financial intermediaries?

- Commercial banks
- Savings & Loans, mutual savings banks, and credit unions
- Life insurance companies
- Mutual funds
- Pension funds

1 - 24

The Top 5 Banking Companies in the World, 12/2001

Bank Name	Country
Citigroup	U.S.
Deutsche Bank AG	Germany
Credit Suisse	Switzerland
BNP Paribas	France
Bank of America	U.S.

1 - 25

What are some types of markets?

- A market is a method of exchanging one asset (usually cash) for another asset.
- Physical assets vs. financial assets
- Spot versus future markets
- Money versus capital markets
- Primary versus secondary markets

usually for goods or service

primary → IPO

secondary - where we would go to buy the stock

1 - 26

How are secondary markets organized?

- By "location"
  - Physical location exchanges
  - Computer/telephone networks
- By the way that orders from buyers and sellers are matched
  - Open outcry auction
  - Dealers (i.e., market makers)
  - Electronic communications networks (ECNs)

1 - 27

Physical Location vs. Computer/telephone Networks

- Physical location exchanges: e.g., NYSE, AMEX, CBOT, Tokyo Stock Exchange
- Computer/telephone: e.g., Nasdaq, government bond markets, foreign exchange markets

Nasdaq - largest

1 - 28

Auction Markets

- NYSE and AMEX are the two largest auction markets for stocks.
- NYSE is a modified auction, with a "specialist."
- Participants have a seat on the exchange, meet face-to-face, and place orders for themselves or for their clients; e.g., CBOT.
- Market orders vs. limit orders

Chicago Board of Trade

1 - 29

Dealer Markets

- "Dealers" keep an inventory of the stock (or other financial asset) and place bid and ask "advertisements," which are prices at which they are willing to buy and sell.
- Computerized quotation system keeps track of bid and ask prices, but does not automatically match buyers and sellers.
- Examples: Nasdaq National Market, Nasdaq SmallCap Market, London SEAQ, German Neuer Markt.

1 - 30

Electronic Communications Networks (ECNs)

- ECNs:
  - Computerized system matches orders from buyers and sellers and automatically executes transaction.
  - Examples: Instinet (US, stocks), Eurex (Swiss-German, futures contracts), SETS (London, stocks).

1 - 31

Over the Counter (OTC) Markets

- In the old days, securities were kept in a safe behind the counter, and passed "over the counter" when they were sold.
- Now the OTC market is the equivalent of a computer bulletin board, which allows potential buyers and sellers to post an offer.
  - No dealers
  - Very poor liquidity

1 - 32

- What do we call the price, or cost, of debt capital?

The interest rate

- What do we call the price, or cost, of equity capital?

Required return = Dividend yield + Capital gain.

1 - 33

What four factors affect the cost of money?

- Production opportunities
- Time preferences for consumption
- Risk
- Expected inflation

capital into benefits

1 - 34

Real versus Nominal Rates

r^* = Real risk-free rate. T-bond rate if no inflation; 1% to 4%.

r = Any nominal rate.

r_{RF} = Rate on Treasury securities.

Nominal or quoted Rate

1 - 35

$$r = r^* + IP + DRP + LP + MRP.$$

Here:

- r = Required rate of return on a debt security.
- r^* = Real risk-free rate.
- IP = Inflation premium.
- DRP = Default risk premium.
- LP = Liquidity premium.
- MRP = Maturity risk premium.

pg. 27 in book
make note of formula

1 - 36

Premiums Added to r* for Different Types of Debt

- ST Treasury: only IP for ST inflation
- LT Treasury: IP for LT inflation, MRP
- ST corporate: ST IP, DRP, LP
- LT corporate: IP, DRP, MRP, LP

1 - 37

What is the "term structure of interest rates"? What is a "yield curve"?

- Term structure: the relationship between interest rates (or yields) and maturities.
- A graph of the term structure is called the yield curve.

1 - 38

How can you construct a hypothetical Treasury yield curve?

- Estimate the inflation premium (IP) for each future year. This is the estimated average inflation over that time period.
- Step 2: Estimate the maturity risk premium (MRP) for each future year.

1 - 39

Assume investors expect inflation to be 5% next year, 6% the following year, and 8% per year thereafter.

Step 1: Find the average expected inflation rate over years 1 to n:

$$IP_n = \frac{\sum_{t=1}^{n} INFL_t}{n}.$$

1 - 40

IP_1 = 5%/1.0 = 5.00%.

IP_{10} = [5 + 6 + 8(8)]/10 = 7.5%.

IP_{20} = [5 + 6 + 8(18)]/20 = 7.75%.

Must earn these IPs to break even versus inflation; that is, these IPs would permit you to earn r* (before taxes).

Interest Premium

1 - 41

Assume the MRP is zero for Year 1 and increases by 0.1% each year.

Step 2: Find MRP based on this equation:

MRP_t = 0.1%(t - 1).

MRP_1 = 0.1% x 0 = 0.0%.

MRP_{10} = 0.1% x 9 = 0.9%.

MRP_{20} = 0.1% x 19 = 1.9%.

1 - 42

Step 3: Add the IPs and MRPs to r*:

r_{RF_t} = r* + IP_t + MRP_t.

r_{RF} = Quoted market interest rate on treasury securities.

Assume r* = 3%:

r_{RF1} = 3% + 5% + 0.0% = 8.0%.

r_{RF10} = 3% + 7.5% + 0.9% = 11.4%.

r_{RF20} = 3% + 7.75% + 1.9% = 12.65%.

1 - 43

Hypothetical Treasury Yield Curve

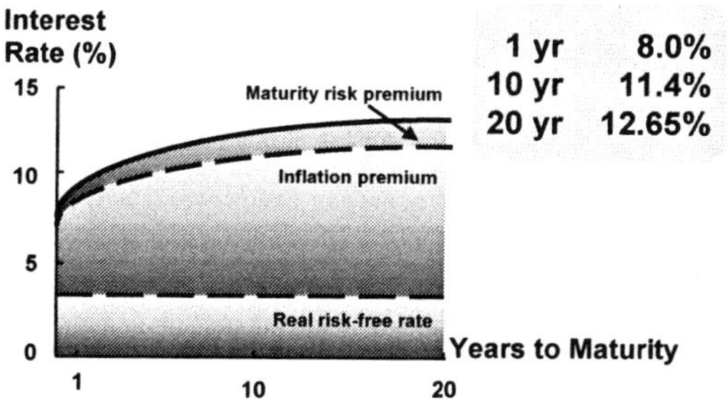

1 - 44

What factors can explain the shape of this yield curve?

- This constructed yield curve is upward sloping.
- This is due to increasing expected inflation and an increasing maturity risk premium.

upward sloping is usual shape

1 - 45

What kind of relationship exists between the Treasury yield curve and the yield curves for corporate issues?

- Corporate yield curves are higher than that of the Treasury bond. However, corporate yield curves are not necessarily parallel to the Treasury curve.
- The spread between a corporate yield curve and the Treasury curve widens as the corporate bond rating decreases.

1 - 46

Hypothetical Treasury and Corporate Yield Curves

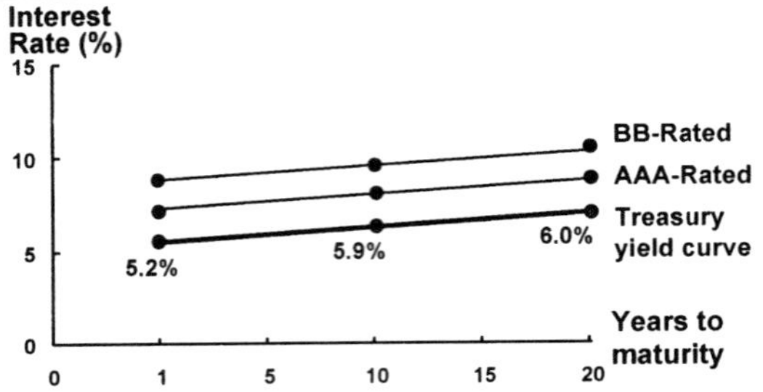

Treasury - Basically Risk Free

AAA = Pretty safe company

BB - good company

1 - 47

What is the Pure Expectations Hypothesis (PEH)?

- Shape of the yield curve depends on the investors' expectations about future interest rates.
- If interest rates are expected to increase, L-T rates will be higher than S-T rates and vice versa. Thus, the yield curve can slope up or down.
- PEH assumes that MRP = 0.

1 - 48

What various types of risks arise when investing overseas?

Country risk: Arises from investing or doing business in a particular country. It depends on the country's economic, political, and social environment.

Exchange rate risk: If investment is denominated in a currency other than the dollar, the investment's value will depend on what happens to exchange rate.

- 3rd world country could be risky

- using exchange rate vs american dollars

1 - 49

What two factors lead to exchange rate fluctuations?

- Changes in relative inflation will lead to changes in exchange rates.
- An increase in country risk will also cause that country's currency to fall.

2-1

Chapter 2
Time Value of Money

- Future value
- Present value
- Rates of return
- Amortization

2-2

Time lines show timing of cash flows.

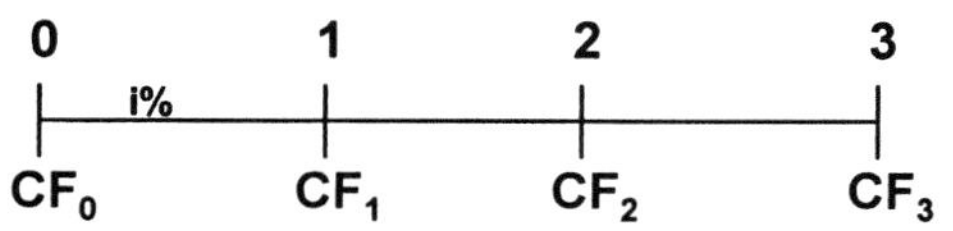

<u>Tick marks</u> at ends of periods, so Time 0 is today; Time 1 is the end of Period 1; or the beginning of Period 2.

2-3

Time line for a $100 lump sum due at the end of Year 2.

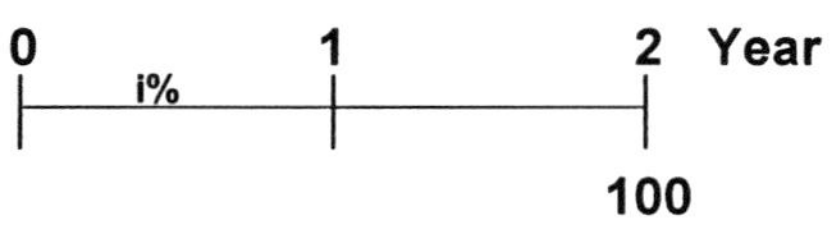

2-4

Time line for an ordinary annuity of $100 for 3 years.

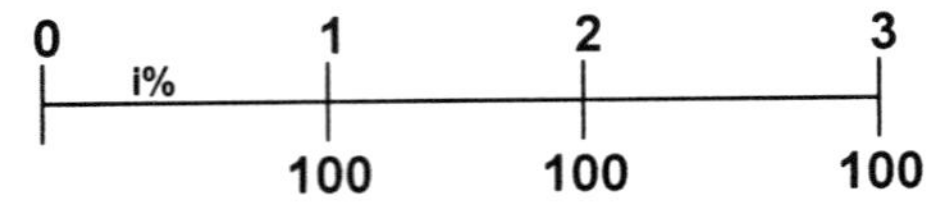

2-5

Time line for uneven CFs: -$50 at t = 0 and $100, $75, and $50 at the end of Years 1 through 3.

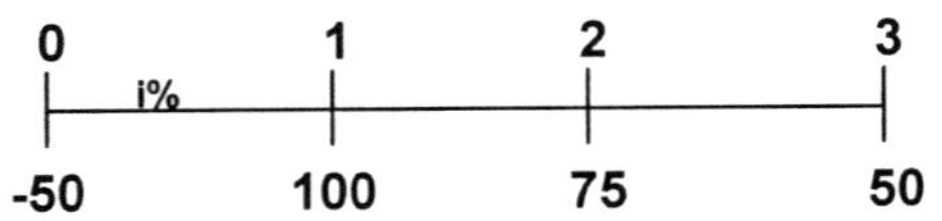

2-6

What's the FV of an initial $100 after 3 years if i = 10%?

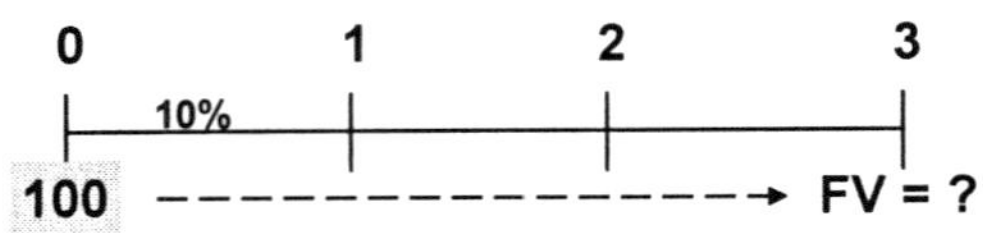

Finding FVs (moving to the right on a time line) is called compounding.

2-7

After 1 year:

$$FV_1 = PV + INT_1 = PV + PV(i)$$
$$= PV(1 + i)$$
$$= \$100(1.10)$$
$$= \$110.00.$$

After 2 years:

$$FV_2 = FV_1(1+i) = PV(1 + i)(1+i)$$
$$= PV(1+i)^2$$
$$= \$100(1.10)^2$$
$$= \$121.00.$$

2-8

After 3 years:

$$FV_3 = FV2(1+i) = PV(1 + i)^2(1+i)$$
$$= PV(1+i)^3$$
$$= \$100(1.10)^3$$
$$= \$133.10.$$

In general,

$$FV_n = PV(1 + i)^n.$$

2-9

Three Ways to Find FVs

- Solve the equation with a regular calculator.
- Use a financial calculator.
- Use a spreadsheet.

2-10

Financial calculator: HP10BII

- Adjust display brightness: hold down ON and push + or -.
- Set number of decimal places to display: Orange Shift key, then DISP key (in orange), then desired decimal places (e.g., 3).
- To temporarily show all digits, hit Orange Shift key, then DISP, then =

2-11

HP10BII (Continued)

- To permantly show all digits, hit ORANGE shift, then DISP, then . (period key)
- Set decimal mode: Hit ORANGE shift, then ./, key. Note: many non-US countries reverse the US use of decimals and commas when writing a number.

2-12

HP10BII: Set Time Value Parameters

- To set END (for cash flows occuring at the end of the year), hit ORANGE shift key, then BEG/END.
- To set 1 payment per period, hit 1, then ORANGE shift key, then P/YR

2-13

Financial Calculator Solution

Financial calculators solve this equation:

$$FV_n + PV(1+i)^n = 0$$

There are 4 variables. If 3 are known, the calculator will solve for the 4th.

2-14

Here's the setup to find FV:

INPUTS	3	10	-100	0	
	N	I/YR	PV	PMT	FV
OUTPUT					133.10

Clearing automatically sets everything to 0, but for safety enter PMT = 0.

Set: P/YR = 1, END.

2-15

Spreadsheet Solution

- Use the FV function: see spreadsheet in *Ch 02 Mini Case.xls.*
  - = FV(Rate, Nper, Pmt, PV)
  - = FV(0.10, 3, 0, -100) = 133.10

2-16

What's the PV of $100 due in 3 years if i = 10%?

Finding PVs is discounting, and it's the reverse of compounding.

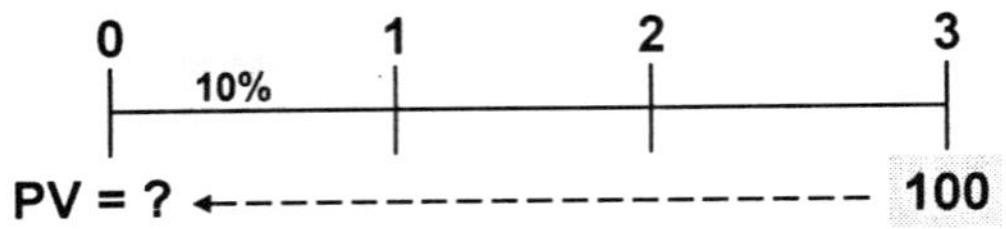

2-17

Solve $FV_n = PV(1 + i)^n$ for PV:

$$PV = \frac{FV_n}{(1+i)^n} = FV_n\left(\frac{1}{1+i}\right)^n$$

$$PV = \$100\left(\frac{1}{1.10}\right)^3$$
$$= \$100(0.7513) = \$75.13.$$

2-18

Financial Calculator Solution

INPUTS	3	10		0	100
	N	I/YR	PV	PMT	FV
OUTPUT			-75.13		

Either PV or FV must be negative. Here PV = -75.13. Put in $75.13 today, take out $100 after 3 years.

2-19

Spreadsheet Solution

- Use the PV function: see spreadsheet.
  - = PV(Rate, Nper, Pmt, FV)
  - = PV(0.10, 3, 0, 100) = -75.13

2-20

Finding the Time to Double

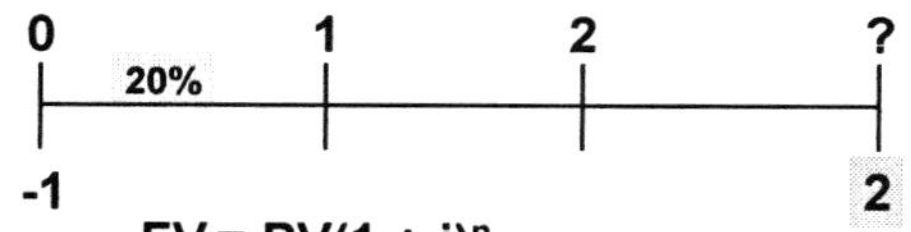

$$FV = PV(1 + i)^n$$
$$\$2 = \$1(1 + 0.20)^n$$
$$(1.2)^n = \$2/\$1 = 2$$
$$nLN(1.2) = LN(2)$$
$$n = LN(2)/LN(1.2)$$
$$n = 0.693/0.182 = 3.8.$$

2-21

Financial Calculator

	N	I/YR	PV	PMT	FV
INPUTS		20	-1	0	2
OUTPUT	3.8				

2-22

Spreadsheet Solution

- Use the NPER function: see spreadsheet.
  - = NPER(Rate, Pmt, PV, FV)
  - = NPER(0.10, 0, -1, 2) = 3.8

2-23

Finding the Interest Rate

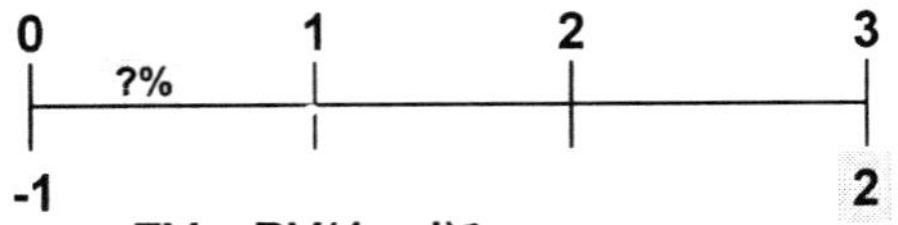

$$FV = PV(1 + i)^n$$
$$\$2 = \$1(1 + i)^3$$
$$(2)^{(1/3)} = (1 + i)$$
$$1.2599 = (1 + i)$$
$$i = 0.2599 = 25.99\%.$$

2-24

Financial Calculator

	N	I/YR	PV	PMT	FV
INPUTS	3		-1	0	2
OUTPUT		25.99			

2-25

Spreadsheet Solution

- Use the RATE function:
  - = RATE(Nper, Pmt, PV, FV)
  - = RATE(3, 0, -1, 2) = 0.2599

2-26

What's the difference between an <u>ordinary annuity</u> and an <u>annuity due</u>?

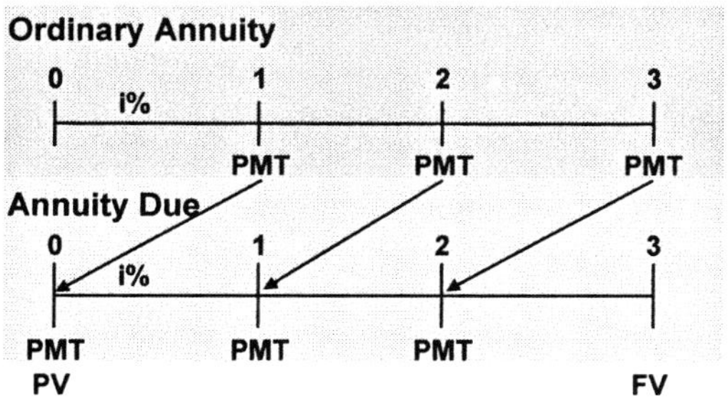

2-27

What's the FV of a 3-year ordinary annuity of $100 at 10%?

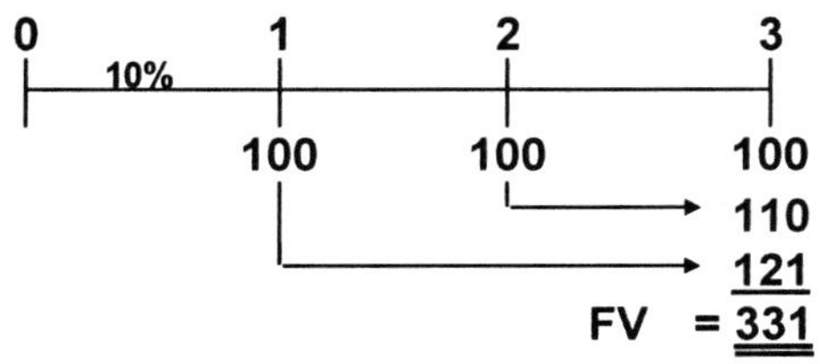

2-28

FV Annuity Formula

- The future value of an annuity with n periods and an interest rate of i can be found with the following formula:

$$=\text{PMT}\,\frac{(1+i)^n-1}{i}$$

$$=100\,\frac{(1+0.10)^3-1}{0.10}=331.$$

2-29

Financial Calculator Formula for Annuities

Financial calculators solve this equation:

$$FV_n+PV(1+i)^n+PMT\,\frac{(1+i)^n-1}{i}=0.$$

There are 5 variables. If 4 are known, the calculator will solve for the 5th.

2-30

Financial Calculator Solution

	N	I/YR	PV	PMT	FV
INPUTS	3	10	0	-100	
OUTPUT					331.00

Have payments but no lump sum PV, so enter 0 for present value.

2-31

Spreadsheet Solution

- Use the FV function: see spreadsheet.
  - = FV(Rate, Nper, Pmt, Pv)
  - = FV(0.10, 3, -100, 0) = 331.00

2-32

What's the PV of this ordinary annuity?

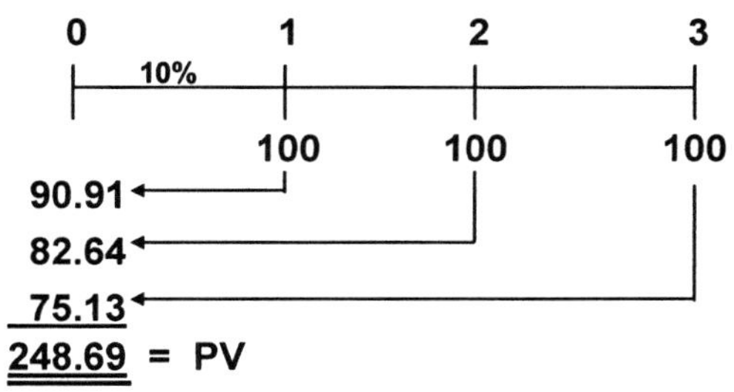

2-33

PV Annuity Formula

- The present value of an annuity with n periods and an interest rate of i can be found with the following formula:

$$= PMT \frac{1 - \frac{1}{(1+i)^n}}{i}$$

$$= 100 \frac{1 - \frac{1}{(1+0.10)^3}}{0.10} = 248.69$$

2-34

Financial Calculator Solution

INPUTS	3	10		100	0
	N	I/YR	PV	PMT	FV
OUTPUT			-248.69		

Have payments but no lump sum FV, so enter 0 for future value.

2-35

Spreadsheet Solution

- Use the PV function: see spreadsheet.
  - = PV(Rate, Nper, Pmt, Fv)
  - = PV(0.10, 3, 100, 0) = -248.69

2-36

Find the FV and PV if the annuity were an annuity due.

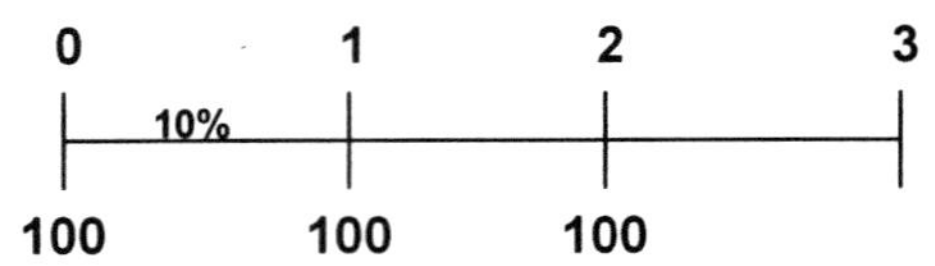

2-37

PV and FV of Annuity Due vs. Ordinary Annuity

- PV of annuity due:
  - = (PV of ordinary annuity) (1+i)
  - = (248.69) (1+ 0.10) = 273.56
- FV of annuity due:
  - = (FV of ordinary annuity) (1+i)
  - = (331.00) (1+ 0.10) = 364.1

2-38

Switch from "End" to "Begin". Then enter variables to find PVA_3 = $273.55.

	N	I/YR	PV	PMT	FV
INPUTS	3	10		100	0
OUTPUT			-273.55		

Then enter PV = 0 and press FV to find FV = $364.10.

2-39

Excel Function for Annuities Due

Change the formula to:

=PV(10%,3,-100,0,1)

The fourth term, 0, tells the function there are no other cash flows. The fifth term tells the function that it is an annuity due. A similar function gives the future value of an annuity due:

=FV(10%,3,-100,0,1)

2-40

What is the PV of this uneven cash flow stream?

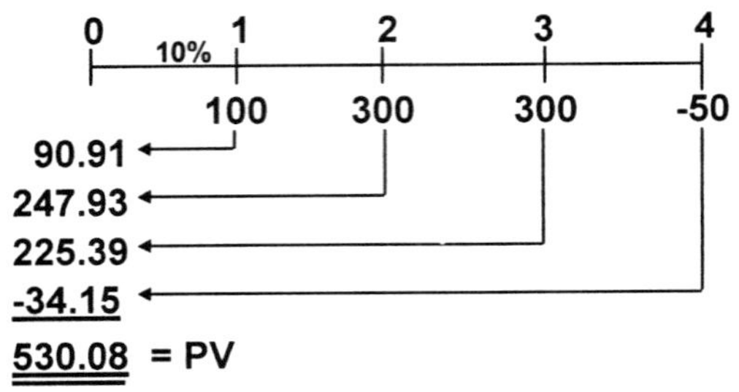

2-41

Financial calculator: HP10BII

- Clear all: Orange Shift key, then C All key (in orange).
- Enter number, then hit the CF_j key.
- Repeat for all cash flows, in order.
- To find NPV: Enter interest rate (I/YR). Then Orange Shift key, then NPV key (in orange).

2-42

Financial calculator: HP10BII (more)

- To see current cash flow in list, hit RCL CF_j CF_j
- To see previous CF, hit RCL CF_j –
- To see subseqent CF, hit RCL CF_j +
- To see CF 0-9, hit RCL CF_j 1 (to see CF 1). To see CF 10-14, hit RCL CF_j . (period) 1 (to see CF 11).

2-43

- Input in "CFLO" register:
  - CF_0 = 0
  - CF_1 = 100
  - CF_2 = 300
  - CF_3 = 300
  - CF_4 = -50
- Enter I = 10%, then press NPV button to get NPV = 530.09. (Here NPV = PV.)

2-44

Spreadsheet Solution

	A	B	C	D	E
1	0	1	2	3	4
2		100	300	300	-50
3	530.09				

Excel Formula in cell A3:

=NPV(10%,B2:E2)

2-45

Nominal rate (i_{Nom})

- Stated in contracts, and quoted by banks and brokers.
- Not used in calculations or shown on time lines
- Periods per year (m) must be given.
- Examples:
  - 8%; Quarterly
  - 8%, Daily interest (365 days)

2-46

Periodic rate (i_{Per})

- $i_{Per} = i_{Nom}/m$, where m is number of compounding periods per year. m = 4 for quarterly, 12 for monthly, and 360 or 365 for daily compounding.
- Used in calculations, shown on time lines.
- Examples:
  - 8% quarterly: iPer = 8%/4 = 2%.
  - 8% daily (365): iPer = 8%/365 = 0.021918%.

2-47

Will the FV of a lump sum be larger or smaller if we compound more often, holding the stated I% constant? Why?

LARGER! If compounding is more frequent than once a year--for example, semiannually, quarterly, or daily--interest is earned on interest more often.

2-48

FV Formula with Different Compounding Periods (e.g., $100 at a 12% nominal rate with semiannual compounding for 5 years)

$$FV_n = PV\left(1 + \frac{i_{Nom}}{m}\right)^{mn}.$$

$$FV_{5S} = \$100\left(1 + \frac{0.12}{2}\right)^{2x5}$$

$$= \$100(1.06)^{10} = \$179.08.$$

2-49

FV of $100 at a 12% nominal rate for 5 years with different compounding

FV(Annual)= $100(1.12)^5 = $176.23.

FV(Semiannual)= $100(1.06)^{10}=$179.08.

FV(Quarterly)= $100(1.03)^{20} = $180.61.

FV(Monthly)= $100(1.01)^{60} = $181.67.

FV(Daily) = $100(1+(0.12/365))^{(5x365)}

= $182.19.

2-50

Effective Annual Rate (EAR = EFF%)

- The EAR is the annual rate which causes PV to grow to the same FV as under multi-period compounding Example: Invest $1 for one year at 12%, semiannual:

$$FV = PV(1 + i_{Nom}/m)^m$$

$$FV = \$1\ (1.06)^2 = 1.1236.$$

- EFF% = 12.36%, because $1 invested for one year at 12% semiannual compounding would grow to the same value as $1 invested for one year at 12.36% annual compounding.

2-51

- An investment with monthly payments is different from one with quarterly payments. Must put on EFF% basis to compare rates of return. Use EFF% only for comparisons.
- Banks say "interest paid daily." Same as compounded daily.

2-52

How do we find EFF% for a nominal rate of 12%, compounded semiannually?

$$EFF\% = \left(1 + \frac{i_{Nom}}{m}\right)^m - 1$$

$$= \left(1 + \frac{0.12}{2}\right)^2 - 1.0$$

$$= (1.06)^2 - 1.0$$

$$= 0.1236 = 12.36\%.$$

2-53

Finding EFF with HP10BII

- Type in nominal rate, then Orange Shift key, then NOM% key (in orange).
- Type in number of periods, then Orange Shift key, then P/YR key (in orange).
- To find effective rate, hit Orange Shift key, then EFF% key (in orange).

2-54

EAR (or EFF%) for a Nominal Rate of of 12%

EAR_{Annual} = 12%.

$EAR_Q = (1 + 0.12/4)^4 - 1 = 12.55\%.$

$EAR_M = (1 + 0.12/12)^{12} - 1 = 12.68\%.$

$EAR_{D(365)} = (1 + 0.12/365)^{365} - 1 = 12.75\%.$

2-55

Can the effective rate ever be equal to the nominal rate?

- Yes, but only if annual compounding is used, i.e., if m = 1.
- If m > 1, EFF% will always be greater than the nominal rate.

2-56

When is each rate used?

i_{Nom}: Written into contracts, quoted by banks and brokers. Not used in calculations or shown on time lines.

2-57

i_{Per}: Used in calculations, shown on time lines.

If i_{Nom} has annual compounding, then $i_{Per} = i_{Nom}/1 = i_{Nom}$.

2-58

EAR = EFF%: Used to compare returns on investments with different payments per year.

(Used for calculations if and only if dealing with annuities where payments don't match interest compounding periods.)

2-59

Amortization

Construct an amortization schedule for a $1,000, 10% annual rate loan with 3 equal payments.

2-60

Step 1: Find the required payments.

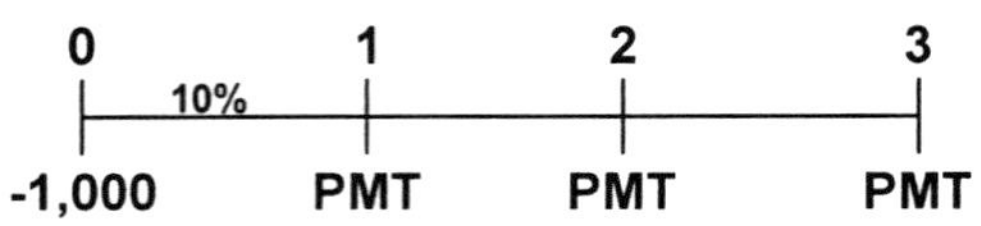

	3	10	-1000		0
INPUTS	N	I/YR	PV	PMT	FV
OUTPUT				402.11	

2-61

Step 2: Find interest charge for Year 1.

INT_t = Beg bal_t (i)
INT_1 = $1,000(0.10) = **$100.**

Step 3: Find repayment of principal in Year 1.

Repmt = PMT - INT
= $402.11 - $100
= **$302.11.**

2-62

Step 4: Find ending balance after Year 1.

End bal = Beg bal - Repmt
= $1,000 - $302.11 = $697.89.

Repeat these steps for Years 2 and 3 to complete the amortization table.

2-63

YR	BEG BAL	PMT	INT	PRIN PMT	END BAL
1	$1,000	$402	$100	$302	$698
2	698	402	70	332	366
3	366	402	37	366	0
TOT		1,206.34	206.34	1,000	

Interest declines. Tax implications.

2-64

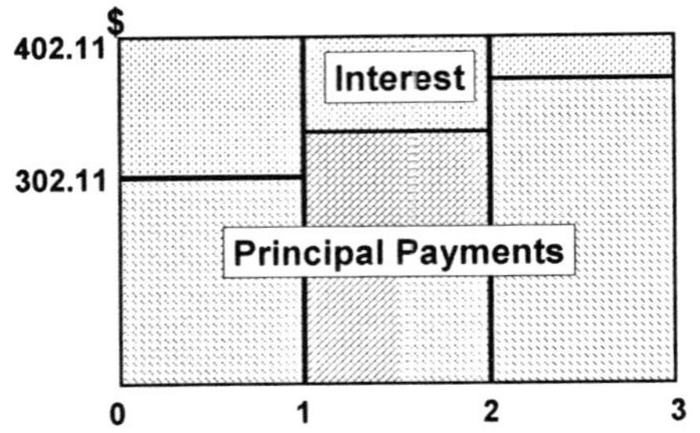

Level payments. Interest declines because outstanding balance declines. Lender earns 10% on loan outstanding, which is falling.

2-65

- Amortization tables are widely used--for home mortgages, auto loans, business loans, retirement plans, and so on. They are very important!
- Financial calculators (and spreadsheets) are great for setting up amortization tables.

2-66

On January 1 you deposit $100 in an account that pays a nominal interest rate of 11.33463%, with daily compounding (365 days).

How much will you have on October 1, or after 9 months (273 days)? (Days given.)

2-67

i_{Per} = 11.33463%/365
= 0.031054% per day.

FV_{273} = 100(1.00031054)^{273}$
= $100(1.08846) = $108.85.

Note: % in calculator, decimal in equation.

2-68

$i_{Per} = i_{Nom}/m$
= 11.33463/365
= 0.031054% per day.

INPUTS	273		-100	0	
	N	I/YR	PV	PMT	FV
OUTPUT					108.85

Enter i in one step.
Leave data in calculator.

2-69

What's the value at the end of Year 3 of the following CF stream if the quoted interest rate is 10%, compounded semiannually?

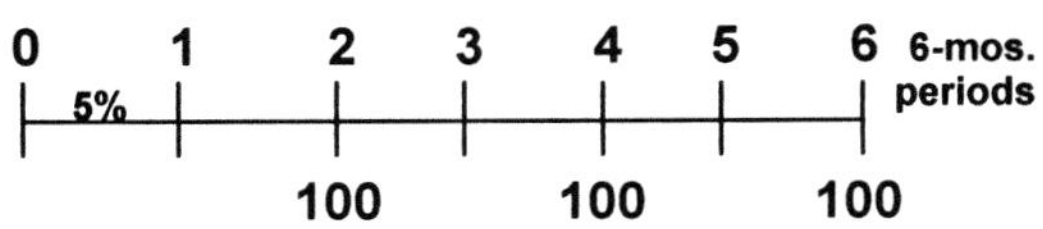

2-70

- Payments occur annually, but compounding occurs each 6 months.
- So we can't use normal annuity valuation techniques.

2-71

1st Method: Compound Each CF

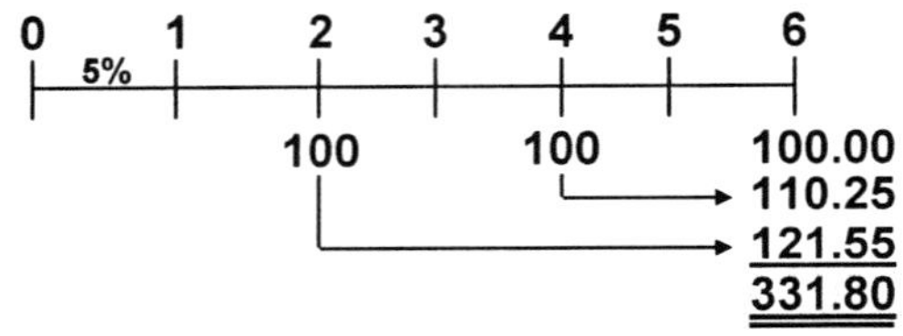

FVA_3 = \$100(1.05)^4 + \$100(1.05)^2 + \$100 = \$331.80.

2-72

2nd Method: Treat as an Annuity

Could you find the FV with a financial calculator?

Yes, by following these steps:

a. Find the EAR for the quoted rate:

$$EAR = \left(1 + \frac{0.10}{2}\right)^2 - 1 = 10.25\%.$$

2-73

b. Use EAR = 10.25% as the annual rate in your calculator:

	N	I/YR	PV	PMT	FV
INPUTS	3	10.25	0	-100	
OUTPUT					331.80

2-74

What's the PV of this stream?

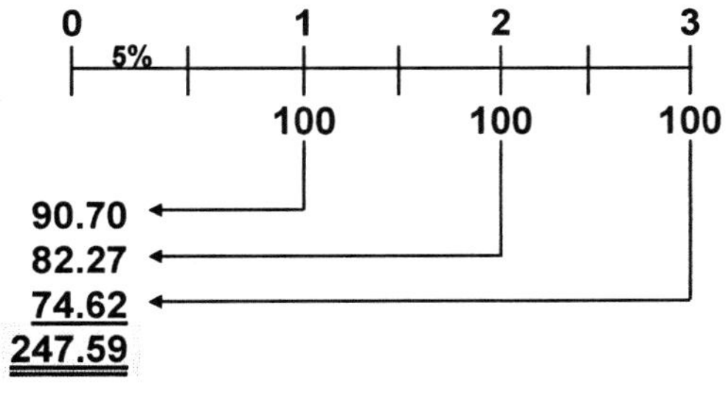

2-75

You are offered a note which pays $1,000 in 15 months (or 456 days) for $850. You have $850 in a bank which pays a 6.76649% nominal rate, with 365 daily compounding, which is a daily rate of 0.018538% and an EAR of 7.0%. You plan to leave the money in the bank if you don't buy the note. The note is riskless.

Should you buy it?

2-76

i_{Per} = 0.018538% per day.

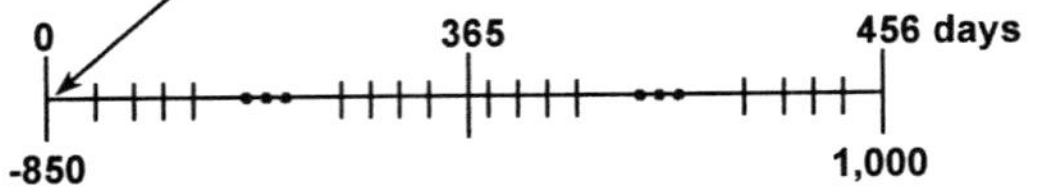

3 Ways to Solve:

1. Greatest future wealth: FV
2. Greatest wealth today: PV
3. Highest rate of return: Highest EFF%

2-77

1. Greatest Future Wealth

Find FV of $850 left in bank for 15 months and compare with note's FV = $1,000.

$$FV_{Bank} = \$850(1.00018538)^{456}$$
$$= \$924.97 \text{ in bank.}$$

Buy the note: $1,000 > $924.97.

2-78

Calculator Solution to FV:

$$i_{Per} = i_{Nom}/m$$
$$= 6.76649\%/365$$
$$= 0.018538\% \text{ per day.}$$

INPUTS	456	↓	-850	0	
	N	I/YR	PV	PMT	FV
OUTPUT					924.97

Enter i_{Per} in one step.

2-79

2. Greatest Present Wealth

Find PV of note, and compare with its $850 cost:

$$PV = \$1{,}000/(1.00018538)^{456} = \$918.95.$$

2-80

	6.76649/365 =				
INPUTS	456	.018538		0	1000
	N	I/YR	PV	PMT	FV
OUTPUT			-918.95		

PV of note is greater than its $850 cost, so buy the note. Raises your wealth.

2-81

3. Rate of Return

Find the EFF% on note and compare with 7.0% bank pays, which is your opportunity cost of capital:

$$FV_n = PV(1 + i)^n$$

$$\$1{,}000 = \$850(1 + i)^{456}$$

Now we must solve for i.

2-82

INPUTS	456		-850	0	1000
	N	I/YR	PV	PMT	FV
OUTPUT		0.035646% per day			

Convert % to decimal:

Decimal = 0.035646/100 = 0.00035646.

EAR = EFF% = $(1.00035646)^{365} - 1$
= 13.89%.

2-83

Using interest conversion:

P/YR = 365
NOM% = 0.035646(365) = 13.01
EFF% = 13.89

Since 13.89% > 7.0% opportunity cost, buy the note.

3 - 1

CHAPTER 3
Financial Statements, Cash Flow, and Taxes

- Balance sheet
- Income statement
- Statement of cash flows
- Accounting income versus cash flow
- MVA and EVA
- Personal taxes
- Corporate taxes

3 - 2

Income Statement

	2003	2004
Sales	3,432,000	5,834,400
COGS	2,864,000	4,980,000
Other expenses	340,000	720,000
Deprec.	18,900	116,960
Tot. op. costs	3,222,900	5,816,960
EBIT	209,100	17,440
Int. expense	62,500	176,000
EBT	146,600	(158,560)
Taxes (40%)	58,640	(63,424)
Net income	87,960	(95,136)

3 - 3

What happened to sales and net income?

- Sales increased by over $2.4 million.
- Costs shot up by more than sales.
- Net income was negative.
- However, the firm received a tax refund since it paid taxes of more than $63,424 during the past two years.

3 - 4

Balance Sheet: Assets

	2003	2004
Cash	9,000	7,282
S-T invest.	48,600	20,000
AR	351,200	632,160
Inventories	715,200	1,287,360
Total CA	1,124,000	1,946,802
Gross FA	491,000	1,202,950
Less: Depr.	146,200	263,160
Net FA	344,800	939,790
Total assets	1,468,800	2,886,592

3 - 5

What effect did the expansion have on the asset section of the balance sheet?

- Net fixed assets almost tripled in size.
- AR and inventory almost doubled.
- Cash and short-term investments fell.

3 - 6

Statement of Retained Earnings: 2004

Balance of ret. earnings, 12/31/2003	203,768
Add: Net income, 2004	(95,136)
Less: Dividends paid, 2004	(11,000)
Balance of ret. earnings, 12/31/2004	97,632

3 - 7

Balance Sheet: Liabilities & Equity

	2003	2004
Accts. payable	145,600	324,000
Notes payable	200,000	720,000
Accruals	136,000	284,960
Total CL	481,600	1,328,960
Long-term debt	323,432	1,000,000
Common stock	460,000	460,000
Ret. earnings	203,768	97,632
Total equity	663,768	557,632
Total L&E	1,468,800	2,886,592

3 - 8

What effect did the expansion have on liabilities & equity?

- CL increased as creditors and suppliers "financed" part of the expansion.
- Long-term debt increased to help finance the expansion.
- The company didn't issue any stock.
- Retained earnings fell, due to the year's negative net income and dividend payment.

3 - 9

Statement of Cash Flows: 2004

Operating Activities	
Net Income	(95,136)
Adjustments:	
Depreciation	116,960
Change in AR	(280,960)
Change in inventories	(572,160)
Change in AP	178,400
Change in accruals	148,960
Net cash provided by ops.	(503,936)

3 - 10

Long-Term Investing Activities

Cash used to acquire FA	(711,950)

Financing Activities

Change in S-T invest.	28,600
Change in notes payable	520,000
Change in long-term debt	676,568
Payment of cash dividends	(11,000)
Net cash provided by fin. act.	1,214,168

3 - 11

Summary of Statement of CF

Net cash provided by ops.	(503,936)
Net cash to acquire FA	(711,950)
Net cash provided by fin. act.	1,214,168
Net change in cash	(1,718)
Cash at beginning of year	9,000
Cash at end of year	7,282

3 - 12

What can you conclude from the statement of cash flows?

- Net CF from operations = -$503,936, because of negative net income and increases in working capital.
- The firm spent $711,950 on FA.
- The firm borrowed heavily and sold some short-term investments to meet its cash requirements.
- Even after borrowing, the cash account fell by $1,718.

3 - 13

What is free cash flow (FCF)? Why is it important?

- FCF is the amount of cash available from operations for distribution to all investors (including stockholders and debtholders) after making the necessary investments to support operations.
- A company's value depends upon the amount of FCF it can generate.

Way to increase shareholders value

3 - 14

What are the five uses of FCF?

1. Pay interest on debt.
2. Pay back principal on debt.
3. Pay dividends.
4. Buy back stock.
5. Buy nonoperating assets (e.g., marketable securities, investments in other companies, etc.)

3 - 15

What are operating current assets?

- Operating current assets are the CA needed to support operations.
  - Op CA include: cash, inventory, receivables.
  - Op CA exclude: short-term investments, because these are not a part of operations.

3 - 16

What are operating current liabilities?

- Operating current liabilities are the CL resulting as a normal part of operations.
  - Op CL include: accounts payable and accruals.
  - Op CA exclude: notes payable, because this is a source of financing, not a part of operations.

3 - 17

What effect did the expansion have on net operating working capital (NOWC)?

$$\text{NOWC} = \text{Operating CA} - \text{Operating CL}$$

$$\begin{aligned} \text{NOWC}_{04} &= (\$7{,}282 + \$632{,}160 + \$1{,}287{,}360) \\ &\quad - (\$324{,}000 + \$284{,}960) \\ &= \$1{,}317{,}842. \end{aligned}$$

$$\text{NOWC}_{03} = \$793{,}800.$$

3 - 18

What effect did the expansion have on total net operating capital (also just called operating capital)?

$$\text{Operating capital} = \text{NOWC} + \text{Net fixed assets.}$$

$$\begin{aligned} \text{Operating capital}_{04} &= \$1{,}317{,}842 + \$939{,}790 \\ &= \$2{,}257{,}632. \end{aligned}$$

$$\text{Operating capital}_{03} = \$1{,}138{,}600.$$

3 - 19

Did the expansion create additional net operating profit after taxes (NOPAT)?

NOPAT = EBIT(1 - Tax rate)

$NOPAT_{04}$ = \$17,440(1 - 0.4)
= \$10,464.

$NOPAT_{03}$ = \$125,460.

3 - 20

What was the free cash flow (FCF) for 2004?

FCF = NOPAT - Net investment in operating capital
= \$10,464 - (\$2,257,632 - \$1,138,600)
= \$10,464 - \$1,119,032
= -\$1,108,568.

How do you suppose investors reacted?

Not very favorably

3 - 21

Return on Invested Capital (ROIC)

ROIC = NOPAT / operating capital

$ROIC_{04}$ = \$10,464 / \$2,257,632 = 0.5%.

$ROIC_{03}$ = 11.0%.

3 - 22

The firm's cost of capital is 10%. Did the growth add value?

- No. The ROIC of 0.5% is less than the WACC of 10%. Investors did not get the return they require.
- Note: High growth usually causes negative FCF (due to investment in capital), but that's ok if ROIC > WACC. For example, Home Depot has high growth, negative FCF, but a high ROIC.

3 - 23

Calculate EVA. Assume the cost of capital (WACC) was 10% for both years.

EVA = NOPAT- (WACC)(Capital)

EVA_{04} = \$10,464 - (0.1)(\$2,257,632)
= \$10,464 - \$225,763
= -\$215,299.

EVA_{03} = \$125,460 - (0.10)(\$1,138,600)
= \$125,460 - \$113,860
= \$11,600.

3 - 24

Stock Price and Other Data

	2003	2004
Stock price	\$8.50	\$2.25
# of shares	100,000	100,000
EPS	\$0.88	-\$0.95
DPS	\$0.22	\$0.11

3 - 25

What is MVA (Market Value Added)?

- MVA = Market Value of the Firm - Book Value of the Firm
- Market Value = (# shares of stock)(price per share) + Value of debt
- Book Value = Total common equity + Value of debt

(More...)

3 - 26

MVA (Continued)

- If the market value of debt is close to the book value of debt, then MVA is:

MVA = Market value of equity – book value of equity

3 - 27

Find 2004 MVA. (Assume market value of debt = book value of debt.)

- Market Value of Equity 2004:
  - (100,000)($6.00) = $600,000.
- Book Value of Equity 2004:
  - $557,632.

MVA_{04} = $600,000 - $557,632 = $42,368.

MVA_{03} = $850,000 - $663,768 = $186,232.

3 - 28

Key Features of the Tax Code

- Corporate Taxes
- Individual Taxes

3 - 29

2003 Corporate Tax Rates

Taxable Income	Tax on Base	Rate*
0 - 50,000	0	15%
50,000 - 75,000	7,500	25%
75,000 - 100,000	13,750	34%
100,000 - 335,000	22,250	39%
...	...	...
Over 18.3M	6.4M	35%

*Plus this percentage on the amount over the bracket base.

3 - 30

Features of Corporate Taxation

- Progressive rate up until $18.3 million taxable income.
  - Below $18.3 million, the marginal rate is not equal to the average rate.
  - Above $18.3 million, the marginal rate and the average rate are 35%.

3 - 31

Features of Corporate Taxes (Cont.)

- A corporation can:
  - deduct its interest expenses but not its dividend payments;
  - carry-back losses for two years, carry-forward losses for 20 years.*
  - exclude 70% of dividend income if it owns less than 20% of the company's stock

*Losses in 2001 and 2002 can be carried back for five years.

3 - 32

Assume a corporation has $100,000 of taxable income from operations, $5,000 of interest income, and $10,000 of dividend income.

What is its tax liability?

3 - 33

Operating income	$100,000
Interest income	5,000
Taxable dividend income	3,000*
Taxable income	$108,000

Tax = $22,250 + 0.39 ($8,000)
= $25,370.

*Dividends - Exclusion
= $10,000 - 0.7($10,000) = $3,000.

3 - 34

Key Features of Individual Taxation

- Individuals face progressive tax rates, from 10% to 35%.
- The rate on long-term (i.e., more than one year) capital gains is 15%. But capital gains are only taxed if you sell the asset.
- Dividends are taxed at the same rate as capital gains.
- Interest on municipal (i.e., state and local government) bonds is not subject to Federal taxation.

3 - 35

Taxable versus Tax Exempt Bonds

State and local government bonds (municipals, or "munis") are generally exempt from federal taxes.

3 - 36

- Exxon bonds at 10% versus California muni bonds at 7%.
- T = Tax rate = 25.0%.
- After-tax interest income:

Exxon = 0.10($5,000)- 0.10($5,000)(0.25)
= 0.10($5,000)(0.73) = $375.

CAL = 0.07($5,000) - 0 = $350.

3 - 37

At what tax rate would you be indifferent between the muni and the corporate bonds?

Solve for T in this equation:

Muni yield = Corp Yield(1-T)

7.00% = 10.0%(1-T)

T = 30.0%.

3 - 38

Implications

- If T > 30%, buy tax exempt munis.
- If T < 30%, buy corporate bonds.
- Only high income, and hence high tax bracket, individuals should buy munis.

4 - 1

CHAPTER 4
Risk and Return: The Basics

- Basic return concepts
- Basic risk concepts
- Stand-alone risk
- Portfolio (market) risk
- Risk and return: CAPM/SML

4 - 2

What are investment returns?

- Investment returns measure the financial results of an investment.
- Returns may be historical or prospective (anticipated).
- Returns can be expressed in:
  - Dollar terms.
  - Percentage terms.

4 - 3

What is the return on an investment that costs $1,000 and is sold after 1 year for $1,100?

- Dollar return:

  $ Received - $ Invested
  $1,100 - $1,000 = $100.

- Percentage return:

  $ Return/$ Invested
  $100/$1,000 = 0.10 = 10%.

4 - 4

What is investment risk?

- Typically, investment returns are not known with certainty.
- Investment risk pertains to the probability of earning a return less than that expected.
- The greater the chance of a return far below the expected return, the greater the risk.

4 - 5

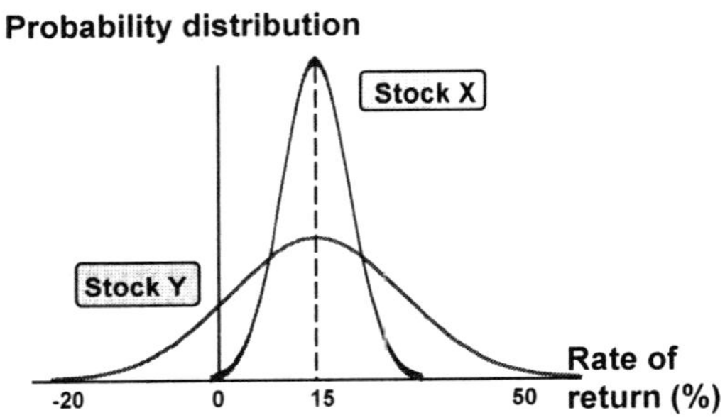

- Which stock is riskier? Why?

4 - 6

Assume the Following Investment Alternatives

Economy	Prob.	T-Bill	Alta	Repo	Am F.	MP
Recession	0.10	8.0%	-22.0%	28.0%	10.0%	-13.0%
Below avg.	0.20	8.0	-2.0	14.7	-10.0	1.0
Average	0.40	8.0	20.0	0.0	7.0	15.0
Above avg.	0.20	8.0	35.0	-10.0	45.0	29.0
Boom	0.10	8.0	50.0	-20.0	30.0	43.0
	1.00					

4 - 7

What is unique about the T-bill return?

- The T-bill will return 8% regardless of the state of the economy.
- Is the T-bill riskless? Explain.

4 - 8

Do the returns of Alta Inds. and Repo Men move with or counter to the economy?

- Alta Inds. moves with the economy, so it is positively correlated with the economy. This is the typical situation.
- Repo Men moves counter to the economy. Such negative correlation is unusual.

4 - 9

Calculate the expected rate of return on each alternative.

$\hat{r}$ = expected rate of return.

$$\hat{r} = \sum_{i=1}^{n} r_i P_i.$$

$\hat{r}_{Alta}$ = 0.10(-22%) + 0.20(-2%) + 0.40(20%) + 0.20(35%) + 0.10(50%) = 17.4%.

4 - 10

	$\hat{r}$
Alta	17.4%
Market	15.0
Am. Foam	13.8
T-bill	8.0
Repo Men	1.7

- Alta has the highest rate of return.
- Does that make it best?

4 - 11

What is the standard deviation of returns for each alternative?

σ = Standard deviation

$$\sigma = \sqrt{\text{Variance}} = \sqrt{\sigma^2} = \sqrt{\sum_{i=1}^{n}\left(r_i - \hat{r}\right)^2 P_i}.$$

4 - 12

$$\sigma = \sqrt{\sum_{i=1}^{n}\left(r_i - \hat{r}\right)^2 P_i}.$$

Alta Inds:

$\sigma = ((-22 - 17.4)^2 0.10 + (-2 - 17.4)^2 0.20 + (20 - 17.4)^2 0.40 + (35 - 17.4)^2 0.20 + (50 - 17.4)^2 0.10)^{1/2} = 20.0\%.$

$\sigma_{T\text{-bills}} = 0.0\%.$ $\sigma_{Repo} = 13.4\%.$
$\sigma_{Alta} = 20.0\%.$ $\sigma_{Am\ Foam} = 18.8\%.$
$\sigma_{Market} = 15.3\%.$

4 - 13

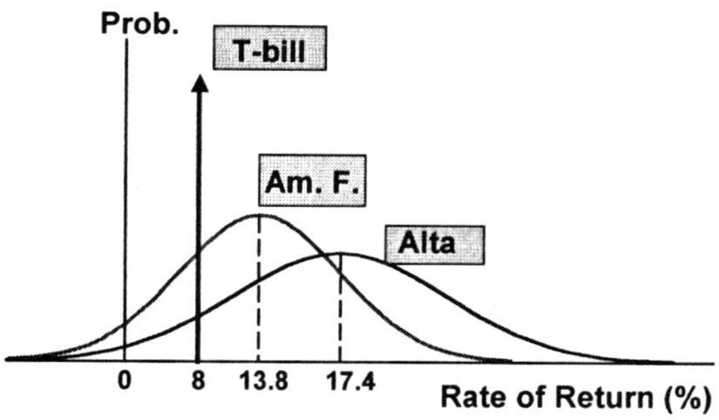

4 - 14

- Standard deviation measures the stand-alone risk of an investment.
- The larger the standard deviation, the higher the probability that returns will be far below the expected return.
- Coefficient of variation is an alternative measure of stand-alone risk.

4 - 15

Expected Return versus Risk

Security	Expected return	Risk, σ
Alta Inds.	17.4%	20.0%
Market	15.0	15.3
Am. Foam	13.8	18.8
T-bills	8.0	0.0
Repo Men	1.7	13.4

4 - 16

Coefficient of Variation:
CV = Standard deviation/expected return

$CV_{T\text{-}BILLS}$ = 0.0%/8.0% = 0.0.

$CV_{Alta\ Inds}$ = 20.0%/17.4% = 1.1.

$CV_{Repo\ Men}$ = 13.4%/1.7% = 7.9.

$CV_{Am.\ Foam}$ = 18.8%/13.8% = 1.4.

CV_{M} = 15.3%/15.0% = 1.0.

4 - 17

Expected Return versus Coefficient of Variation

Security	Expected return	Risk: σ	Risk: CV
Alta Inds	17.4%	20.0%	1.1
Market	15.0	15.3	1.0
Am. Foam	13.8	18.8	1.4
T-bills	8.0	0.0	0.0
Repo Men	1.7	13.4	7.9

4 - 18

Return vs. Risk (Std. Dev.):
Which investment is best?

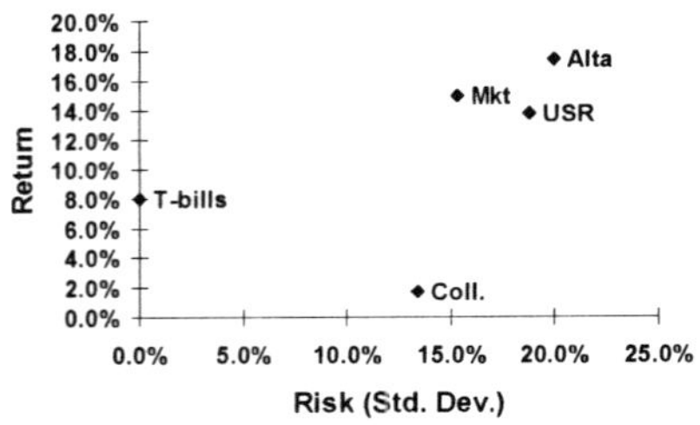

4 - 19

Portfolio Risk and Return

Assume a two-stock portfolio with \$50,000 in Alta Inds. and \$50,000 in Repo Men.

Calculate $\hat{r}_p$ and σ_p.

4 - 20

Portfolio Return, $\hat{r}_p$

$\hat{r}_p$ is a weighted average:

$$\hat{r}_p = \sum_{i=1}^{n} w_i \hat{r}_i.$$

$\hat{r}_p$ = 0.5(17.4%) + 0.5(1.7%) = 9.6%.

$\hat{r}_p$ is between $\hat{r}_{Alta}$ and $\hat{r}_{Repo}$.

4 - 21

Alternative Method

		Estimated Return		
Economy	Prob.	Alta	Repo	Port.
Recession	0.10	-22.0%	28.0%	3.0%
Below avg.	0.20	-2.0	14.7	6.4
Average	0.40	20.0	0.0	10.0
Above avg.	0.20	35.0	-10.0	12.5
Boom	0.10	50.0	-20.0	15.0

$\hat{r}_p$ = (3.0%)0.10 + (6.4%)0.20 + (10.0%)0.40 + (12.5%)0.20 + (15.0%)0.10 = 9.6%.

(More...)

- σ_p = ((3.0 - 9.6)^{2}0.10 + (6.4 - 9.6)^{2}0.20 + (10.0 - 9.6)^{2}0.40 + (12.5 - 9.6)^{2}0.20 + (15.0 - 9.6)^{2}0.10)$^{1/2}$ = 3.3%.
- σ_p is much lower than:
  - either stock (20% and 13.4%).
  - average of Alta and Repo (16.7%).
- The portfolio provides average return but much lower risk. The key here is negative correlation.

Two-Stock Portfolios

- Two stocks can be combined to form a riskless portfolio if ρ = -1.0.
- Risk is not reduced at all if the two stocks have ρ = +1.0.
- In general, stocks have $\rho \approx$ 0.65, so risk is lowered but not eliminated.
- Investors typically hold many stocks.
- What happens when ρ = 0?

What would happen to the risk of an average 1-stock portfolio as more randomly selected stocks were added?

- σ_p would decrease because the added stocks would not be perfectly correlated, but $\hat{r}_p$ would remain relatively constant.

4 - 25

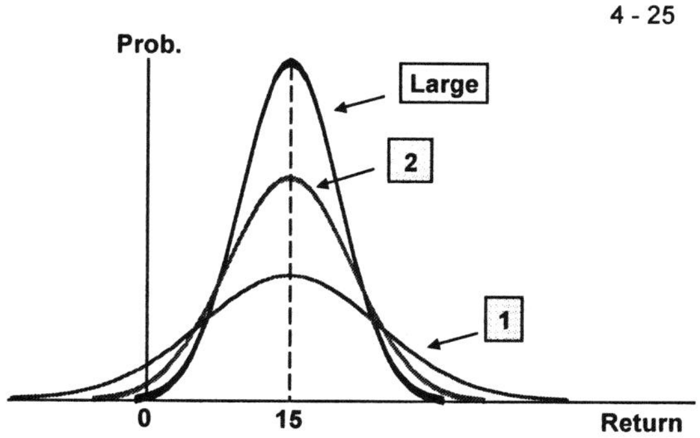

$\sigma_1 \approx 35\%$; $\sigma_{Large} \approx 20\%$.

4 - 26

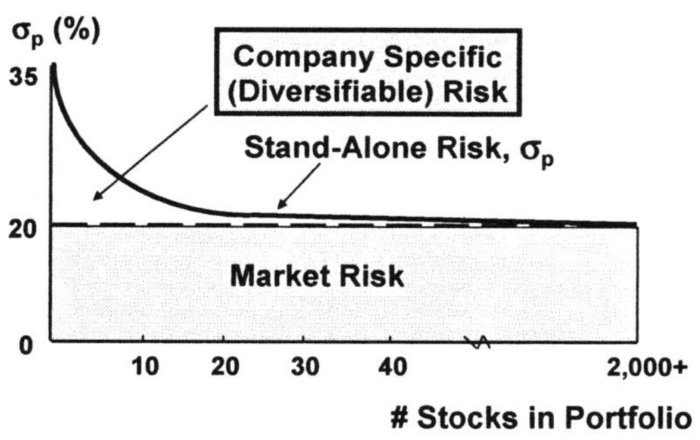

4 - 27

Stand-alone risk = Market risk + Diversifiable risk.

Market risk is that part of a security's stand-alone risk that *cannot* be eliminated by diversification.

Firm-specific, or diversifiable, risk is that part of a security's stand-alone risk that *can* be eliminated by diversification.

4 - 28

Conclusions

- As more stocks are added, each new stock has a smaller risk-reducing impact on the portfolio.
- σ_p falls very slowly after about 40 stocks are included. The lower limit for σ_p is about 20% = σ_M .
- By forming well-diversified portfolios, investors can eliminate about half the riskiness of owning a single stock.

4 - 29

Can an investor holding one stock earn a return commensurate with its risk?

- No. Rational investors will minimize risk by holding portfolios.
- They bear only market risk, so prices and returns reflect this lower risk.
- The one-stock investor bears higher (stand-alone) risk, so the return is less than that required by the risk.

4 - 30

How is market risk measured for individual securities?

- Market risk, which is relevant for stocks held in well-diversified portfolios, is defined as the contribution of a security to the overall riskiness of the portfolio.
- It is measured by a stock's beta coefficient. For stock i, its beta is:

$$b_i = (\rho_{iM}\ \sigma_i) / \sigma_M$$

4 - 31

How are betas calculated?

- In addition to measuring a stock's contribution of risk to a portfolio, beta also which measures the stock's volatility relative to the market.

4 - 32

Using a Regression to Estimate Beta

- Run a regression with returns on the stock in question plotted on the Y axis and returns on the market portfolio plotted on the X axis.
- The slope of the regression line, which measures relative volatility, is defined as the stock's beta coefficient, or b.

4 - 33

Use the historical stock returns to calculate the beta for PQU.

Year	Market	PQU
1	25.7%	40.0%
2	8.0%	-15.0%
3	-11.0%	-15.0%
4	15.0%	35.0%
5	32.5%	10.0%
6	13.7%	30.0%
7	40.0%	42.0%
8	10.0%	-10.0%
9	-10.8%	-25.0%
10	-13.1%	25.0%

4 - 34

Calculating Beta for PQU

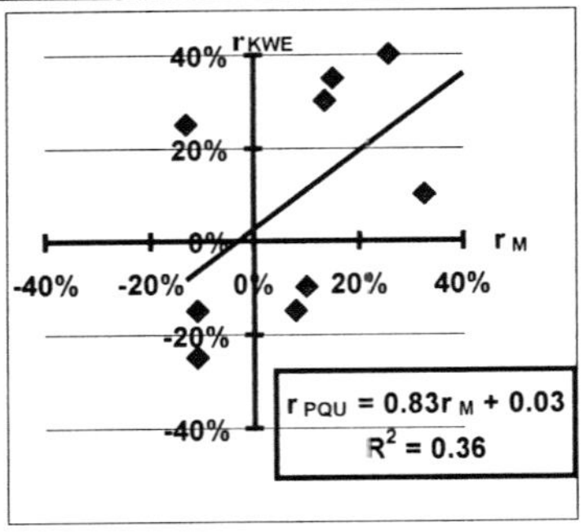

4 - 35

What is beta for PQU?

- The regression line, and hence beta, can be found using a calculator with a regression function or a spreadsheet program. In this example, b = 0.83.

4 - 36

Calculating Beta in Practice

- Many analysts use the S&P 500 to find the market return.
- Analysts typically use four or five years' of monthly returns to establish the regression line.
- Some analysts use 52 weeks of weekly returns.

4 - 37

How is beta interpreted?

- If b = 1.0, stock has average risk.
- If b > 1.0, stock is riskier than average.
- If b < 1.0, stock is less risky than average.
- Most stocks have betas in the range of 0.5 to 1.5.
- Can a stock have a negative beta?

4 - 38

Finding Beta Estimates on the Web

- Go to www.thomsonfn.com.
- Enter the ticker symbol for a "Stock Quote", such as IBM or Dell, then click GO.
- When the quote comes up, select Company Earnings, then GO.

4 - 39

Expected Return versus Market Risk

Security	Expected return	Risk, b
Alta	17.4%	1.29
Market	15.0	1.00
Am. Foam	13.8	0.68
T-bills	8.0	0.00
Repo Men	1.7	-0.86

- Which of the alternatives is best?

4 - 40

Use the SML to calculate each alternative's required return.

- The Security Market Line (SML) is part of the Capital Asset Pricing Model (CAPM).
- SML: $r_i = r_{RF} + (RP_M)b_i$.
- Assume $r_{RF} = 8\%$; $\hat{r}_M = r_M = 15\%$.
- $RP_M = (r_M - r_{RF}) = 15\% - 8\% = 7\%$.

4 - 41

Required Rates of Return

$$
\begin{aligned}
r_{Alta} &= 8.0\% + (7\%)(1.29) \\
&= 8.0\% + 9.0\% &= 17.0\%. \\
r_M &= 8.0\% + (7\%)(1.00) &= 15.0\%. \\
r_{Am.\,F.} &= 8.0\% + (7\%)(0.68) &= 12.8\%. \\
r_{T\text{-}bill} &= 8.0\% + (7\%)(0.00) &= 8.0\%. \\
r_{Repo} &= 8.0\% + (7\%)(-0.86) &= 2.0\%.
\end{aligned}
$$

4 - 42

Expected versus Required Returns

	$\hat{r}$	r	
Alta	17.4%	17.0%	Undervalued
Market	15.0	15.0	Fairly valued
Am. F.	13.8	12.8	Undervalued
T-bills	8.0	8.0	Fairly valued
Repo	1.7	2.0	Overvalued

4 - 43

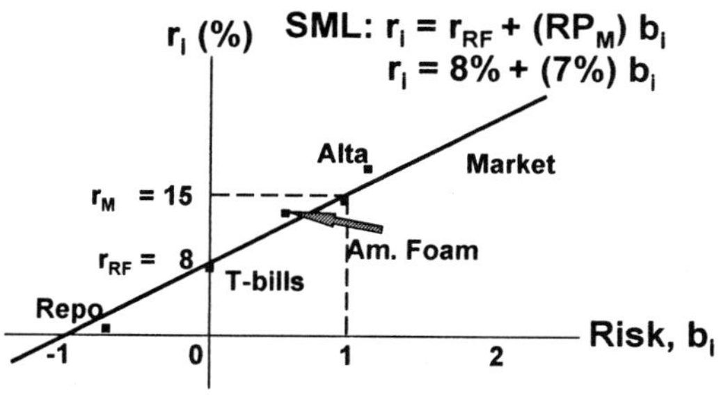

SML and Investment Alternatives

4 - 44

Calculate beta for a portfolio with 50% Alta and 50% Repo

$$b_p = \text{Weighted average}$$
$$= 0.5(b_{Alta}) + 0.5(b_{Repo})$$
$$= 0.5(1.29) + 0.5(-0.86)$$
$$= 0.22.$$

4 - 45

What is the required rate of return on the Alta/Repo portfolio?

$$r_p = \text{Weighted average } r$$
$$= 0.5(17\%) + 0.5(2\%) = 9.5\%.$$

Or use SML:

$$r_p = r_{RF} + (RP_M)\, b_p$$
$$= 8.0\% + 7\%(0.22) = 9.5\%.$$

4 - 46

Impact of Inflation Change on SML

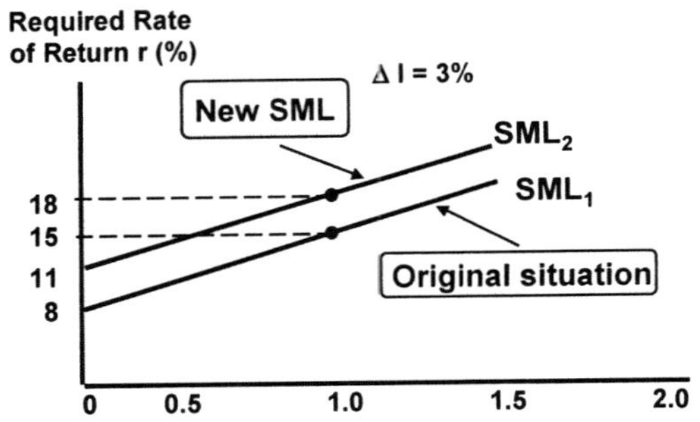

4 - 47

Impact of Risk Aversion Change

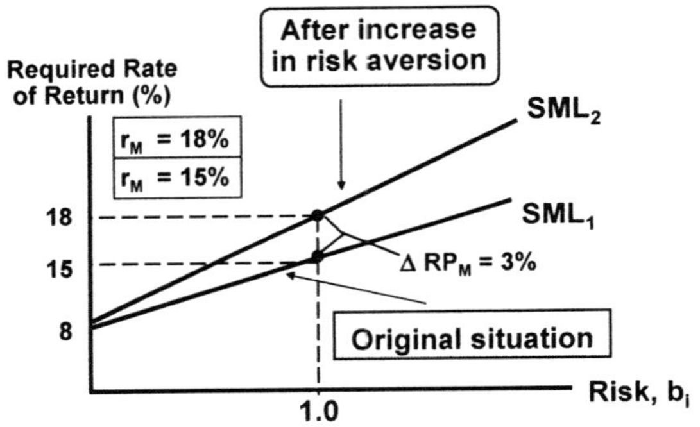

4 - 48

Has the CAPM been completely confirmed or refuted through empirical tests?

- No. The statistical tests have problems that make empirical verification or rejection virtually impossible.
  - Investors' required returns are based on future risk, but betas are calculated with historical data.
  - Investors may be concerned about both stand-alone and market risk.

5 - 1

CHAPTER 5
Risk and Return: Portfolio Theory and Asset Pricing Models

- **Portfolio Theory**
- **Capital Asset Pricing Model (CAPM)**
  - **Efficient frontier**
  - **Capital Market Line (CML)**
  - **Security Market Line (SML)**
  - **Beta calculation**
- **Arbitrage pricing theory**
- **Fama-French 3-factor model**

5 - 2

Portfolio Theory

- **Suppose Asset A has an expected return of 10 percent and a standard deviation of 20 percent. Asset B has an expected return of 16 percent and a standard deviation of 40 percent. If the correlation between A and B is 0.6, what are the expected return and standard deviation for a portfolio comprised of 30 percent Asset A and 70 percent Asset B?**

5 - 3

Portfolio Expected Return

$$\begin{aligned}\hat{r}_P &= w_A \hat{r}_A + (1 - w_A)\hat{r}_B \\ &= 0.3(0.1) + 0.7(0.16) \\ &= 0.142 = 14.2\%.\end{aligned}$$

Portfolio Standard Deviation

$$\sigma_p = \sqrt{W_A^2\sigma_A^2 + (1-W_A)^2\sigma_B^2 + 2W_A(1-W_A)\rho_{AB}\sigma_A\sigma_B}$$
$$= \sqrt{0.3^2(0.2^2) + 0.7^2(0.4^2) + 2(0.3)(0.7)(0.4)(0.2)(0.4)}$$
$$= 0.309$$

Attainable Portfolios: ρ_{AB} = 0.4

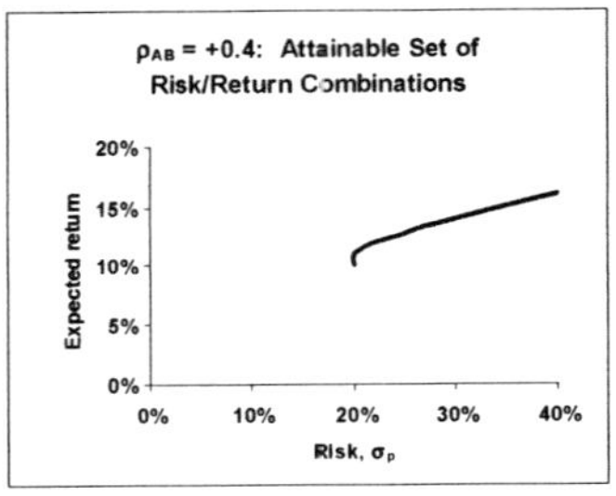

Attainable Portfolios: ρ_{AB} = +1

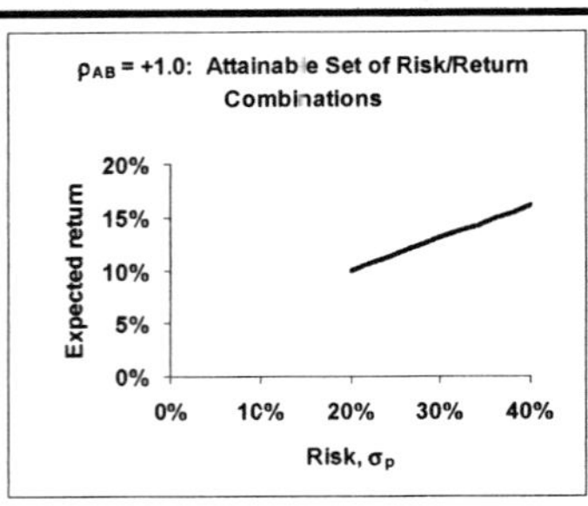

5 - 7

Attainable Portfolios: ρ_{AB} = -1

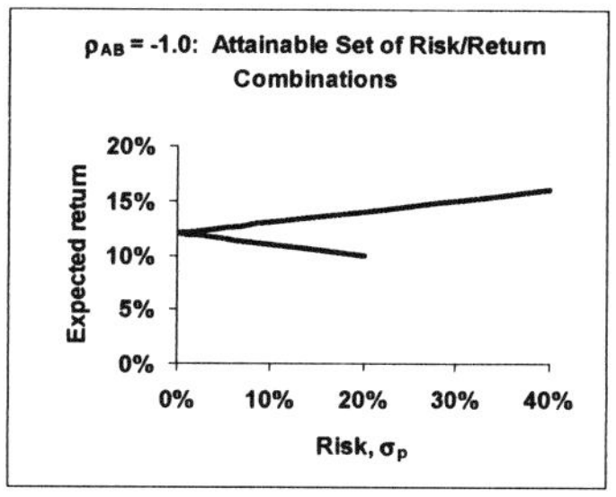

5 - 8

Attainable Portfolios with Risk-Free Asset (Expected risk-free return = 5%)

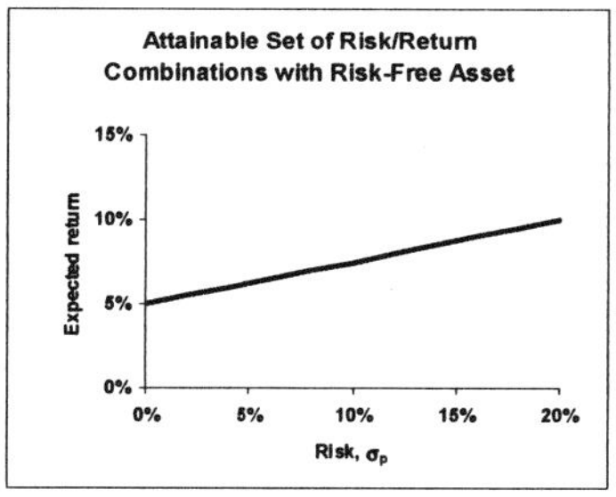

5 - 9

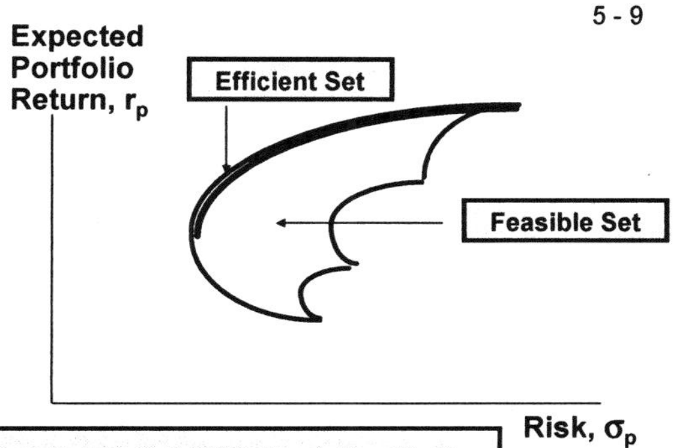

Feasible and Efficient Portfolios

5 - 10

- The feasible set of portfolios represents all portfolios that can be constructed from a given set of stocks.
- An efficient portfolio is one that offers:
  - the most return for a given amount of risk, or
  - the least risk for a give amount of return.
- The collection of efficient portfolios is called the efficient set or efficient frontier.

5 - 11

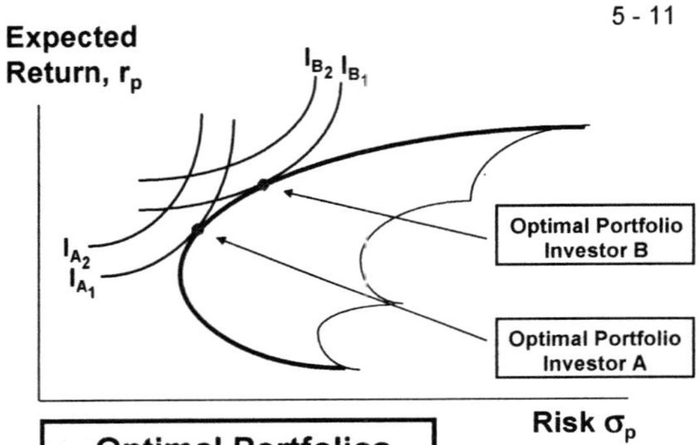

Optimal Portfolios

5 - 12

- Indifference curves reflect an investor's attitude toward risk as reflected in his or her risk/return tradeoff function. They differ among investors because of differences in risk aversion.
- An investor's optimal portfolio is defined by the tangency point between the efficient set and the investor's indifference curve.

5 - 13

What is the CAPM?

- The CAPM is an equilibrium model that specifies the relationship between risk and required rate of return for assets held in well-diversified portfolios.
- It is based on the premise that only one factor affects risk.
- What is that factor?

5 - 14

What are the assumptions of the CAPM?

- Investors all think in terms of a single holding period.
- All investors have identical expectations.
- Investors can borrow or lend unlimited amounts at the risk-free rate.

(More...)

5 - 15

- All assets are perfectly divisible.
- There are no taxes and no transactions costs.
- All investors are price takers, that is, investors' buying and selling won't influence stock prices.
- Quantities of all assets are given and fixed.

5 - 16

What impact does r_{RF} have on the efficient frontier?

- When a risk-free asset is added to the feasible set, investors can create portfolios that combine this asset with a portfolio of risky assets.
- The straight line connecting r_{RF} with M, the tangency point between the line and the old efficient set, becomes the new efficient frontier.

5 - 17

Efficient Set with a Risk-Free Asset

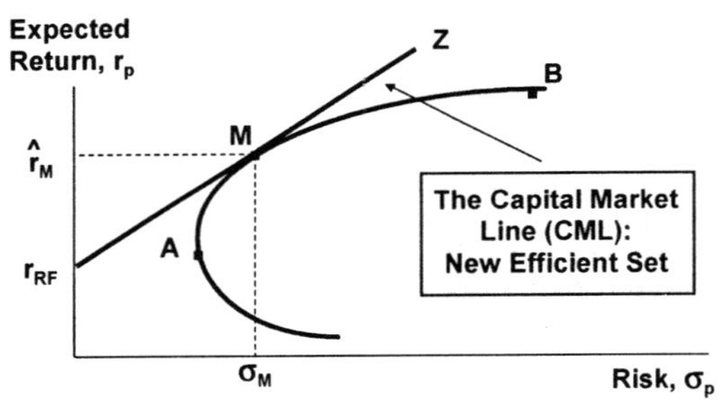

5 - 18

What is the Capital Market Line?

- The Capital Market Line (CML) is all linear combinations of the risk-free asset and Portfolio M.
- Portfolios below the CML are inferior.
  - The CML defines the new efficient set.
  - All investors will choose a portfolio on the CML.

5 - 19

The CML Equation

$$\hat{r}_p = r_{RF} + \left[\frac{\hat{r}_M - r_{RF}}{\sigma_M} \right] \sigma_p.$$

Intercept (r_{RF}) — Slope (bracketed term) — Risk measure (σ_p)

5 - 20

What does the CML tell us?

- The expected rate of return on any efficient portfolio is equal to the risk-free rate plus a risk premium.
- The optimal portfolio for any investor is the point of tangency between the CML and the investor's indifference curves.

5 - 21

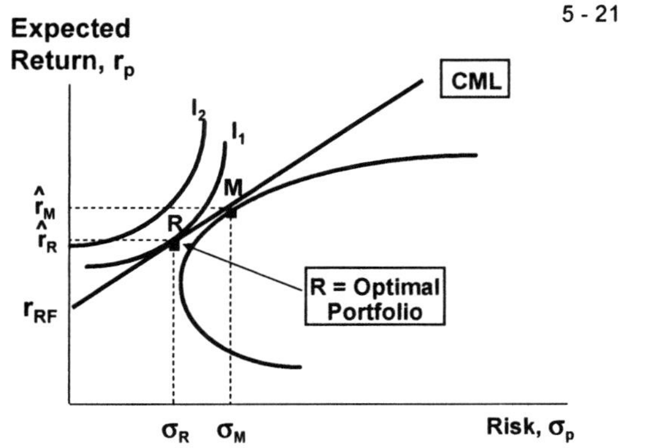

5 - 22

What is the Security Market Line (SML)?

- The CML gives the risk/return relationship for efficient portfolios.
- The Security Market Line (SML), also part of the CAPM, gives the risk/return relationship for individual stocks.

5 - 23

The SML Equation

- The measure of risk used in the SML is the beta coefficient of company i, b_i.
- The SML equation:

$$r_i = r_{RF} + (RP_M)\ b_i$$

5 - 24

How are betas calculated?

- Run a regression line of past returns on Stock i versus returns on the market.
- The regression line is called the characteristic line.
- The slope coefficient of the characteristic line is defined as the beta coefficient.

5 - 25

Illustration of beta calculation

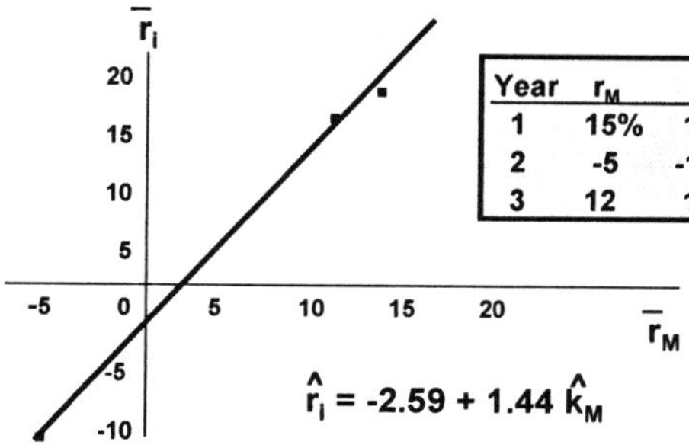

Year	r_M	r_i
1	15%	18%
2	-5	-10
3	12	16

$$\hat{r}_i = -2.59 + 1.44\ \hat{k}_M$$

5 - 26

Method of Calculation

- Analysts use a computer with statistical or spreadsheet software to perform the regression.
  - At least 3 year's of monthly returns or 1 year's of weekly returns are used.
  - Many analysts use 5 years of monthly returns.

(More...)

5 - 27

- If beta = 1.0, stock is average risk.
- If beta > 1.0, stock is riskier than average.
- If beta < 1.0, stock is less risky than average.
- Most stocks have betas in the range of 0.5 to 1.5.

Interpreting Regression Results

- The R^2 measures the percent of a stock's variance that is explained by the market. The typical R^2 is:
  - 0.3 for an individual stock
  - over 0.9 for a well diversified portfolio

Interpreting Regression Results (Continued)

- The 95% confidence interval shows the range in which we are 95% sure that the true value of beta lies. The typical range is:
  - from about 0.5 to 1.5 for an individual stock
  - from about .92 to 1.08 for a well diversified portfolio

What is the relationship between stand-alone, market, and diversifiable risk.

$$\sigma_j^2 = b_j^2 \sigma_M^2 + \sigma_{e_j}^2.$$

σ_j^2 = variance
= stand-alone risk of Stock j.

$b_j^2 \sigma_M^2$ = market risk of Stock j.

$\sigma_{e_j}^2$ = variance of error term
= diversifiable risk of Stock j.

5 - 31

What are two potential tests that can be conducted to verify the CAPM?

- Beta stability tests
- Tests based on the slope of the SML

5 - 32

Tests of the SML indicate:

- A more-or-less linear relationship between realized returns and market risk.
- Slope is less than predicted.
- Irrelevance of diversifiable risk specified in the CAPM model can be questioned.

(More...)

5 - 33

- Betas of individual securities are not good estimators of future risk.
- Betas of portfolios of 10 or more randomly selected stocks are reasonably stable.
- Past portfolio betas are good estimates of future portfolio volatility.

5 - 34

Are there problems with the CAPM tests?

- Yes.
  - Richard Roll questioned whether it was even conceptually possible to test the CAPM.
  - Roll showed that it is virtually impossible to prove investors behave in accordance with CAPM theory.

5 - 35

What are our conclusions regarding the CAPM?

- It is impossible to verify.
- Recent studies have questioned its validity.
- Investors seem to be concerned with both market risk and stand-alone risk. Therefore, the SML may not produce a correct estimate of r_i.

(More...)

5 - 36

- CAPM/SML concepts are based on expectations, yet betas are calculated using historical data. A company's historical data may not reflect investors' expectations about future riskiness.
- Other models are being developed that will one day replace the CAPM, but it still provides a good framework for thinking about risk and return.

5 - 37

What is the difference between the CAPM and the Arbitrage Pricing Theory (APT)?

- The CAPM is a single factor model.
- The APT proposes that the relationship between risk and return is more complex and may be due to multiple factors such as GDP growth, expected inflation, tax rate changes, and dividend yield.

5 - 38

Required Return for Stock i under the APT

$$r_i = r_{RF} + (r_1 - r_{RF})b_1 + (r_2 - r_{RF})b_2 + \ldots + (r_j - r_{RF})b_j.$$

r_j = required rate of return on a portfolio sensitive only to economic Factor j.

b_j = sensitivity of Stock i to economic Factor j.

5 - 39

What is the status of the APT?

- The APT is being used for some real world applications.
- Its acceptance has been slow because the model does not specify what factors influence stock returns.
- More research on risk and return models is needed to find a model that is theoretically sound, empirically verified, and easy to use.

5 - 40

Fama-French 3-Factor Model

- Fama and French propose three factors:
  - The excess market return, r_M-r_{RF}.
  - the return on, S, a portfolio of small firms (where size is based on the market value of equity) minus the return on B, a portfolio of big firms. This return is called r_{SMB}, for S minus B.

5 - 41

Fama-French 3-Factor Model (Continued)

- the return on, H, a portfolio of firms with high book-to-market ratios (using market equity and book equity) minus the return on L, a portfolio of firms with low book-to-market ratios. This return is called r_{HML}, for H minus L.

5 - 42

Required Return for Stock i under the Fama-French 3-Factor Model

$r_i = r_{RF} + (r_M - r_{RF})b_i + (r_{SMB})c_i + (r_{HMB})d_i$

b_i = sensitivity of Stock i to the market return.

c_j = sensitivity of Stock i to the size factor.

d_j = sensitivity of Stock i to the book-to-market factor.

5 - 43

Required Return for Stock i: b_i=0.9, r_{RF}=6.8%, the market risk premium is 6.3%, c_i=-0.5, the expected value for the size factor is 4%, d_i=-0.3, and the expected value for the book-to-market factor is 5%.

$r_i = r_{RF} + (r_M - r_{RF})b_i + (r_{SMB})c_i + (r_{HMB})d_i$

$r_i = 6.8\% + (6.3\%)(0.9) + (4\%)(-0.5) + (5\%)(-0.3)$
$= 8.97\%$

5 - 44

CAPM Required Return for Stock i

CAPM:

$r_i = r_{RF} + (r_M - r_{RF})b_i$

$r_i = 6.8\% + (6.3\%)(0.9)$
$= 12.47\%$

Fama-French (previous slide):

$r_i = 8.97\%$

6 - 1

CHAPTER 6
Bonds and Their Valuation

- Key features of bonds
- Bond valuation
- Measuring yield
- Assessing risk

6 - 2

Key Features of a Bond

1. Par value: Face amount; paid at maturity. Assume $1,000.

2. Coupon interest rate: Stated interest rate. Multiply by par value to get dollars of interest. Generally fixed.

(More...)

6 - 3

3. Maturity: Years until bond must be repaid. Declines.

4. Issue date: Date when bond was issued.

5. Default risk: Risk that issuer will not make interest or principal payments.

6 - 4

How does adding a call provision affect a bond?

- Issuer can refund if rates decline. That helps the issuer but hurts the investor.
- Therefore, borrowers are willing to pay more, and lenders require more, on callable bonds.
- Most bonds have a deferred call and a declining call premium.

6 - 5

What's a sinking fund?

- Provision to pay off a loan over its life rather than all at maturity.
- Similar to amortization on a term loan.
- Reduces risk to investor, shortens average maturity.
- But not good for investors if rates decline after issuance.

6 - 6

Sinking funds are generally handled in 2 ways

1. Call x% at par per year for sinking fund purposes.
2. Buy bonds on open market.

Company would call if r_d is below the coupon rate and bond sells at a premium. Use open market purchase if r_d is above coupon rate and bond sells at a discount.

6 - 7

Financial Asset Valuation

0	1	2	...	n
r				
Value	CF_1	CF_2		CF_n

$$PV = \frac{CF_1}{(1+r)^1} + \frac{CF_2}{(1+r)^2} + \dots + \frac{CF_n}{(1+r)^n}.$$

6 - 8

- **The discount rate (r_i) is the <u>opportunity cost of capital</u>, i.e., the rate that could be earned on alternative investments of equal risk.**

$$r_i = r^* + IP + LP + MRP + DRP$$

for debt securities.

6 - 9

What's the value of a 10-year, 10% coupon bond if r_d = 10%?

0	1	2	...	10
10%				
V = ?	100	100		100 + 1,000

$$V_B = \frac{\$100}{(1+r_d)^1} + \dots + \frac{\$100}{(1+r_d)^{10}} + \frac{\$1,000}{(1+r_d)^{10}}$$

$= \$90.91 + \dots + \$38.55 + \$385.54$
$= \$1,000.$

6 - 10

The bond consists of a 10-year, 10% annuity of $100/year plus a $1,000 lump sum at t = 10:

PV annuity	=	$ 614.46
PV maturity value	=	385.54
Value of bond	=	$1,000.00

INPUTS	10	10		100	1000
	N	I/YR	PV	PMT	FV
OUTPUT			-1,000		

6 - 11

What would happen if expected inflation rose by 3%, causing r = 13%?

INPUTS	10	13		100	1000
	N	I/YR	PV	PMT	FV
OUTPUT			-837.21		

When r_d rises, above the coupon rate, the bond's value falls below par, so it sells at a discount.

6 - 12

What would happen if inflation fell, and r_d declined to 7%?

INPUTS	10	7		100	1000
	N	I/YR	PV	PMT	FV
OUTPUT			-1,210.71		

If coupon rate > r_d, price rises above par, and bond sells at a premium.

6 - 13

Suppose the bond was issued 20 years ago and now has 10 years to maturity. What would happen to its value over time if the required rate of return remained at 10%, or at 13%, or at 7%?

6 - 14

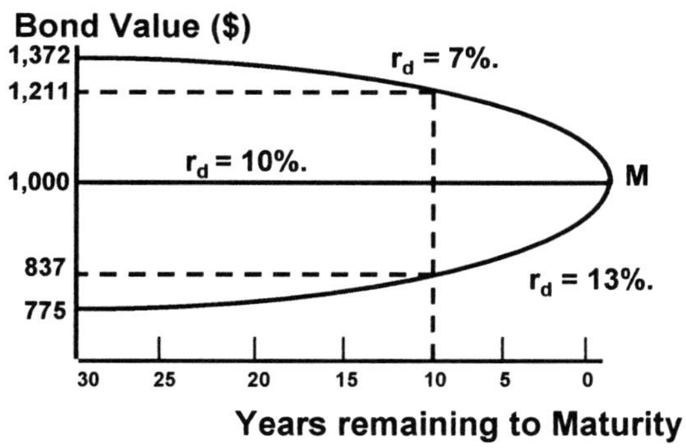

6 - 15

- At maturity, the value of any bond must equal its par value.
- The value of a premium bond would decrease to $1,000.
- The value of a discount bond would increase to $1,000.
- A par bond stays at $1,000 if r_d remains constant.

6 - 16

What's "yield to maturity"?

- YTM is the rate of return earned on a bond held to maturity. Also called "promised yield."

6 - 17

What's the YTM on a 10-year, 9% annual coupon, $1,000 par value bond that sells for $887?

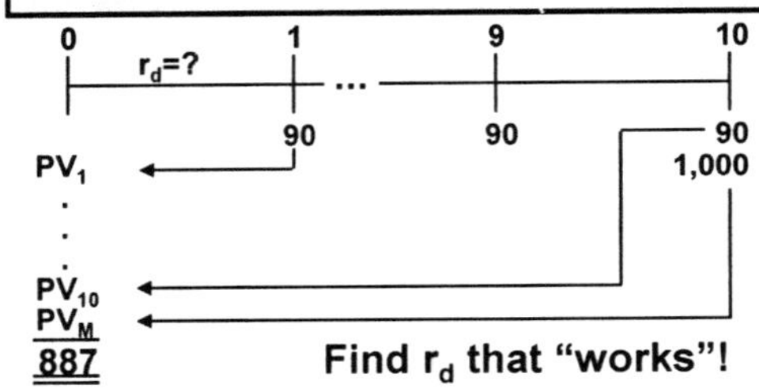

6 - 18

Find r_d

$$V_B = \frac{INT}{(1+r_d)^1} + \cdots + \frac{INT}{(1+r_d)^N} + \frac{M}{(1+r_d)^N}$$

$$887 = \frac{90}{(1+r_d)^1} + \cdots + \frac{90}{(1+r_d)^{10}} + \frac{1{,}000}{(1+r_d)^{10}}$$

	N	I/YR	PV	PMT	FV
INPUTS	10		-887	90	1000
OUTPUT		10.91			

6 - 19

- If coupon rate < r_d, bond sells at a discount.
- If coupon rate = r_d, bond sells at its par value.
- If coupon rate > r_d, bond sells at a premium.
- If r_d rises, price falls.
- Price = par at maturity.

6 - 20

Find YTM if price were $1,134.20.

	10		-1134.2	90	1000
INPUTS	N	I/YR	PV	PMT	FV
OUTPUT		7.08			

Sells at a premium. Because coupon = 9% > r_d = 7.08%, bond's value > par.

6 - 21

Definitions

$$\text{Current yield} = \frac{\text{Annual coupon pmt}}{\text{Current price}}$$

$$\text{Capital gains yield} = \frac{\text{Change in price}}{\text{Beginning price}}$$

$$\text{Exp total return} = \text{YTM} = \text{Exp Curr yld} + \text{Exp cap gains yld}$$

6 - 22

Find current yield and capital gains yield for a 9%, 10-year bond when the bond sells for $887 and YTM = 10.91%.

$$\text{Current yield} = \frac{\$90}{\$887}$$

$$= 0.1015 = \boxed{10.15\%.}$$

6 - 23

YTM = Current yield + Capital gains yield.

Cap gains yield = YTM - Current yield
= 10.91% - 10.15%
= **0.76%.**

Could also find values in Years 1 and 2, get difference, and divide by value in Year 1. Same answer.

6 - 24

What's interest rate (or price) risk? Does a 1-year or 10-year 10% bond have more risk?

Interest rate risk: Rising r_d causes bond's price to fall.

r_d	1-year	Change	10-year	Change
5%	$1,048		$1,386	
		4.8%		38.6%
10%	1,000		1,000	
		4.4%		25.1%
15%	956		749	

6 - 25

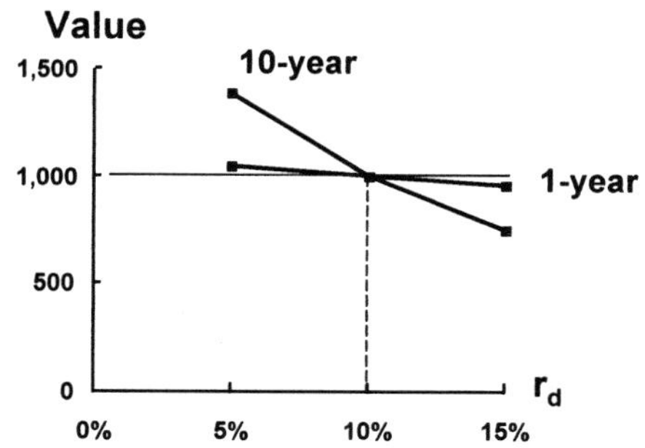

6 - 26

What is reinvestment rate risk?

The risk that CFs will have to be reinvested in the future at lower rates, reducing income.

Illustration: Suppose you just won $500,000 playing the lottery. You'll invest the money and live off the interest. You buy a 1-year bond with a YTM of 10%.

6 - 27

Year 1 income = $50,000. At year-end get back $500,000 to reinvest.

If rates fall to 3%, income will drop from $50,000 to $15,000. Had you bought 30-year bonds, income would have remained constant.

6 - 28

- Long-term bonds: High interest rate risk, low reinvestment rate risk.
- Short-term bonds: Low interest rate risk, high reinvestment rate risk.
- Nothing is riskless!

6 - 29

True or False: "All 10-year bonds have the same price and reinvestment rate risk."

False! Low coupon bonds have less reinvestment rate risk but more price risk than high coupon bonds.

6 - 30

Semiannual Bonds

1. Multiply years by 2 to get periods = 2n.
2. Divide nominal rate by 2 to get periodic rate = $r_d/2$.
3. Divide annual INT by 2 to get PMT = INT/2.

INPUTS	2n	$r_d/2$	OK	INT/2	OK
	N	I/YR	PV	PMT	FV
OUTPUT					

6 - 31

Find the value of 10-year, 10% coupon, semiannual bond if r_d = 13%.

	2(10)	13/2		100/2	
INPUTS	20	6.5		50	1000
	N	I/YR	PV	PMT	FV
OUTPUT			-834.72		

6 - 32

Spreadsheet Functions for Bond Valuation

- See Ch 06 Mini Case.xls for details.
  - PRICE
  - YIELD

6 - 33

You could buy, for $1,000, either a 10%, 10-year, annual payment bond or an equally risky 10%, 10-year semiannual bond. Which would you prefer?

The semiannual bond's EFF% is:

$$EFF\% = \left(1+\frac{i_{Nom}}{m}\right)^m - 1 = \left(1+\frac{0.10}{2}\right)^2 - 1 = 10.25\%.$$

EFR

10.25% > 10% EFF% on annual bond, so buy semiannual bond.

6 - 34

If $1,000 is the proper price for the semiannual bond, what is the proper price for the annual payment bond?

- Semiannual bond has r_{Nom} = 10%, with EFF% = 10.25%. Should earn same EFF% on annual payment bond, so:

	N	I/YR	PV	PMT	FV
INPUTS	10	10.25		100	1000
OUTPUT			-984.80		

6 - 35

- At a price of $984.80, the annual and semiannual bonds would be in equilibrium, because investors would earn EFF% = 10.25% on either bond.

6 - 36

A 10-year, 10% semiannual coupon, $1,000 par value bond is selling for $1,135.90 with an 8% yield to maturity. It can be called after 5 years at $1,050.

What's the bond's nominal yield to call (YTC)?

	N	I/YR	PV	PMT	FV
INPUTS	10		-1135.9	50	1050
OUTPUT		3.765 x 2 = 7.53%			

6 - 37

r_{Nom} = 7.53% is the rate brokers would quote. Could also calculate EFF% to call:

EFF% = $(1.03765)^2$ - 1 = 7.672%.

This rate could be compared to monthly mortgages, and so on.

6 - 38

If you bought bonds, would you be more likely to earn YTM or YTC?

- Coupon rate = 10% vs. YTC = r_d = 7.53%. Could raise money by selling new bonds which pay 7.53%.
- Could thus replace bonds which pay $100/year with bonds that pay only $75.30/year.
- Investors should expect a call, hence YTC = 7.5%, not YTM = 8%.

6 - 39

- In general, if a bond sells at a premium, then (1) coupon > r_d, so (2) a call is likely.
- So, expect to earn:
  - YTC on premium bonds.
  - YTM on par & discount bonds.

6 - 40

- Disney recently issued 100-year bonds with a YTM of 7.5%--this represents the promised return. The expected return was less than 7.5% when the bonds were issued.
- If issuer defaults, investors receive less than the promised return. Therefore, the expected return on corporate and municipal bonds is less than the promised return.

6 - 41

Bond Ratings Provide One Measure of Default Risk

	Investment Grade				Junk Bonds			
Moody's	Aaa	Aa	A	Baa	Ba	B	Caa	C
S&P	AAA	AA	A	BBB	BB	B	CCC	D

6 - 42

What factors affect default risk and bond ratings?

- Financial performance
  - Debt ratio
  - Coverage ratios, such as interest coverage ratio or EBITDA coverage ratio
  - Current ratios

(More...)

6 - 43

- Provisions in the bond contract
  - Secured versus unsecured debt
  - Senior versus subordinated debt
  - Guarantee provisions
  - Sinking fund provisions
  - Debt maturity

(More...)

6 - 44

- Other factors
  - Earnings stability
  - Regulatory environment
  - Potential product liability
  - Accounting policies

6 - 45

Bankruptcy

- Two main chapters of Federal Bankruptcy Act:
  - Chapter 11, Reorganization
  - Chapter 7, Liquidation
- Typically, company wants Chapter 11, creditors may prefer Chapter 7.

6 - 46

- If company can't meet its obligations, it files under Chapter 11. That stops creditors from foreclosing, taking assets, and shutting down the business.
- Company has 120 days to file a reorganization plan.
  - Court appoints a "trustee" to supervise reorganization.
  - Management usually stays in control.

6 - 47

- Company must demonstrate in its reorganization plan that it is "worth more alive than dead."

Otherwise, judge will order liquidation under Chapter 7.

6 - 48

- If the company is liquidated, here's the payment priority:
  1. Secured creditors from sales of secured assets.
  2. Trustee's costs
  3. Wages, subject to limits
  4. Taxes
  5. Unfunded pension liabilities
  6. Unsecured creditors
  7. Preferred stock
  8. Common stock

6 - 49

- In a liquidation, unsecured creditors generally get zero. This makes them more willing to participate in reorganization even though their claims are greatly scaled back.
- Various groups of creditors vote on the reorganization plan. If both the majority of the creditors and the judge approve, company "emerges" from bankruptcy with lower debts, reduced interest charges, and a chance for success.

7 - 1

CHAPTER 7
Stocks and Their Valuation

- Features of common stock
- Determining common stock values
- Efficient markets
- Preferred stock

7 - 2

Common Stock: Owners, Directors, and Managers

- Represents ownership.
- Ownership implies control.
- Stockholders elect directors.
- Directors hire management.
- Since managers are "agents" of shareholders, their goal should be: Maximize stock price.

7 - 3

What's classified stock? How might classified stock be used?

- Classified stock has special provisions.
- Could classify existing stock as founders' shares, with voting rights but dividend restrictions.
- New shares might be called "Class A" shares, with voting restrictions but full dividend rights.

don't give up total control of company = "classified stock"

7 - 4

What is tracking stock?

- The dividends of tracking stock are tied to a particular division, rather than the company as a whole.
  - Investors can separately value the divisions.
  - Its easier to compensate division managers with the tracking stock.
- But tracking stock usually has no voting rights, and the financial disclosure for the division is not as regulated as for the company.

7 - 5

When is a stock sale an initial public offering (IPO)?

- A firm "goes public" through an IPO when the stock is first offered to the public.
- Prior to an IPO, shares are typically owned by the firm's managers, key employees, and, in many situations, venture capital providers.

IPOs are hard to buy

7 - 6

What is a seasoned equity offering (SEO)?

- A seasoned equity offering occurs when a company with public stock issues additional shares.
- After an IPO or SEO, the stock trades in the secondary market, such as the NYSE or Nasdaq.

7 - 7

Different Approaches for Valuing Common Stock

- Dividend growth model
- Using the multiples of comparable firms
- Free cash flow method (covered in Chapter 15)

7 - 8

Stock Value = PV of Dividends

$$\hat{P}_0 = \frac{D_1}{(1+r_s)^1} + \frac{D_2}{(1+r_s)^2} + \frac{D_3}{(1+r_s)^3} + \ldots + \frac{D_\infty}{(1+r_s)^\infty}$$

What is a constant growth stock?

One whose dividends are expected to grow forever at a constant rate, g.

7 - 9

For a constant growth stock,

$$D_1 = D_0(1+g)^1$$
$$D_2 = D_0(1+g)^2$$
$$D_t = D_t(1+g)^t$$

If g is constant, then:

$$\hat{P}_0 = \frac{D_0(1+g)}{r_s - g} = \frac{D_1}{r_s - g}$$

company that is expected to grow

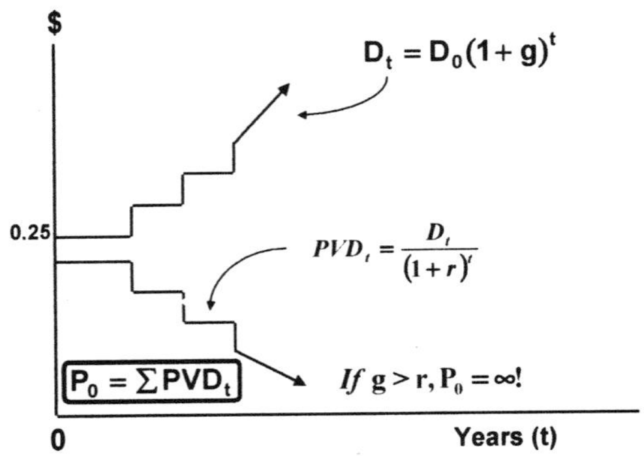

What happens if $g > r_s$?

$$\hat{P}_0 = \frac{D_1}{r_s - g} \text{ requires } r_s > g.$$

- If $r_s < g$, get negative stock price, which is nonsense.
- We can't use model unless (1) $g < r_s$ and (2) g is expected to be constant forever. Because g must be a long-term growth rate, it cannot be $> r_s$.

Assume beta = 1.2, r_{RF} = 7%, and RP_M = 5%. What is the required rate of return on the firm's stock?

Use the SML to calculate r_s:

$$r_s = r_{RF} + (RP_M)b_{Firm}$$
$$= 7\% + (5\%)(1.2)$$
$$= 13\%.$$

7 - 13

D_0 was \$2.00 and g is a constant 6%. Find the expected dividends for the next 3 years, and their PVs. r_s = 13%.

0 (g=6%)	1	2	3	4
D_0=2.00	2.12	2.2472	2.3820	

Discounted at 13%:

1.8761 ← 2.12

1.7599 ← 2.2472

1.6508 ← 2.3820

7 - 14

What's the stock's market value? D_0 = 2.00, r_s = 13%, g = 6%.

Constant growth model:

$$\hat{P}_0 = \frac{D_0(1+g)}{r_s - g} = \frac{D_1}{r_s - g}$$

$$= \frac{\$2.12}{0.13 - 0.06} = \frac{\$2.12}{0.07} \ \$30.29.$$

7 - 15

What is the stock's market value one year from now, $\hat{P}_1$?

- D_1 will have been paid, so expected dividends are D_2, D_3, D_4 and so on. Thus,

$$P_1 = \frac{D_2}{r_s - g}$$

$$= \frac{\$2.2427}{0.07} = \$32.10$$

7 - 16

Find the expected dividend yield and capital gains yield during the first year.

$$\text{Dividend yield} = \frac{D_1}{P_0} = \frac{\$2.12}{\$30.29} = 7.0\%.$$

$$\text{CG Yield} = \frac{\hat{P}_1 - P_0}{P_0} = \frac{\$32.10 - \$30.29}{\$30.29}$$

$$= 6.0\%.$$

7 - 17

Find the total return during the first year.

- Total return = Dividend yield + Capital gains yield.
- Total return = 7% + 6% = 13%.
- Total return = 13% = r_s.
- For constant growth stock:

  Capital gains yield = 6% = g.

7 - 18

Rearrange model to rate of return form:

$$\hat{P}_0 = \frac{D_1}{r_s - g} \text{ to } \hat{r}_s = \frac{D_1}{P_0} + g.$$

Then, $\hat{r}_s$ = \$2.12/\$30.29 + 0.06
= 0.07 + 0.06 = 13%.

7 - 19

What would P_0 be if g = 0?

The dividend stream would be a perpetuity.

0	r_s=13%	1	2	3
		2.00	2.00	2.00

$$\hat{P}_0 = \frac{PMT}{r} = \frac{\$2.00}{0.13} = \$15.38.$$

7 - 20

If we have supernormal growth of 30% for 3 years, then a long-run constant g = 6%, what is $\hat{P}_0$? r is still 13%.

- **Can no longer use constant growth model.**
- **However, growth becomes constant after 3 years.**

7 - 21

Nonconstant growth followed by constant growth:

0		1		2		3		4
	r_s=13%, g = 30%		g = 30%		g = 30%		g = 6%	
D_0 = 2.00		2.60		3.38		4.394		4.6576

2.3009 ← 2.60

2.6470 ← 3.38

3.0453 ← 4.394

46.1135 ← $\hat{P}_3 = \frac{\$4.6576}{0.13 - 0.06} = \$66.5371$

54.1067 = $\hat{P}_0$

7 - 22

What is the expected dividend yield and capital gains yield at t = 0? At t = 4?

At t = 0:

$$\text{Dividend yield} = \frac{D_1}{P_0} = \frac{\$2.60}{\$54.11} = 4.8\%.$$

CG Yield = 13.0% - 4.8% = 8.2%.

(More...)

7 - 23

- During nonconstant growth, dividend yield and capital gains yield are not constant.
- If current growth is greater than g, current capital gains yield is greater than g.
- After t = 3, g = constant = 6%, so the t t = 4 capital gains gains yield = 6%.
- Because r_s = 13%, the t = 4 dividend yield = 13% - 6% = 7%.

7 - 24

Is the stock price based on short-term growth?

- The current stock price is \$54.11.
- The PV of dividends beyond year 3 is \$46.11 ($\hat{P}_3$ discounted back to t = 0).
- The percentage of stock price due to "long-term" dividends is:

$$\frac{\$46.11}{\$54.11} = 85.2\%.$$

7 - 25

If most of a stock's value is due to long-term cash flows, why do so many managers focus on quarterly earnings?

- Sometimes changes in quarterly earnings are a signal of future changes in cash flows. This would affect the current stock price.
- Sometimes managers have bonuses tied to quarterly earnings.

more important to focus on long term

7 - 26

Suppose g = 0 for t = 1 to 3, and then g is a constant 6%. What is $\hat{P}_0$?

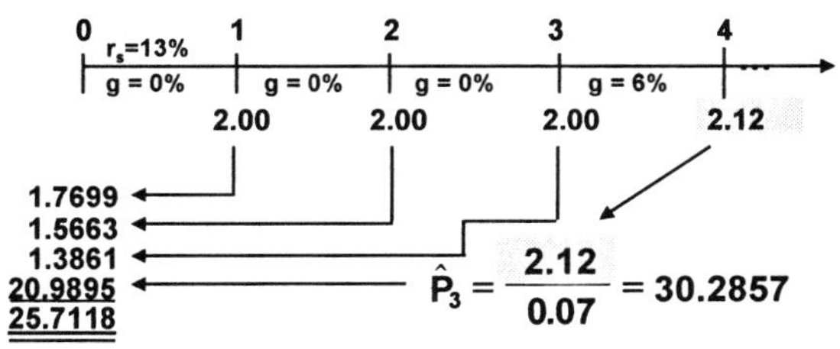

7 - 27

What is dividend yield and capital gains yield at t = 0 and at t = 3?

$$t = 0: \frac{D_1}{P_0} = \frac{2.00}{\$25.72} = 7.8\%.$$

CGY = 13.0% - 7.8% = 5.2%.

t = 3: Now have constant growth with g = capital gains yield = 6% and dividend yield = 7%.

7 - 28

If g = -6%, would anyone buy the stock? If so, at what price?

Firm still has earnings and still pays dividends, so $\hat{P}_0 > 0$:

$$\hat{P}_0 = \frac{D_0(1+g)}{r_s - g} = \frac{D_1}{r_s - g}$$

$$= \frac{\$2.00(0.94)}{0.13 - (-0.06)} = \frac{\$1.88}{0.19} = \$9.89.$$

7 - 29

What are the annual dividend and capital gains yield?

Capital gains yield = g = -6.0%.

Dividend yield = 13.0% - (-6.0%)
= 19.0%.

Both yields are constant over time, with the high dividend yield (19%) offsetting the negative capital gains yield.

7 - 30

Using the Stock Price Multiples to Estimate Stock Price

- Analysts often use the P/E multiple (the price per share divided by the earnings per share) or the P/CF multiple (price per share divided by cash flow per share, which is the earnings per share plus the dividends per share) to value stocks.
- Example:
  - Estimate the average P/E ratio of comparable firms. This is the P/E multiple.
  - Multiply this average P/E ratio by the expected earnings of the company to estimate its stock price.

7 - 31

Using Entity Multiples

- The entity value (V) is:
  - the market value of equity (# shares of stock multiplied by the price per share)
  - plus the value of debt.
- Pick a measure, such as EBITDA, Sales, Customers, Eyeballs, etc.
- Calculate the average entity ratio for a sample of comparable firms. For example,
  - V/EBITDA
  - V/Customers

7 - 32

Using Entity Multiples (Continued)

- Find the entity value of the firm in question. For example,
  - Multiply the firm's sales by the V/Sales multiple.
  - Multiply the firm's # of customers by the V/Customers ratio
- The result is the total value of the firm.
- Subtract the firm's debt to get the total value of equity.
- Divide by the number of shares to get the price per share.

7 - 33

Problems with Market Multiple Methods

- It is often hard to find comparable firms.
- The average ratio for the sample of comparable firms often has a wide range.
  - For example, the average P/E ratio might be 20, but the range could be from 10 to 50. How do you know whether your firm should be compared to the low, average, or high performers?

7 - 34

Why are stock prices volatile?

$$\hat{P}_0 = \frac{D_1}{r_s - g}$$

- $r_s = r_{RF} + (RP_M)b_i$ could change.
  - Inflation expectations
  - Risk aversion
  - Company risk
- g could change.

7 - 35

Stock value vs. changes in r_s and g

D_1 = \$2, r_s = 10%, and g = 5%:
$P_0 = D_1 / (r_s - g)$ = \$2 / (0.10 - 0.05) = \$40.

What if r_s or g change?

r_s	g 4%	g 5%	g 6%
9%	40.00	50.00	66.67
10%	33.33	40.00	50.00
11%	28.57	33.33	40.00

Input changes will effect the value of the stock

7 - 36

Are volatile stock prices consistent with rational pricing?

- Small changes in expected g and r_s cause large changes in stock prices.
- As new information arrives, investors continually update their estimates of g and r_s.
- If stock prices aren't volatile, then this means there isn't a good flow of information.

7 - 37

What is market equilibrium?

In equilibrium, stock prices are stable. There is no general tendency for people to buy versus to sell.

The expected price, $\hat{P}$, must equal the actual price, P. In other words, the fundamental value must be the same as the price.

(More...)

7 - 38

In equilibrium, expected returns must equal required returns:

SML line

$$\hat{r}_s = D_1/P_0 + g = r_s = r_{RF} + (r_M - r_{RF})b.$$

7 - 39

How is equilibrium established?

If $\hat{r}_s = \frac{\hat{D}_1}{P_0} + g > r_s$, **then P_0 is "too low."**

If the price is lower than the fundamental value, then the stock is a "bargain."

Buy orders will exceed sell orders, the price will be bid up, and D_1/P_0 falls until

$$D_1/P_0 + g = \hat{r}_s = r_s.$$

7 - 40

Why do stock prices change?

$$\hat{P}_0 = \frac{D_1}{r_i - g}$$

- $r_i = r_{RF} + (r_M - r_{RF})b_i$ could change.
  - Inflation expectations
  - Risk aversion
  - Company risk
- g could change.

markets are efficient

7 - 41

What's the Efficient Market Hypothesis (EMH)?

Securities are normally in equilibrium and are "fairly priced." One cannot "beat the market" except through good luck or inside information.

(More…)

7 - 42

1. Weak-form EMH:
   Can't profit by looking at past trends. A recent decline is no reason to think stocks will go up (or down) in the future. Evidence supports weak-form EMH, but "technical analysis" is still used.

7 - 43

2. Semistrong-form EMH:
   All publicly available information is reflected in stock prices, so it doesn't pay to pore over annual reports looking for undervalued stocks. Largely true.

7 - 44

3. Strong-form EMH:
   All information, even inside information, is embedded in stock prices. Not true--insiders can gain by trading on the basis of insider information, but that's illegal.

7 - 45

Markets are generally efficient because:

1. 100,000 or so trained analysts--MBAs, CFAs, and PhDs--work for firms like Fidelity, Merrill, Morgan, and Prudential.
2. These analysts have similar access to data and megabucks to invest.
3. Thus, news is reflected in P_0 almost instantaneously.

7 - 46

Preferred Stock

- Hybrid security.
- Similar to bonds in that preferred stockholders receive a fixed dividend which must be paid before dividends can be paid on common stock.
- However, unlike bonds, preferred stock dividends can be omitted without fear of pushing the firm into bankruptcy.

7 - 47

What's the expected return on preferred stock with V_{ps} = \$50 and annual dividend = \$5?

$$V_{ps} = \$50 = \frac{\$5}{\hat{r}_{ps}}$$

$$\hat{r}_{ps} = \frac{\$5}{\$50} = 0.10 = 10.0\%.$$

8 - 1

CHAPTER 8
Financial Options and Their Valuation

- Financial options
- Black-Scholes Option Pricing Model

8 - 2

What is a financial option?

An option is a contract which gives its holder the right, but not the obligation, to buy (or sell) an asset at some predetermined price within a specified period of time.

8 - 3

What is the single most important characteristic of an option?

- It does not obligate its owner to take any action. It merely gives the owner the right to buy or sell an asset.

8 - 4

Option Terminology

- Call option: An option to buy a specified number of shares of a security within some future period.
- Put option: An option to sell a specified number of shares of a security within some future period.
- Exercise (or strike) price: The price stated in the option contract at which the security can be bought or sold.

8 - 5

- Option price: The market price of the option contract.
- Expiration date: The date the option matures.
- Exercise value: The value of a call option if it were exercised today = Current stock price - Strike price.

  Note: The exercise value is zero if the stock price is less than the strike price.

8 - 6

- Covered option: A call option written against stock held in an investor's portfolio.
- Naked (uncovered) option: An option sold without the stock to back it up.
- In-the-money call: A call whose exercise price is less than the current price of the underlying stock.

8 - 7

- Out-of-the-money call: A call option whose exercise price exceeds the current stock price.
- LEAPS: Long-term Equity AnticiPation Securities that are similar to conventional options except that they are long-term options with maturities of up to 2 1/2 years.

8 - 8

Consider the following data:

Exercise price = $25.

Stock Price	Call Option Price
$25	$ 3.00
30	7.50
35	12.00
40	16.50
45	21.00
50	25.50

8 - 9

Create a table which shows (a) stock price, (b) strike price, (c) exercise value, (d) option price, and (e) premium of option price over the exercise value.

Price of Stock (a)	Strike Price (b)	Exercise Value of Option (a) - (b)
$25.00	$25.00	$0.00
30.00	25.00	5.00
35.00	25.00	10.00
40.00	25.00	15.00
45.00	25.00	20.00
50.00	25.00	25.00

8 - 10

Table (Continued)

Exercise Value of Option (c)	Mkt. Price of Option (d)	Premium (d) - (c)
$ 0.00	$ 3.00	$ 3.00
5.00	7.50	2.50
10.00	12.00	2.00
15.00	16.50	1.50
20.00	21.00	1.00
25.00	25.50	0.50

8 - 11

Call Premium Diagram

8 - 12

What happens to the premium of the option price over the exercise value as the stock price rises?

- The premium of the option price over the exercise value declines as the stock price increases.
- This is due to the declining degree of leverage provided by options as the underlying stock price increases, and the greater loss potential of options at higher option prices.

8 - 13

What are the assumptions of the Black-Scholes Option Pricing Model?

- The stock underlying the call option provides no dividends during the call option's life.
- There are no transactions costs for the sale/purchase of either the stock or the option.
- R_{RF} is known and constant during the option's life.

(More...)

8 - 14

- Security buyers may borrow any fraction of the purchase price at the short-term risk-free rate.
- No penalty for short selling and sellers receive immediately full cash proceeds at today's price.
- Call option can be exercised only on its expiration date.
- Security trading takes place in continuous time, and stock prices move randomly in continuous time.

8 - 15

What are the three equations that make up the OPM?

$$V = P[N(d_1)] - Xe^{-r_{RF}t}[N(d_2)].$$

$$d_1 = \frac{\ln(P/X) + [r_{RF} + (\sigma^2/2)]t}{\sigma\sqrt{t}}.$$

$$d_2 = d_1 - \sigma\sqrt{t}.$$

8 - 16

What is the value of the following call option according to the OPM? Assume: P = \$27; X = \$25; r_{RF} = 6%; t = 0.5 years: σ^2 = 0.11

$V = \$27[N(d_1)] - \$25e^{-(0.06)(0.5)}[N(d_2)].$

$$d_1 = \frac{\ln(\$27/\$25) + [(0.06 + 0.11/2)](0.5)}{(0.3317)(0.7071)}$$

$= 0.5736.$

$d_2 = d_1 - (0.3317)(0.7071) = d_1 - 0.2345$

$= 0.5736 - 0.2345 = 0.3391.$

8 - 17

$N(d_1) = N(0.5736) = 0.5000 + 0.2168$
$= 0.7168.$

$N(d_2) = N(0.3391) = 0.5000 + 0.1327$
$= 0.6327.$

Note: Values obtained from Excel using NORMSDIST function.

$V = \$27(0.7168) - \$25e^{-0.03}(0.6327)$
$= \$19.3536 - \$25(0.97045)(0.6327)$
$= \$4.0036.$

8 - 18

What impact do the following parameters have on a call option's value?

- Current stock price: Call option value increases as the current stock price increases.
- Exercise price: As the exercise price increases, a call option's value decreases.

8 - 19

- Option period: As the expiration date is lengthened, a call option's value increases (more chance of becoming in the money.)
- Risk-free rate: Call option's value tends to increase as r_{RF} increases (reduces the PV of the exercise price).
- Stock return variance: Option value increases with variance of the underlying stock (more chance of becoming in the money).

8 - 20

Put-Call Parity

- Portfolio 1:
  - Put option,
  - Share of stock, P
- Portfolio 2:
  - Call option, V
  - PV of exercise price, X

8 - 21

Payoff at Expiration if P<X

- Portfolio 1:
  - Put: X-P
  - Stock: P
  - Total: X
- Porfolio 2:
  - Call: 0
  - Cash: X
  - Total: X

8 - 22

Payoff at Expiration if P≥X

- Portfolio 1:
  - Put: 0
  - Stock: P
  - Total: P
- Porfolio 2:
  - Call: P-X
  - Cash: X
  - Total: P

8 - 23

Payoffs are Equal, Values Must Be Equal. Put-Call Parity Relationship

Put + Stock = Call + PV of Exercise Price

$$\text{Put} + P = V + Xe^{-r_{RF}t}$$

$$\text{Put} = V - P + Xe^{-r_{RF}t}$$

9 - 1

CHAPTER 9
The Cost of Capital

- Cost of Capital Components
  - Debt
  - Preferred
  - Common Equity
- WACC

3 types of long-term capital

9 - 2

What types of long-term capital do firms use?

- Long-term debt
- Preferred stock
- Common equity

9 - 3

Capital components are sources of funding that come from investors.

Accounts payable, accruals, and deferred taxes are not sources of funding that come from investors, so they are not included in the calculation of the cost of capital.

We do adjust for these items when calculating the cash flows of a project, but not when calculating the cost of capital.

9 - 4

Should we focus on before-tax or after-tax capital costs?

- Tax effects associated with financing can be incorporated either in capital budgeting cash flows or in cost of capital.
- Most firms incorporate tax effects in the cost of capital. Therefore, focus on after-tax costs.
- Only cost of debt is affected.

9 - 5

Should we focus on historical (embedded) costs or new (marginal) costs?

The cost of capital is used primarily to make decisions which involve raising and investing new capital. So, we should focus on marginal costs.

9 - 6

Cost of Debt

- Method 1: Ask an investment banker what the coupon rate would be on new debt.
- Method 2: Find the bond rating for the company and use the yield on other bonds with a similar rating.
- Method 3: Find the yield on the company's debt, if it has any.

3 ways

9 - 7

A 15-year, 12% semiannual bond sells for $1,153.72. What's r_d?

0	1	2	...	30
i = ?				
-1,153.72	60	60		60 + 1,000

INPUTS	30		-1153.72	60	1000
	N	I/YR	PV	PMT	FV
OUTPUT		5.0% x 2 = r_d = 10%			

9 - 8

Component Cost of Debt

- Interest is tax deductible, so the after tax (AT) cost of debt is:

$$r_{d\,AT} = r_{d\,BT}(1 - T)$$
$$= 10\%(1 - 0.40) = 6\%.$$

- Use nominal rate.
- Flotation costs small, so ignore.

9 - 9

What's the cost of preferred stock? P_P = $113.10; 10%Q; Par = $100; F = $2.

Use this formula:

$$r_{ps} = \frac{D_{ps}}{P_n} = \frac{0.1(\$100)}{\$113.10 - \$2.00}$$

$$= \frac{\$10}{\$111.10} = 0.090 = 9.0\%.$$

Floatation Cost = expenses associated with issuing that type of stock.

9 - 10

Picture of Preferred

0	r_{ps} = ?	1	2	...	∞
-111.1		2.50	2.50		2.50

$$\$111.10 = \frac{D_Q}{r_{Per}} = \frac{\$2.50}{r_{Per}}.$$

$$r_{Per} = \frac{\$2.50}{\$111.10} = 2.25\%; r_{ps(Nom)} = 2.25\%(4) = 9\%.$$

why issue preferred stock?

depends on company

9 - 11

Note:

- Flotation costs for preferred are significant, so are reflected. Use net price.
- Preferred dividends are not deductible, so no tax adjustment. Just r_{ps}.
- Nominal r_{ps} is used.

9 - 12

Is preferred stock more or less risky to investors than debt?

- More risky; company not required to pay preferred dividend.
- However, firms want to pay preferred dividend. Otherwise, (1) cannot pay common dividend, (2) difficult to raise additional funds, and (3) preferred stockholders may gain control of firm.

9 - 13

Why is yield on preferred lower than r_d?

- Corporations own most preferred stock, because 70% of preferred dividends are nontaxable to corporations.
- Therefore, preferred often has a lower B-T yield than the B-T yield on debt.
- The A-T yield to investors and A-T cost to the issuer are higher on preferred than on debt, which is consistent with the higher risk of preferred.

9 - 14

Example:

r_{ps} = 9% r_d = 10%   T = 40%

$r_{ps, AT} = r_{ps} - r_{ps}(1 - 0.7)(T)$

= 9% - 9%(0.3)(0.4) = 7.92%

$r_{d, AT}$ = 10% - 10%(0.4) = 6.00%

A-T Risk Premium on Preferred = 1.92%

debt has to pay Tax

9 - 15

What are the two ways that companies can raise common equity?

- Directly, by issuing new shares of common stock.
- Indirectly, by reinvesting earnings that are not paid out as dividends (i.e., retaining earnings).

9 - 16

Why is there a cost for reinvested earnings?

- Earnings can be reinvested or paid out as dividends.
- Investors could buy other securities, earn a return.
- Thus, there is an opportunity cost if earnings are reinvested.

9 - 17

- Opportunity cost: The return stockholders could earn on alternative investments of equal risk.
- They could buy similar stocks and earn r_s, or company could repurchase its own stock and earn r_s. So, r_s, is the cost of reinvested earnings and it is the cost of equity.

9 - 18

Three ways to determine the cost of equity, r_s:

1. CAPM: $r_s = r_{RF} + (r_M - r_{RF})b$
   $= r_{RF} + (RP_M)b.$
2. DCF: $r_s = D_1/P_0 + g.$
3. Own-Bond-Yield-Plus-Risk Premium:

   $r_s = r_d + \text{Bond RP}.$

9 - 19

What's the cost of equity based on the CAPM?
r_{RF} = 7%, RP_M = 6%, b = 1.2.

$r_s = r_{RF} + (r_M - r_{RF})b.$

$= 7.0\% + (6.0\%)1.2 = 14.2\%.$

9 - 20

Issues in Using CAPM

- Most analysts use the rate on a long-term (10 to 20 years) government bond as an estimate of r_{RF}. For a current estimate, go to www.bloomberg.com, select "U.S. Treasuries" from the section on the left under the heading "Market."

More…

9 - 21

Issues in Using CAPM (Continued)

- Most analysts use a rate of 5% to 6.5% for the market risk premium (RP_M)
- Estimates of beta vary, and estimates are "noisy" (they have a wide confidence interval). For an estimate of beta, go to www.bloomberg.com and enter the ticker symbol for STOCK QUOTES.

can't tell if true or not unless you are there

9 - 22

**What's the DCF cost of equity, r_s?
Given: D_0 = \$4.19; P_0 = \$50; g = 5%.**

$$r_s = \frac{D_1}{P_0} + g = \frac{D_0(1+g)}{P_0} + g$$

$$= \frac{\$4.19(1.05)}{\$50} + 0.05$$

$$= 0.088 + 0.05$$

$$= 13.8\%.$$

9 - 23

Estimating the Growth Rate

- **Use the historical growth rate if you believe the future will be like the past.**
- **Obtain analysts' estimates: Value Line, Zack's, Yahoo!.Finance.**
- **Use the earnings retention model, illustrated on next slide.**

9 - 24

Suppose the company has been earning 15% on equity (ROE = 15%) and retaining 35% (dividend payout = 65%), and this situation is expected to continue.

What's the expected future g?

9 - 25

Retention growth rate:

g = ROE(Retention rate)

g = 0.35(15%) = 5.25%.

This is close to g = 5% given earlier. Think of bank account paying 15% with retention ratio = 0. What is g of account balance? If retention ratio is 100%, what is g?

9 - 26

Could DCF methodology be applied if g is not constant?

- YES, nonconstant g stocks are expected to have constant g at some point, generally in 5 to 10 years.
- But calculations get complicated. See "FM11 Ch 9 Tool Kit.xls".

9 - 27

Find r_s using the own-bond-yield-plus-risk-premium method. (r_d = 10%, RP = 4%.)

$r_s = r_d + RP$
$= 10.0\% + 4.0\% = 14.0\%$

- This RP $\neq$ CAPM RP_M.
- Produces ballpark estimate of r_s. Useful check.

9 - 28

What's a reasonable final estimate of r_s?

Method	Estimate
CAPM	14.2%
DCF	13.8%
r_d + RP	14.0%
Average	14.0%

9 - 29

Determining the Weights for the WACC

- The weights are the percentages of the firm that will be financed by each component.
- If possible, always use the target weights for the percentages of the firm that will be financed with the various types of capital.

9 - 30

Estimating Weights for the Capital Structure

- If you don't know the targets, it is better to estimate the weights using current market values than current book values.
- If you don't know the market value of debt, then it is usually reasonable to use the book values of debt, especially if the debt is short-term.

(More...)

9 - 31

Estimating Weights (Continued)

- Suppose the stock price is $50, there are 3 million shares of stock, the firm has $25 million of preferred stock, and $75 million of debt.

(More...)

9 - 32

- V_{ce} = $50 (3 million) = $150 million.
- V_{ps} = $25 million.
- V_d = $75 million.
- Total value = $150 + $25 + $75 = $250 million.
- w_{ce} = $150/$250 = 0.6
- w_{ps} = $25/$250 = 0.1
- w_d = $75/$250 = 0.3

9 - 33

What's the WACC?

$$WACC = w_d r_d(1 - T) + w_{ps} r_{ps} + w_{ce} r_s$$

$$= 0.3(10\%)(0.6) + 0.1(9\%) + 0.6(14\%)$$

$$= 1.8\% + 0.9\% + 8.4\% = 11.1\%.$$

9 - 34

WACC Estimates for Some Large U. S. Corporations

Company	WACC	w_d
Intel (INTC)	16.0	2.0%
Dell Computer (DELL	12.5	9.1%
BellSouth (BLS)	10.3	39.8%
Wal-Mart (WMT)	8.8	33.3%
Walt Disney (DIS)	8.7	35.5%
Coca-Cola (KO)	6.9	33.8%
H.J. Heinz (HNZ)	6.5	74.9%
Georgia-Pacific (GP)	5.9	69.9%

9 - 35

What factors influence a company's WACC?

- Market conditions, especially interest rates and tax rates.
- The firm's capital structure and dividend policy.
- The firm's investment policy. Firms with riskier projects generally have a higher WACC.

9 - 36

Should the company use the composite WACC as the hurdle rate for each of its divisions?

- NO! The composite WACC reflects the risk of an average project undertaken by the firm.
- Different divisions may have different risks. The division's WACC should be adjusted to reflect the division's risk and capital structure.

9 - 37

What procedures are used to determine the risk-adjusted cost of capital for a particular division?

- Estimate the cost of capital that the division would have if it were a stand-alone firm.
- This requires estimating the division's beta, cost of debt, and capital structure.

9 - 38

Methods for Estimating Beta for a Division or a Project

1. Pure play. Find several publicly traded companies exclusively in project's business.

   Use average of their betas as proxy for project's beta.

   Hard to find such companies.

9 - 39

2. Accounting beta. Run regression between project's ROA and S&P index ROA.

   Accounting betas are correlated (0.5 – 0.6) with market betas.

   But normally can't get data on new projects' ROAs before the capital budgeting decision has been made.

difficult to use because can't get the information

9 - 40

Find the division's market risk and cost of capital based on the CAPM, given these inputs:

- Target debt ratio = 10%.
- r_d = 12%.
- r_{RF} = 7%.
- Tax rate = 40%.
- $beta_{Division}$ = 1.7.
- Market risk premium = 6%.

9 - 41

- Beta = 1.7, so division has more market risk than average.
- Division's required return on equity:

$$r_s = r_{RF} + (r_M - r_{RF})b_{Div.}$$
$$= 7\% + (6\%)1.7 = 17.2\%.$$

$$WACC_{Div.} = w_d r_d(1 - T) + w_c r_s$$
$$= 0.1(12\%)(0.6) + 0.9(17.2\%)$$
$$= 16.2\%.$$

9 - 42

How does the division's WACC compare with the firm's overall WACC?

- Division WACC = 16.2% versus company WACC = 11.1%.
- "Typical" projects within this division would be accepted if their returns are above 16.2%.

9 - 43

Divisional Risk and the Cost of Capital

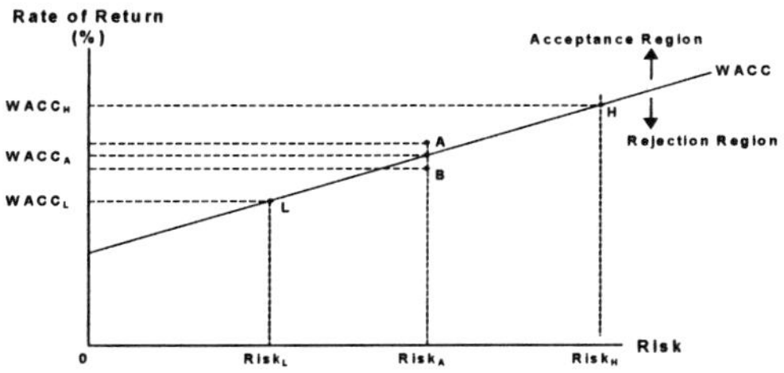

9 - 44

What are the three types of project risk?

- Stand-alone risk
- Corporate risk
- Market risk

9 - 45

How is each type of risk used?

- Stand-alone risk is easiest to calculate.
- Market risk is theoretically best in most situations.
- However, creditors, customers, suppliers, and employees are more affected by corporate risk.
- Therefore, corporate risk is also relevant.

9 - 46

A Project-Specific, Risk-Adjusted Cost of Capital

- Start by calculating a divisional cost of capital.
- Estimate the risk of the project using the techniques in Chapter 11.
- Use judgment to scale up or down the cost of capital for an individual project relative to the divisional cost of capital.

9 - 47

Why is the cost of internal equity from reinvested earnings cheaper than the cost of issuing new common stock?

1. When a company issues new common stock they also have to pay flotation costs to the underwriter.
2. Issuing new common stock may send a negative signal to the capital markets, which may depress stock price.

9 - 48

Estimate the cost of new common equity: P_0=\$50, D_0=\$4.19, g=5%, and F=15%.

$$r_e = \frac{D_0(1+g)}{P_0(1-F)} + g$$

$$= \frac{\$4.19(1.05)}{\$50(1-0.15)} + 5.0\%$$

$$= \frac{\$4.40}{\$42.50} + 5.0\% = 15.4\%.$$

account for flotation cost

9 - 49

Estimate the cost of new 30-year debt: Par=$1,000, Coupon=10%paid annually, and F=2%.

- Using a financial calculator:
  - N = 30
  - PV = 1000(1-.02) = 980
  - PMT = -(.10)(1000)(1-.4) = -60
  - FV = -1000
- Solving for I: 6.15%

= 6.147

9 - 50

Comments about flotation costs:

- Flotation costs depend on the risk of the firm and the type of capital being raised.
- The flotation costs are highest for common equity. However, since most firms issue equity infrequently, the per-project cost is fairly small.
- We will frequently ignore flotation costs when calculating the WACC.

9 - 51

Four Mistakes to Avoid

1. When estimating the cost of debt, don't use the coupon rate on existing debt. Use the current interest rate on new debt.
2. When estimating the risk premium for the CAPM approach, don't subtract the *current* long-term T-bond rate from the *historical* average return on common stocks. (More ...)

9 - 52

For example, if the historical r_M has been about 12.2% and inflation drives the current r_{RF} up to 10%, the current market risk premium is not 12.2% - 10% = 2.2%!

(More ...)

9 - 53

3. Don't use book weights to estimate the weights for the capital structure.

Use the target capital structure to determine the weights.

If you don't know the target weights, then use the current market value of equity, and never the book value of equity.

If you don't know the market value of debt, then the book value of debt often is a reasonable approximation, especially for short-term debt.

(More...)

9 - 54

4. Always remember that capital components are sources of funding that come from investors.

Accounts payable, accruals, and deferred taxes are not sources of funding that come from investors, so they are not included in the calculation of the WACC.

We do adjust for these items when calculating the cash flows of the project, but not when calculating the WACC.

10 - 1

Chapter 10: The Basics of Capital Budgeting: Evaluating Cash Flows

- Overview and "vocabulary"
- Methods
  - Payback, discounted payback
  - NPV
  - IRR, MIRR
- Unequal lives
- Economic life

10 - 2

What is capital budgeting?

- Analysis of potential projects.
- Long-term decisions; involve large expenditures.
- Very important to firm's future.

10 - 3

Steps in Capital Budgeting

- Estimate cash flows (inflows & outflows).
- Assess risk of cash flows.
- Determine r = WACC for project.
- Evaluate cash flows.

10 - 4

What is the difference between independent and mutually exclusive projects?

Projects are:

- independent, if the cash flows of one are unaffected by the acceptance of the other.
- mutually exclusive, if the cash flows of one can be adversely impacted by the acceptance of the other.

Franchise L
Breakfast/Lunch
Franchise D
Served Dinner

10 - 5

What is the payback period?

The number of years required to recover a project's cost,

or how long does it take to get the business's money back?

10 - 6

Payback for Franchise L (Long: Most CFs in out years)

	0	1	2	2.4	3
CF_t	-100	10	60	100	80
Cumulative	-100	-90	-30	0	50

$Payback_L$ = 2 + 30/80 = 2.375 years

10 - 7

Franchise S (Short: CFs come quickly)

	0	1	1.6	2	3
CF_t	-100	70	100	50	20
Cumulative	-100	-30	0	20	40

$\text{Payback}_S = 1 + 30/50 = 1.6 \text{ years}$

except S not L

Exclusiveness of project does not matter in this case

10 - 8

Strengths of Payback:

1. Provides an indication of a project's risk and liquidity.
2. Easy to calculate and understand.

Weaknesses of Payback:

1. Ignores the TVM.
2. Ignores CFs occurring after the payback period.

10 - 9

Discounted Payback: Uses discounted rather than raw CFs.

	0 (10%)	1	2	3
CF_t	-100	10	60	80
$PVCF_t$	-100	9.09	49.59	60.11
Cumulative	-100	-90.91	-41.32	18.79

Discounted payback = 2 + 41.32/60.11 = 2.7 yrs

Recover invest. + cap. costs in 2.7 yrs.

10 - 10

NPV: Sum of the PVs of inflows and outflows.

$$NPV = \sum_{t=0}^{n} \frac{CF_t}{(1+r)^t}.$$

Cost often is CF_0 and is negative.

$$NPV = \sum_{t=1}^{n} \frac{CF_t}{(1+r)^t} - CF_0.$$

10 - 11

What's Franchise L's NPV?

Project L:

	0	1	2	3
10%	-100.00	10	60	80

9.09

49.59

60.11

18.79 = NPV_L

NPV_S = $19.98.

10 - 12

Calculator Solution

Enter in CFLO for L:

-100 [CF_0]

10 [CF_1]

60 [CF_2]

80 [CF_3]

10 [I] [NPV] = 18.78 = NPV_L

10 - 13

Rationale for the NPV Method

NPV = PV inflows - Cost
= Net gain in wealth.

Accept project if NPV > 0.

Choose between mutually exclusive projects on basis of higher NPV. Adds most value.

Above zero, more than enough to cover cost of project

10 - 14

Using NPV method, which franchise(s) should be accepted?

- If Franchise S and L are mutually exclusive, accept S because $NPV_s > NPV_L$.
- If S & L are independent, accept both; NPV > 0.

10 - 15

Internal Rate of Return: IRR

0	1	2	3
CF_0	CF_1	CF_2	CF_3
Cost	←	Inflows	→

IRR is the discount rate that forces PV inflows = cost. This is the same as forcing NPV = 0.

10 - 16

NPV: Enter r, solve for NPV.

$$\sum_{t=0}^{n} \frac{CF_t}{(1+r)^t} = NPV .$$

IRR: Enter NPV = 0, solve for IRR.

$$\sum_{t=0}^{n} \frac{CF_t}{(1+IRR)^t} = 0.$$

10 - 17

What's Franchise L's IRR?

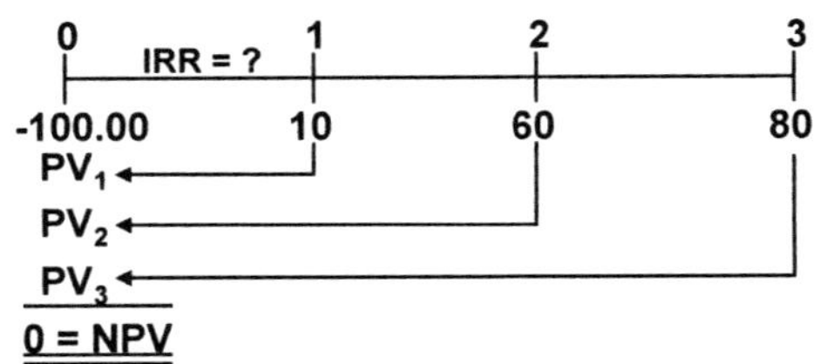

Enter CFs in CFLO, then press IRR:
IRR_L = 18.13%. IRR_S = 23.56%.

10 - 18

Find IRR if CFs are constant:

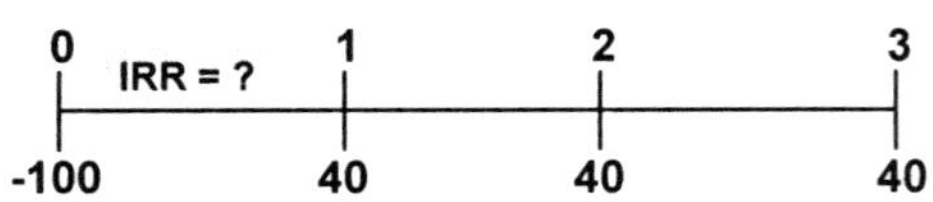

	N	I/YR	PV	PMT	FV
INPUTS	3		-100	40	0
OUTPUT		9.70%			

Or, with CFLO, enter CFs and press IRR = 9.70%.

10 - 19

Rationale for the IRR Method

If IRR > WACC, then the project's rate of return is greater than its cost-- some return is left over to boost stockholders' returns.

<u>Example</u>: WACC = 10%, IRR = 15%. Profitable.

10 - 20

Decisions on Projects S and L per IRR

- If S and L are independent, accept both. IRRs > r = 10%.
- If S and L are mutually exclusive, accept S because $IRR_S > IRR_L$.

10 - 21

Construct NPV Profiles

Enter CFs in CFLO and find NPV_L and NPV_S at different discount rates:

r	NPV_L	NPV_S
0	50	40
5	33	29
10	19	20
15	7	12
20	(4)	5

10 - 22

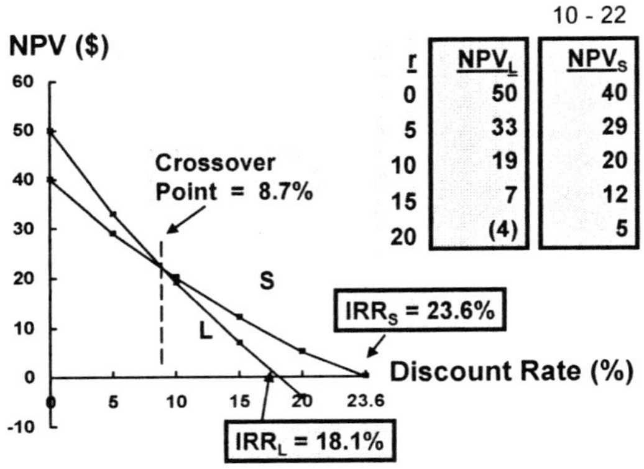

r	NPV_L	NPV_S
0	50	40
5	33	29
10	19	20
15	7	12
20	(4)	5

10 - 23

NPV and IRR always lead to the same accept/reject decision for independent projects:

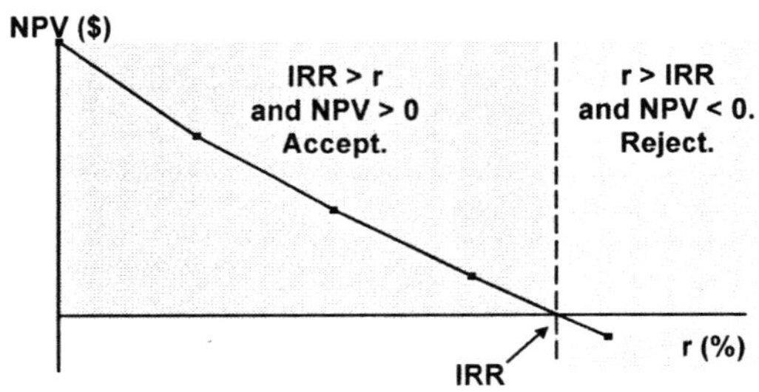

10 - 24

Mutually Exclusive Projects

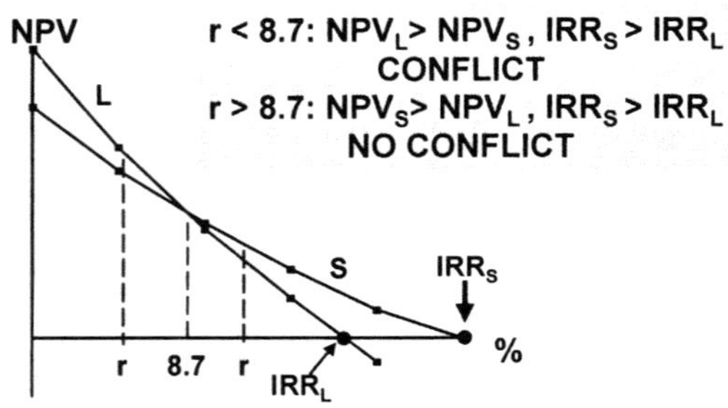

10 - 25

To Find the Crossover Rate

1. Find cash flow differences between the projects. See data at beginning of the case.
2. Enter these differences in CFLO register, then press IRR. Crossover rate = 8.68%, rounded to 8.7%.
3. Can subtract S from L or vice versa, but better to have first CF negative.
4. If profiles don't cross, one project dominates the other.

10 - 26

Two Reasons NPV Profiles Cross

1. Size (scale) differences. Smaller project frees up funds at t = 0 for investment. The higher the opportunity cost, the more valuable these funds, so high r favors small projects.
2. Timing differences. Project with faster payback provides more CF in early years for reinvestment. If r is high, early CF especially good, $NPV_S > NPV_L$.

Longer term projects will have steeper lines.

10 - 27

Reinvestment Rate Assumptions

- NPV assumes reinvest at r (opportunity cost of capital).
- IRR assumes reinvest at IRR.
- Reinvest at opportunity cost, r, is more realistic, so NPV method is best. NPV should be used to choose between mutually exclusive projects.

Managers prefer to use IRR

10 - 28

Managers like rates--prefer IRR to NPV comparisons. Can we give them a better IRR?

Yes, MIRR is the discount rate which causes the PV of a project's terminal value (TV) to equal the PV of costs. TV is found by compounding inflows at WACC.

Thus, MIRR assumes cash inflows are reinvested at WACC.

10 - 29

MIRR for Franchise L (r = 10%)

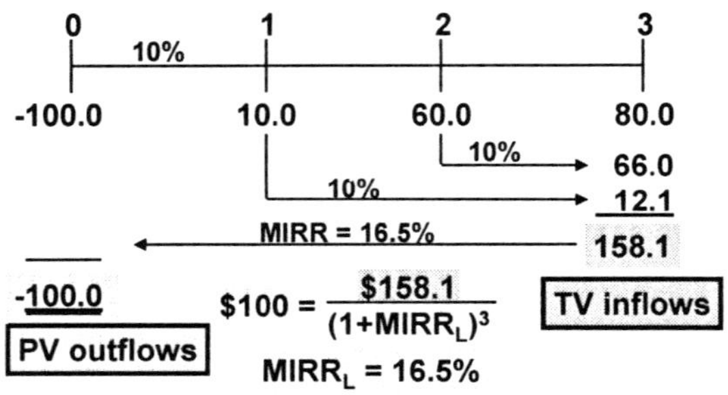

$$\$100 = \frac{\$158.1}{(1+MIRR_L)^3}$$

$MIRR_L = 16.5\%$

10 - 30

To find TV with 10B, enter in CFLO:

$CF_0 = 0$, $CF_1 = 10$, $CF_2 = 60$, $CF_3 = 80$
I = 10

NPV = 118.78 = PV of inflows.

Enter PV = -118.78, N = 3, I = 10, PMT = 0.
Press FV = 158.10 = FV of inflows.

Enter FV = 158.10, PV = -100, PMT = 0, N = 3.
Press I = 16.50% = MIRR.

10 - 31

Why use MIRR versus IRR?

MIRR correctly assumes reinvestment at opportunity cost = WACC. MIRR also avoids the problem of multiple IRRs.

Managers like rate of return comparisons, and MIRR is better for this than IRR.

NPV is the best to use

10 - 32

Normal Cash Flow Project:

Cost (negative CF) followed by a series of positive cash inflows. One change of signs.

Nonnormal Cash Flow Project:

Two or more changes of signs. Most common: Cost (negative CF), then string of positive CFs, then cost to close project. Nuclear power plant, strip mine.

10 - 33

Inflow (+) or Outflow (-) in Year

0	1	2	3	4	5	N	NN
-	+	+	+	+	+	N	
-	+	+	+	+	-		NN
-	-	-	+	+	+	N	
+	+	+	-	-	-	N	
-	+	+	-	+	-		NN

Non normal cash flows use modified when have non normal cash flows

10 - 34

Pavilion Project: NPV and IRR?

Enter CFs in CFLO, enter I = 10.

NPV = -386.78

IRR = ERROR. Why?

10 - 35

We got IRR = ERROR because there are 2 IRRs. Nonnormal CFs--two sign changes. Here's a picture:

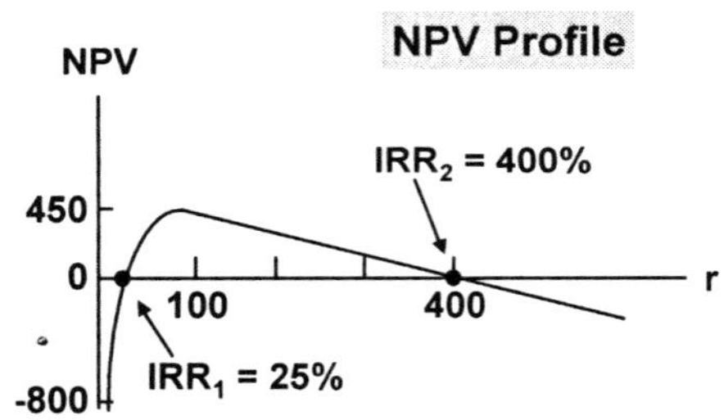

10 - 36

Logic of Multiple IRRs

1. At very low discount rates, the PV of CF_2 is large & negative, so NPV < 0.
2. At very high discount rates, the PV of both CF_1 and CF_2 are low, so CF_0 dominates and again NPV < 0.
3. In between, the discount rate hits CF_2 harder than CF_1, so NPV > 0.
4. Result: 2 IRRs.

10 - 37

Could find IRR with calculator:

1. Enter CFs as before.
2. Enter a "guess" as to IRR by storing the guess. Try 10%:

   10 ■ STO

   ■ IRR = 25% = lower IRR

   Now guess large IRR, say, 200:

   200 ■ STO

   ■ IRR = 400% = upper IRR

10 - 38

When there are nonnormal CFs and more than one IRR, use MIRR:

0	1	2
-800,000	5,000,000	-5,000,000

PV outflows @ 10% = -4,932,231.40.

TV inflows @ 10% = 5,500,000.00.

MIRR = 5.6%

10 - 39

Accept Project P?

NO. Reject because MIRR = 5.6% < r = 10%.

Also, if MIRR < r, NPV will be negative: NPV = -$386,777.

10 - 40

S and L are mutually exclusive and will be repeated. r = 10%. Which is better? (000s)

	0	1	2	3	4
Project S:	(100)	60	60		
Project L:	(100)	33.5	33.5	33.5	33.5

10 - 41

	S	L
CF_0	-100,000	-100,000
CF_1	60,000	33,500
N_j	2	4
I	10	10
NPV	4,132	6,190

$NPV_L > NPV_S$. But is L better? Can't say yet. Need to perform common life analysis.

10 - 42

- Note that Project S could be repeated after 2 years to generate additional profits.
- Can use either <u>replacement chain</u> or <u>equivalent annual annuity</u> analysis to make decision.

10 - 43

Replacement Chain Approach (000s)

Franchise S with Replication:

	0	1	2	3	4
Franchise S:	(100)	60	60		
			(100)	60	60
	(100)	60	(40)	60	60

NPV = $7,547.

10 - 44

Or, use NPVs:

0	1	2	3	4
4,132		4,132		
3,415 ←	10%	(discounted from year 2)		
7,547				

Compare to Franchise L NPV = $6,190.

10 - 45

If the cost to repeat S in two years rises to $105,000, which is best? (000s)

	0	1	2	3	4
Franchise S:	(100)	60	60		
			(105)	60	60
			(45)		

NPV_S = $3,415 < NPV_L = $6,190.
Now choose L.

extending the two projects to compare apples to apples

extending the project S to 4 years

10 - 46

Consider another project with a 3-year life. If terminated prior to Year 3, the machinery will have positive salvage value.

Year	CF	Salvage Value
0	($5,000)	$5,000
1	2,100	3,100
2	2,000	2,000
3	1,750	0

10 - 47

CFs Under Each Alternative (000s)

	0	1	2	3
1. No termination	(5)	2.1	2	1.75
2. Terminate 2 years	(5)	2.1	4	
3. Terminate 1 year	(5)	5.2		

10 - 48

Assuming a 10% cost of capital, what is the project's optimal, or economic life?

$NPV_{(no)}$ = -$123.

$NPV_{(2)}$ = $215.

$NPV_{(1)}$ = -$273.

10 - 49

Conclusions

- The project is acceptable only if operated for 2 years.
- A project's engineering life does not always equal its economic life.

10 - 50

Choosing the Optimal Capital Budget

- Finance theory says to accept all positive NPV projects.
- Two problems can occur when there is not enough internally generated cash to fund all positive NPV projects:
  - An increasing marginal cost of capital.
  - Capital rationing

10 - 51

Increasing Marginal Cost of Capital

- Externally raised capital can have large flotation costs, which increase the cost of capital.
- Investors often perceive large capital budgets as being risky, which drives up the cost of capital.

(More...)

10 - 52

- If external funds will be raised, then the NPV of all projects should be estimated using this higher marginal cost of capital.

10 - 53

Capital Rationing

- Capital rationing occurs when a company chooses not to fund all positive NPV projects.
- The company typically sets an upper limit on the total amount of capital expenditures that it will make in the upcoming year.

(More...)

10 - 54

Reason: Companies want to avoid the direct costs (i.e., flotation costs) and the indirect costs of issuing new capital.

Solution: Increase the cost of capital by enough to reflect all of these costs, and then accept all projects that still have a positive NPV with the higher cost of capital.

(More...)

10 - 55

Reason: Companies don't have enough managerial, marketing, or engineering staff to implement all positive NPV projects.

Solution: Use linear programming to maximize NPV subject to not exceeding the constraints on staffing.

(More...)

10 - 56

Reason: Companies believe that the project's managers forecast unreasonably high cash flow estimates, so companies "filter" out the worst projects by limiting the total amount of projects that can be accepted.

Solution: Implement a post-audit process and tie the managers' compensation to the subsequent performance of the project.

11 - 1

CHAPTER 11
Cash Flow Estimation and Risk Analysis

- Estimating cash flows:
  - Relevant cash flows
  - Working capital treatment
  - Inflation
- Risk Analysis: Sensitivity Analysis, Scenario Analysis, and Simulation Analysis

11 - 2

Proposed Project

- Cost: $200,000 + $10,000 shipping + $30,000 installation.
- Depreciable cost $240,000.
- Economic life = 4 years.
- Salvage value = $25,000.
- MACRS 3-year class.

11 - 3

- Annual unit sales = 1,250.
- Unit sales price = $200.
- Unit costs = $100.
- Net operating working capital (NOWC) = 12% of sales.
- Tax rate = 40%.
- Project cost of capital = 10%.

11 - 4

Incremental Cash Flow for a Project

- **Project's incremental cash flow is:**
  - **Corporate cash flow with the project**

    Minus
  - **Corporate cash flow without the project.**

incremental is solely from project

11 - 5

Should you subtract interest expense or dividends when calculating CF?

- **NO. We discount project cash flows with a cost of capital that is the rate of return required by all investors (not just debtholders or stockholders), and so we should discount the total amount of cash flow available to all investors.**
- **They are part of the costs of capital. If we subtracted them from cash flows, we would be double counting capital costs.**

11 - 6

Suppose $100,000 had been spent last year to improve the production line site. Should this cost be included in the analysis?

- **NO. This is a <u>sunk cost</u>. Focus on incremental investment and operating cash flows.**

11 - 7

Suppose the plant space could be leased out for $25,000 a year. Would this affect the analysis?

- **Yes. Accepting the project means we will not receive the $25,000. This is an <u>opportunity cost</u> and it should be charged to the project.**
- **A.T. opportunity cost = $25,000 (1 - T) = $15,000 annual cost.**

11 - 8

If the new product line would decrease sales of the firm's other products by $50,000 per year, would this affect the analysis?

- **Yes. The effects on the other projects' CFs are "externalities".**
- **Net CF loss per year on other lines would be a cost to this project.**
- **Externalities will be positive if new projects are complements to existing assets, negative if substitutes.**

11 - 9

What is the depreciation basis?

Basis = Cost
+ Shipping
+ Installation
$240,000

11 - 10

Annual Depreciation Expense (000s)

Year	%	x Basis	= Depr.
1	0.33	$240	$ 79.2
2	0.45		108.0
3	0.15		36.0
4	0.07		16.8

11 - 11

Annual Sales and Costs

	Year 1	Year 2	Year 3	Year 4
Units	1250	1250	1250	1250
Unit price	$200	$206	$212.18	$218.55
Unit cost	$100	$103	$106.09	$109.27
Sales	$250,000	$257,500	$265,225	$273,188
Costs	$125,000	$128,750	$132,613	$136,588

11 - 12

Why is it important to include inflation when estimating cash flows?

- Nominal r > real r. The cost of capital, r, includes a premium for inflation.
- Nominal CF > real CF. This is because nominal cash flows incorporate inflation.
- If you discount real CF with the higher nominal r, then your NPV estimate is too low.

Continued...

Nominal cost

11 - 13

Inflation (Continued)

- Nominal CF should be discounted with nominal r, and real CF should be discounted with real r.
- It is more realistic to find the nominal CF (i.e., increase cash flow estimates with inflation) than it is to reduce the nominal r to a real r.

Nominal paired with Real

11 - 14

Operating Cash Flows (Years 1 and 2)

	Year 1	Year 2
Sales	$250,000	$257,500
Costs	$125,000	$128,750
Depr.	$79,200	$108,000
EBIT	$45,800	$20,750
Taxes (40%)	$18,320	$8,300
NOPAT	$27,480	$12,450
+ Depr.	$79,200	$108,000
Net Op. CF	$106,680	$120,450

Add back depreciation for Net Op CF.
Depreciation is for Tax purposes

11 - 15

Operating Cash Flows (Years 3 and 4)

	Year 3	Year 4
Sales	$265,225	$273,188
Costs	$132,613	$136,588
Depr.	$36,000	$16,800
EBIT	$96,612	$119,800
Taxes (40%)	$38,645	$47,920
NOPAT	$57,967	$71,880
+ Depr.	$36,000	$16,800
Net Op. CF	$93,967	$88,680

11 - 16

Cash Flows due to Investments in Net Operating Working Capital (NOWC)

	Sales	NOWC (% of sales)	CF
Year 0		$30,000	-$30,000
Year 1	$250,000	$30,900	-$900
Year 2	$257,500	$31,827	-$927
Year 3	$265,225	$32,783	-$956
Year 4	$273,188		$32,783

11 - 17

Salvage Cash Flow at t = 4 (000s)

Salvage value	$25
Tax on SV	(10)
Net terminal CF	$15

11 - 18

What if you terminate a project before the asset is fully depreciated?

Cash flow from sale = Sale proceeds
- taxes paid.

Taxes are based on difference between sales price and tax basis, where:

Basis = Original basis - Accum. deprec.

11 - 19

Example: If Sold After 3 Years (000s)

- Original basis = $240.
- After 3 years = $16.8 remaining.
- Sales price = $25.
- Tax on sale = 0.4($25-$16.8) = $3.28.
- Cash flow = $25-$3.28=$21.72.

Depreciated out the amount of the three years to get the 16.8 Remaining

11 - 20

Net Cash Flows for Years 1-3

	Year 0	Year 1	Year 2
Init. Cost	-$240,000	0	0
Op. CF	0	$106,680	$120,450
NOWC CF	-$30,000	-$900	-$927
Salvage CF	0	0	0
Net CF	-$270,000	$105,780	$119,523

11 - 21

Net Cash Flows for Years 4-5

	Year 3	Year 4
Init. Cost	0	0
Op CF	$93,967	$88,680
NOWC CF	-$956	$32,783
Salvage CF	0	$15,000
Net CF	$93,011	$136,463

11 - 22

Project Net CFs on a Time Line

0	1	2	3	4
(270,000)	105,780	119,523	93,011	136,463

Enter CFs in CFLO register and I = 10.

NPV = $88,030.

IRR = 23.9%.

11 - 23

What is the project's MIRR? (000s)

0	1	2	3	4
(270,000)	105,780	119,523	93,011	136,463
			→	102,312
		→		144,623
	→			140,793
(270,000) ←		MIRR = ?		524,191

motified internal Rate of Return

11 - 24

Calculator Solution

1. Enter positive CFs in CFLO: I = 10; Solve for NPV = $358,029.581.
2. Use TVM keys: PV = -358,029.581, N = 4, I = 10; PMT = 0; Solve for FV = 524,191. (TV of inflows)
3. Use TVM keys: N = 4; FV = 524,191; PV = -270,000; PMT= 0; Solve for I = 18.0.

MIRR = 18.0%.

11 - 25

What is the project's payback? (000s)

0	1	2	3	4
(270)*	106	120	93	136

Cumulative:

(270)	(164)	(44)	49	185

Payback = 2 + 44/93 = 2.5 years.

11 - 26

What does "risk" mean in capital budgeting?

- Uncertainty about a project's future profitability.
- Measured by σ_{NPV}, σ_{IRR}, beta.
- Will taking on the project increase the firm's and stockholders' risk?

11 - 27

Is risk analysis based on historical data or subjective judgment?

- Can sometimes use historical data, but generally cannot.
- So risk analysis in capital budgeting is usually based on subjective judgments.

11 - 28

What three types of risk are relevant in capital budgeting?

- Stand-alone risk
- Corporate risk
- Market (or beta) risk

11 - 29

How is each type of risk measured, and how do they relate to one another?

1. Stand-Alone Risk:
   - The project's risk if it were the firm's only asset and there were no shareholders.
   - Ignores both firm and shareholder diversification.
   - Measured by the σ or CV of NPV, IRR, or MIRR.

11 - 30

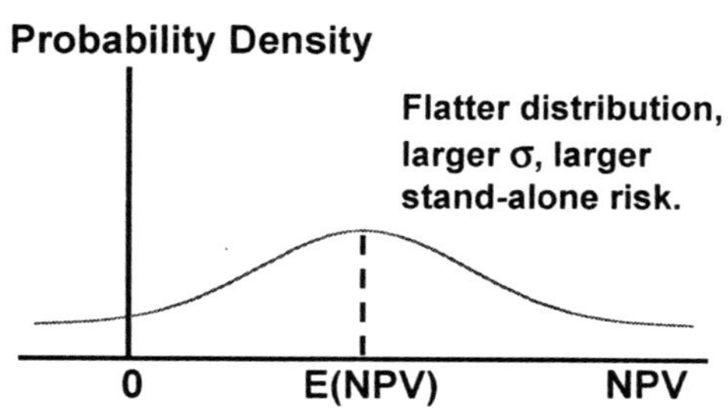

Such graphics are increasingly used by corporations.

11 - 31

2. Corporate Risk:
- Reflects the project's effect on corporate earnings stability.
- Considers firm's other assets (diversification within firm).
- Depends on:
  - project's σ, and
  - its correlation, ρ, with returns on firm's other assets.
- Measured by the project's corporate beta.

11 - 32

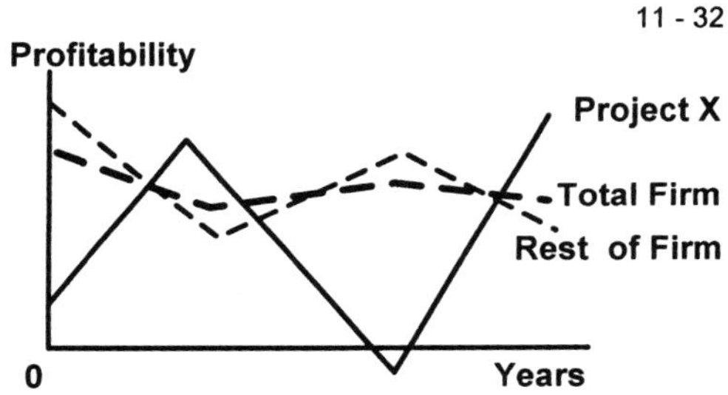

1. Project X is negatively correlated to firm's other assets.
2. If $\rho < 1.0$, some diversification benefits.
3. If $\rho = 1.0$, no diversification effects.

11 - 33

3. Market Risk:
- Reflects the project's effect on a well-diversified stock portfolio.
- Takes account of stockholders' other assets.
- Depends on project's σ and correlation with the stock market.
- Measured by the project's market beta.

11 - 34

How is each type of risk used?

- Market risk is theoretically best in most situations.
- However, creditors, customers, suppliers, and employees are more affected by corporate risk.
- Therefore, corporate risk is also relevant.

Continued...

11 - 35

- Stand-alone risk is easiest to measure, more intuitive.
- Core projects are highly correlated with other assets, so stand-alone risk generally reflects corporate risk.
- If the project is highly correlated with the economy, stand-alone risk also reflects market risk.

11 - 36

What is sensitivity analysis?

- Shows how changes in a variable such as unit sales affect NPV or IRR.
- Each variable is fixed except one. Change this one variable to see the effect on NPV or IRR.
- Answers "what if" questions, e.g. "What if sales decline by 30%?"

Be familiar with the concept

11 - 37

Sensitivity Analysis

Change from Base Level	Resulting NPV (000s) r	Unit Sales	Salvage
-30%	$113	$17	$85
-15%	$100	$52	$86
0%	$88	$88	$88
15%	$76	$124	$90
30%	$65	$159	$91

11 - 38

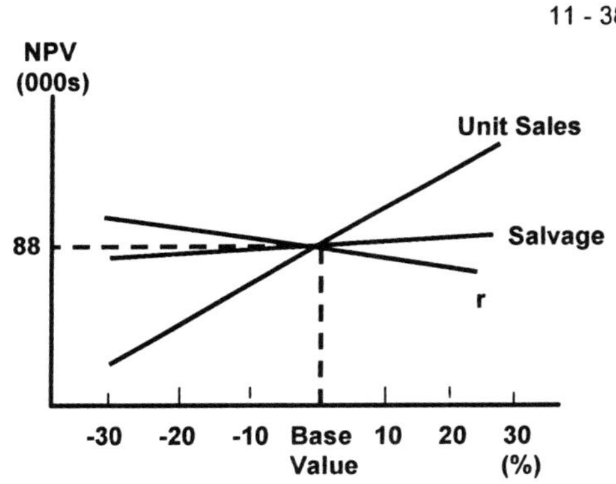

11 - 39

Results of Sensitivity Analysis

- Steeper sensitivity lines show greater risk. Small changes result in large declines in NPV.
- Unit sales line is steeper than salvage value or r, so for this project, should worry most about accuracy of sales forecast.

11 - 40

What are the weaknesses of sensitivity analysis?

- Does not reflect diversification.
- Says nothing about the likelihood of change in a variable, i.e. a steep sales line is not a problem if sales won't fall.
- Ignores relationships among variables.

What about Forecast Errors?

11 - 41

Why is sensitivity analysis useful?

- Gives some idea of stand-alone risk.
- Identifies dangerous variables.
- Gives some breakeven information.

11 - 42

What is scenario analysis?

- Examines several possible situations, usually worst case, most likely case, and best case.
- Provides a range of possible outcomes.

Don't worry about calculating just understand concept

11 - 43

Best scenario: 1,600 units @ $240
Worst scenario: 900 units @ $160

Scenario	Probability	NPV(000)
Best	0.25	$ 279
Base	0.50	88
Worst	0.25	-49

E(NPV) = $101.5

σ(NPV) = 75.7

CV(NPV) = σ(NPV)/E(NPV) = 0.75

11 - 44

Are there any problems with scenario analysis?

- Only considers a few possible out- comes.
- Assumes that inputs are perfectly correlated--all "bad" values occur together and all "good" values occur together.
- Focuses on stand-alone risk, although subjective adjustments can be made.

11 - 45

What is a simulation analysis?

- A computerized version of scenario analysis which uses continuous probability distributions.
- Computer selects values for each variable based on given probability distributions.

(More...)

11 - 46

- NPV and IRR are calculated.
- Process is repeated many times (1,000 or more).
- End result: Probability distribution of NPV and IRR based on sample of simulated values.
- Generally shown graphically.

11 - 47

Simulation Example

- Assume a:
  - Normal distribution for unit sales:
    - Mean = 1,250
    - Standard deviation = 200
  - Triangular distribution for unit price:
    - Lower bound = $160
    - Most likely = $200
    - Upper bound = $250

11 - 48

Simulation Process

- Pick a random variable for unit sales and sale price.
- Substitute these values in the spreadsheet and calculate NPV.
- Repeat the process many times, saving the input variables (units and price) and the output (NPV).

11 - 49

Simulation Results (1000 trials)
(See Ch 11 Mini Case Simulation.xls)

	Units	Price	NPV
Mean	1260	$202	$95,914
St. Dev.	201	$18	$59,875
CV			0.62
Max	1883	$248	$353,238
Min	685	$163	($45,713)
Prob NPV>0			97%

11 - 50

Interpreting the Results

- Inputs are consistent with specificied distributions.
  - Units: Mean = 1260, St. Dev. = 201.
  - Price: Min = $163, Mean = $202, Max = $248.
- Mean NPV = $95,914. Low probability of negative NPV (100% - 97% = 3%).

11 - 51

Histogram of Results

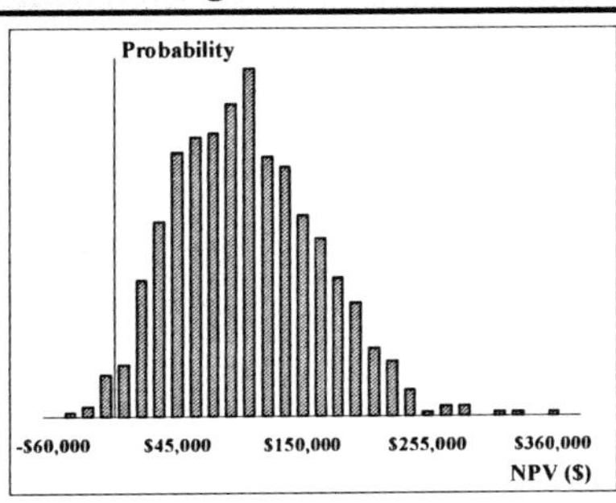

11 - 52

What are the advantages of simulation analysis?

- Reflects the probability distributions of each input.
- Shows range of NPVs, the expected NPV, σ_{NPV}, and CV_{NPV}.
- Gives an intuitive graph of the risk situation.

11 - 53

What are the disadvantages of simulation?

- Difficult to specify probability distributions and correlations.
- If inputs are bad, output will be bad: "Garbage in, garbage out."

(More...)

11 - 54

- Sensitivity, scenario, and simulation analyses do not provide a decision rule. They do not indicate whether a project's expected return is sufficient to compensate for its risk.
- Sensitivity, scenario, and simulation analyses all ignore diversification. Thus they measure only stand-alone risk, which may not be the most relevant risk in capital budgeting.

All ignore diversification

11 - 55

If the firm's average project has a CV of 0.2 to 0.4, is this a high-risk project? What type of risk is being measured?

- CV from scenarios = 0.74, CV from simulation = 0.62. Both are > 0.4, this project has high risk.
- CV measures a project's stand-alone risk.
- High stand-alone risk usually indicates high corporate and market risks.

11 - 56

With a 3% risk adjustment, should our project be accepted?

- Project r = 10% + 3% = 13%.
- That's 30% above base r.
- NPV = $65,371.
- Project remains acceptable after accounting for differential (higher) risk.

11 - 57

Should subjective risk factors be considered?

- Yes. A numerical analysis may not capture all of the risk factors inherent in the project.
- For example, if the project has the potential for bringing on harmful lawsuits, then it might be riskier than a standard analysis would indicate.

what about a lawsuits

12 - 1

CHAPTER 12
Real Options

- Real options
- Decision trees
- Application of financial options to real options

12 - 2

What is a real option?

- Real options exist when managers can influence the size and risk of a project's cash flows by taking different actions during the project's life in response to changing market conditions.
- Alert managers always look for real options in projects.
- Smarter managers try to create real options.

12 - 3

What is the single most important characteristic of an option?

- It does not obligate its owner to take any action. It merely gives the owner the right to buy or sell an asset.

12 - 4

How are real options different from financial options?

- Financial options have an underlying asset that is traded--usually a security like a stock.
- A real option has an underlying asset that is not a security--for example a project or a growth opportunity, and it isn't traded.

(More...)

12 - 5

How are real options different from financial options?

- The payoffs for financial options are specified in the contract.
- Real options are "found" or created inside of projects. Their payoffs can be varied.

12 - 6

What are some types of real options?

- Investment timing options
- Growth options
  - Expansion of existing product line
  - New products
  - New geographic markets

12 - 7

Types of real options (Continued)

- Abandonment options
  - Contraction
  - Temporary suspension
- Flexibility options

12 - 8

Five Procedures for Valuing Real Options

1. DCF analysis of expected cash flows, ignoring the option.
2. Qualitative assessment of the real option's value.
3. Decision tree analysis.
4. Standard model for a corresponding financial option.
5. Financial engineering techniques.

12 - 9

Analysis of a Real Option: Basic Project

- Initial cost = \$70 million, Cost of Capital = 10%, risk-free rate = 6%, cash flows occur for 3 years.

Demand	Probability	Annual Cash Flow
High	30%	\$45
Average	40%	\$30
Low	30%	\$15

12 - 10

Approach 1: DCF Analysis

- E(CF) =.3($45)+.4($30)+.3($15)
  = $30.
- PV of expected CFs = ($30/1.1) + ($30/1.1^2) + ($30/1/1^3) = $74.61 million.
- Expected NPV = $74.61 - $70
  = $4.61 million

12 - 11

Investment Timing Option

- If we immediately proceed with the project, its expected NPV is $4.61 million.
- However, the project is very risky:
  - If demand is high, NPV = $41.91 million.*
  - If demand is low, NPV = -$32.70 million.*

* See *FM11 Ch 12 Mini Case.xls* for calculations.

12 - 12

Investment Timing (Continued)

- If we wait one year, we will gain additional information regarding demand.
- If demand is low, we won't implement project.
- If we wait, the up-front cost and cash flows will stay the same, except they will be shifted ahead by a year.

12 - 13

Procedure 2: Qualitative Assessment

- The value of any real option increases if:
  - the underlying project is very risky
  - there is a long time before you must exercise the option
- This project is risky and has one year before we must decide, so the option to wait is probably valuable.

12 - 14

Procedure 3: Decision Tree Analysis (Implement only if demand is not low.)

		Cost	Future Cash Flows			NPV this
0	Prob.	1	2	3	4	Scenario[a]
	30%	-$70	$45	$45	$45	
$0	40%	-$70	$30	$30	$30	
	30%	$0	$0	$0	$0	

Discount the cost of the project at the risk-free rate, since the cost is known. Discount the operating cash flows at the cost of capital.
Example: $35.70 = -$70/1.06 + $45/1.1^2 + $45/1.1^3 + $45/1.1^3.
See *Ch 12 Mini Case.xls* for calculations.

12 - 15

Use these scenarios, with their given probabilities, to find the project's expected NPV if we wait.

E(NPV) = [0.3($35.70)]+[0.4($1.79)]
+ [0.3 ($0)]

E(NPV) = $11.42.

12 - 16

Decision Tree with Option to Wait vs. Original DCF Analysis

- Decision tree NPV is higher ($11.42 million vs. $4.61).
- In other words, the option to wait is worth $11.42 million. If we implement project today, we gain $4.61 million but lose the option worth $11.42 million.
- Therefore, we should wait and decide next year whether to implement project, based on demand.

12 - 17

The Option to Wait Changes Risk

- The cash flows are less risky under the option to wait, since we can avoid the low cash flows. Also, the cost to implement may not be risk-free.
- Given the change in risk, perhaps we should use different rates to discount the cash flows.
- But finance theory doesn't tell us how to estimate the right discount rates, so we normally do sensitivity analysis using a range of different rates.

12 - 18

Procedure 4: Use the existing model of a financial option.

- The option to wait resembles a financial call option-- we get to "buy" the project for $70 million in one year if value of project in one year is greater than $70 million.
- This is like a call option with an exercise price of $70 million and an expiration date of one year.

12 - 19

Inputs to Black-Scholes Model for Option to Wait

- X = exercise price = cost to implement project = $70 million.
- r_{RF} = risk-free rate = 6%.
- t = time to maturity = 1 year.
- P = current stock price = Estimated on following slides.
- σ^2 = variance of stock return = Estimated on following slides.

12 - 20

Estimate of P

- For a financial option:
  - P = current price of stock = PV of all of stock's expected future cash flows.
  - Current price is unaffected by the exercise cost of the option.
- For a real option:
  - P = PV of all of project's future expected cash flows.
  - P does not include the project's cost.

12 - 21

Step 1: Find the PV of future CFs at option's exercise year.

0	Prob.	1	2	3	4	PV at Year 1
	30%		$45	$45	$45	$111.91
	40%		$30	$30	$30	$74.61
	30%		$15	$15	$15	$37.30

(Columns 2–4 are headed "Future Cash Flows".)

Example: $111.91 = $45/1.1 + $45/1.1^2 + $45/1.1^3.
See *Ch 12 Mini Case.xls* for calculations.

12 - 22

Step 2: Find the expected PV at the current date, Year 0.

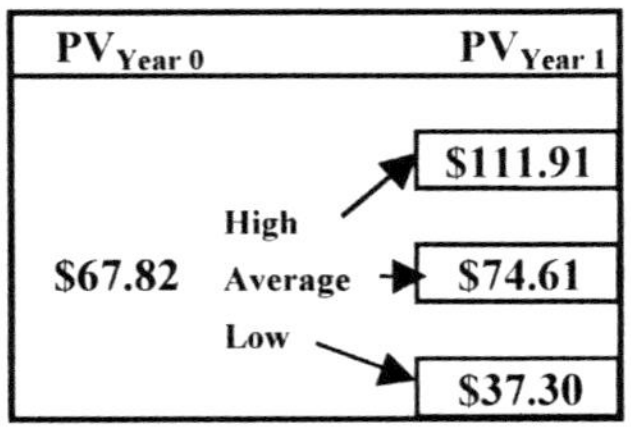

PV_{2004}=PV of Exp. PV_{2005} = [(0.3* $111.91) +(0.4*$74.61) +(0.3*$37.3)]/1.1 = $67.82.

See *Ch 12 Mini Case.xls* for calculations.

12 - 23

The Input for P in the Black-Scholes Model

- The input for price is the present value of the project's expected future cash flows.
- Based on the previous slides,

  P = $67.82.

12 - 24

Estimating σ^2 for the Black-Scholes Model

- For a financial option, σ^2 is the variance of the stock's rate of return.
- For a real option, σ^2 is the variance of the project's rate of return.

12 - 25

Three Ways to Estimate σ^2

- Judgment.
- The direct approach, using the results from the scenarios.
- The indirect approach, using the expected distribution of the project's value.

12 - 26

Estimating σ^2 with Judgment

- The typical stock has σ^2 of about 12%.
- A project should be riskier than the firm as a whole, since the firm is a portfolio of projects.
- The company in this example has σ^2 = 10%, so we might expect the project to have σ^2 between 12% and 19%.

12 - 27

Estimating σ^2 with the Direct Approach

- Use the previous scenario analysis to estimate the return from the present until the option must be exercised. Do this for each scenario
- Find the variance of these returns, given the probability of each scenario.

12 - 28

Find Returns from the Present until the Option Expires

$PV_{Year\ 0}$		$PV_{Year\ 1}$	Return
	High	$111.91	65.0%
$67.82	Average	$74.61	10.0%
	Low	$37.30	-45.0%

Example: 65.0% = ($111.91- $67.82) / $67.82.
See *Ch 12 Mini Case.xls* for calculations.

12 - 29

Use these scenarios, with their given probabilities, to find the expected return and variance of return.

E(Ret.)=0.3(0.65)+0.4(0.10)+0.3(-0.45)

E(Ret.)= 0.10 = 10%.

σ^2 = 0.3(0.65-0.10)^2 + 0.4(0.10-0.10)^2 + 0.3(-0.45-0.10)^2

σ^2 = 0.182 = 18.2%.

12 - 30

Estimating σ^2 with the Indirect Approach

- From the scenario analysis, we know the project's expected value and the variance of the project's expected value at the time the option expires.
- The questions is: "Given the current value of the project, how risky must its expected return be to generate the observed variance of the project's value at the time the option expires?"

12 - 31

The Indirect Approach (Cont.)

- From option pricing for financial options, we know the probability distribution for returns (it is lognormal).
- This allows us to specify a variance of the rate of return that gives the variance of the project's value at the time the option expires.

12 - 32

Indirect Estimate of σ^2

- Here is a formula for the variance of a stock's return, if you know the coefficient of variation of the expected stock price at some time, t, in the future:

$$\sigma^2 = \frac{\ln[CV^2 + 1]}{t}$$

We can apply this formula to the real option.

12 - 33

From earlier slides, we know the value of the project for each scenario at the expiration date.

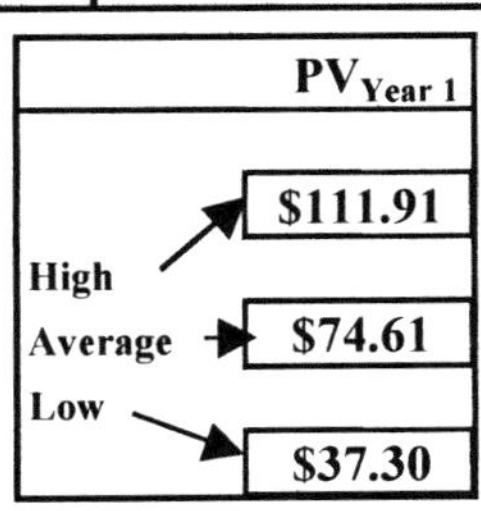

12 - 34

Use these scenarios, with their given probabilities, to find the project's expected PV and σ_{PV}.

E(PV)=.3($111.91)+.4($74.61)+.3($37.3)

E(PV)= $74.61.

σ_{PV} = [.3($111.91-$74.61)^2
+ .4($74.61-$74.61)^2
+ .3($37.30-$74.61)^2]$^{1/2}$

σ_{PV} = $28.90.

12 - 35

Find the project's expected coefficient of variation, CV_{PV}, at the time the option expires.

CV_{PV} = $28.90 /$74.61 = 0.39.

12 - 36

Now use the formula to estimate σ^2.

- From our previous scenario analysis, we know the project's CV, 0.39, at the time it the option expires (t=1 year).

$$\sigma^2 = \frac{\ln[0.39^2 + 1]}{1} = 14.2\%$$

12 - 37

The Estimate of σ^2

- Subjective estimate:
  - 12% to 19%.
- Direct estimate:
  - 18.2%.
- Indirect estimate:
  - 14.2%
- For this example, we chose 14.2%, but we recommend doing sensitivity analysis over a range of σ^2.

12 - 38

Use the Black-Scholes Model: P = \$67.83; X = \$70; r_{RF} = 6%; t = 1 year: $\sigma^2 = 0.142$

$$V = \$67.83[N(d_1)] - \$70e^{-(0.06)(1)}[N(d_2)].$$

$$d_1 = \frac{\ln(\$67.83/\$70)+[(0.06 + 0.142/2)](1)}{(0.142)^{0.5}(1)^{.05}}$$

$$= 0.2641.$$

$$d_2 = d_1 - (0.142)^{0.5}(1)^{.05} = d_1 - 0.3768$$

$$= 0.2641 - 0.3768 = -0.1127.$$

12 - 39

$N(d_1) = N(0.2641) = 0.6041$

$N(d_2) = N(-0.1127) = 0.4551$

$$V = \$67.83(0.6041) - \$70e^{-0.06}(0.4551)$$

$$= \$40.98 - \$70(0.9418)(0.4551)$$

$$= \$10.98.$$

Note: Values of $N(d_i)$ obtained from Excel using NORMSDIST function. See *Ch 12 Mini Case.xls* for details.

12 - 40

Step 5: Use financial engineering techniques.

- Although there are many existing models for financial options, sometimes none correspond to the project's real option.
- In that case, you must use financial engineering techniques, which are covered in later finance courses.
- Alternatively, you could simply use decision tree analysis.

12 - 41

Other Factors to Consider When Deciding When to Invest

- Delaying the project means that cash flows come later rather than sooner.
- It might make sense to proceed today if there are important advantages to being the first competitor to enter a market.
- Waiting may allow you to take advantage of changing conditions.

12 - 42

A New Situation: Cost is $75 Million, No Option to Wait

Cost Year 0	Prob.	Future Cash Flows Year 1	Year 2	Year 3	NPV this Scenario
	30%	$45	$45	$45	$36.91
-$75	40%	$30	$30	$30	-$0.39
	30%	$15	$15	$15	-$37.70

Example: $36.91 = -$75 + $45/1.1 + $45/1.1 + $45/1.1.
See *Ch 12 Mini Case.xls* for calculations.

12 - 43

Expected NPV of New Situation

- E(NPV) = [0.3($36.91)]+[0.4(-$0.39)]
  + [0.3 (-$37.70)]
- E(NPV) = -$0.39.

- The project now looks like a loser.

12 - 44

Growth Option: You can replicate the original project after it ends in 3 years.

- NPV = NPV Original + NPV Replication
  $= -\$0.39 + -\$0.39/(1+0.10)^3$
  $= -\$0.39 + -\$0.30 = -\$0.69.$
- Still a loser, but you would implement Replication only if demand is high.

Note: the NPV would be even lower if we separately discounted the $75 million cost of Replication at the risk-free rate.

12 - 45

Decision Tree Analysis

Cost Year 0	Prob.	Future Cash Flows 1	2	3	4	5	6	NPV this Scenario
	30%	$45	$45	-$30	$45	$45	$45	$58.02
-$75	40%	$30	$30	$30	$0	$0	$0	-$0.39
	30%	$15	$15	$15	$0	$0	$0	-$37.70

Notes: The Year 3 CF includes the cost of the project if it is optimal to replicate. The cost is discounted at the risk-free rate, other cash flows are discounted at the cost of capital. See *Ch 12 Mini Case.xls* for all calculations.

12 - 46

Expected NPV of Decision Tree

- E(NPV) = [0.3($58.02)]+[0.4(-$0.39)] + [0.3 (-$37.70)]
- E(NPV) = $5.94.
- The growth option has turned a losing project into a winner!

12 - 47

Financial Option Analysis: Inputs

- X = exercise price = cost of implement project = $75 million.
- r_{RF} = risk-free rate = 6%.
- t = time to maturity = 3 years.

12 - 48

Estimating P: First, find the value of future CFs at exercise year.

Cost Year 0	Prob.	1	2	3	4	5	6	PV at Year 3	Prob. x NPV
	30%				$45	$45	$45	$111.91	$33.57
	40%				$30	$30	$30	$74.61	$29.84
	30%				$15	$15	$15	$37.30	$11.19

Example: $111.91 = $45/1.1 + $45/1.1² + $45/1.1³.
See *Ch 12 Mini Case.xls* for calculations.

12 - 49

Now find the expected PV at the current date, Year 0.

$PV_{Year\ 0}$		Year 1	Year 2	$PV_{Year\ 3}$
	High →			\$111.91
\$56.05	Average →			\$74.61
	Low →			\$37.30

$PV_{Year\ 0}$=PV of Exp. $PV_{Year\ 3}$ = [(0.3* \$111.91) +(0.4*\$74.61) +(0.3*\$37.3)]/1.1³ = \$56.05.
See *Ch 12 Mini Case.xls* for calculations.

12 - 50

The Input for P in the Black-Scholes Model

- The input for price is the present value of the project's expected future cash flows.
- Based on the previous slides,

P = \$56.05.

12 - 51

Estimating σ^2: Find Returns from the Present until the Option Expires

$PV_{Year\ 0}$		Year 1	Year 2	$PV_{Year\ 3}$	Annual Return
	High →			\$111.91	25.9%
\$56.05	Average →			\$74.61	10.0%
	Low →			\$37.30	-12.7%

Example: 25.9% = (\$111.91/\$56.05)$^{(1/3)}$ - 1.
See *Ch 12 Mini Case.xls* for calculations.

12 - 52

Use these scenarios, with their given probabilities, to find the expected return and variance of return.

E(Ret.)=0.3(0.259)+0.4(0.10)+0.3(-0.127)

E(Ret.)= 0.080 = 8.0%.

$\sigma^2 = 0.3(0.259-0.08)^2 + 0.4(0.10-0.08)^2$
$+ 0.3(-0.1275-0.08)^2$

$\sigma^2 =$ 0.023 = 2.3%.

12 - 53

Why is σ^2 so much lower than in the investment timing example?

- σ^2 has fallen, because the dispersion of cash flows for replication is the same as for the original project, even though it begins three years later. This means the rate of return for the replication is less volatile.
- We will do sensitivity analysis later.

12 - 54

Estimating σ^2 with the Indirect Method

- From earlier slides, we know the value of the project for each scenario at the expiration date.

	$PV_{Year\ 3}$
High	\$111.91
Average	\$74.61
Low	\$37.30

12 - 55

Use these scenarios, with their given probabilities, to find the project's expected PV and σ_{PV}.

E(PV)=.3($111.91)+.4($74.61)+.3($37.3)

E(PV)= $74.61.

σ_{PV} = [.3($111.91-$74.61)^2
+ .4($74.61-$74.61)^2
+ .3($37.30-$74.61)^2]$^{1/2}$

σ_{PV} = $28.90.

12 - 56

Now use the indirect formula to estimate σ^2.

- CV_{PV} = $28.90 /$74.61 = 0.39.
- The option expires in 3 years, t=3.

$$\sigma^2 = \frac{\ln[0.39^2 + 1]}{3} = 4.7\%$$

12 - 57

Use the Black-Scholes Model:
P = $56.06; X = $75; r_{RF} = 6%;
t = 3 years: σ^2 = 0.047

V = $56.06[N($d_1$)] - 75e^{-(0.06)(3)}$[N(d_2)].

$$d_1 = \frac{\ln(\$56.06/\$75)+[(0.06 + 0.047/2)](3)}{(0.047)^{0.5}(3)^{.05}}$$

= -0.1085.

$d_2 = d_1 - (0.047)^{0.5}(3)^{.05} = d_1 - 0.3755$
= -0.1085 - 0.3755 =- 0.4840.

12 - 58

$N(d_1) = N(0.2641) = 0.4568$
$N(d_2) = N(-0.1127) = 0.3142$

$V = \$56.06(0.4568) - \$75e^{(-0.06)(3)}(0.3142)$
$= \$5.92.$

Note: Values of $N(d_i)$ obtained from Excel using NORMSDIST function. See *Ch 12 Mini Case.xls* for calculations.

12 - 59

Total Value of Project with Growth Opportunity

Total value = NPV of Original Project + Value of growth option
=-\$0.39 + \$5.92
= \$5.5 million.

12 - 60

Sensitivity Analysis on the Impact of Risk (using the Black-Scholes model)

- **If risk, defined by σ^2, goes up, then value of growth option goes up:**
  - **σ^2 = 4.7%, Option Value = \$5.92**
  - **σ^2 = 14.2%, Option Value = \$12.10**
  - **σ^2 = 50%, Option Value = \$24.08**
- **Does this help explain the high value many dot.com companies had before 2002?**

13 - 1

CHAPTER 13
Analysis of Financial Statements

- Ratio analysis
- Du Pont system
- Effects of improving ratios
- Limitations of ratio analysis
- Qualitative factors

13 - 2

Income Statement

	2004	2005E
Sales	5,834,400	7,035,600
COGS	4,980,000	5,800,000
Other expenses	720,000	612,960
Deprec.	116,960	120,000
Tot. op. costs	5,816,960	6,532,960
EBIT	17,440	502,640
Int. expense	176,000	80,000
EBT	(158,560)	422,640
Taxes (40%)	(63,424)	169,056
Net income	(95,136)	253,584

13 - 3

Balance Sheets: Assets

	2004	2005E
Cash	7,282	14,000
S-T invest.	20,000	71,632
AR	632,160	878,000
Inventories	1,287,360	1,716,480
Total CA	1,946,802	2,680,112
Net FA	939,790	836,840
Total assets	2,886,592	3,516,952

13 - 4

Balance Sheets: Liabilities & Equity

	2004	2005E
Accts. payable	324,000	359,800
Notes payable	720,000	300,000
Accruals	284,960	380,000
Total CL	1,328,960	1,039,800
Long-term debt	1,000,000	500,000
Common stock	460,000	1,680,936
Ret. earnings	97,632	296,216
Total equity	557,632	1,977,152
Total L&E	2,886,592	3,516,952

13 - 5

Other Data

	2004	2005E
Stock price	$6.00	$12.17
# of shares	100,000	250,000
EPS	-$0.95	$1.01
DPS	$0.11	$0.22
Book val. per share	$5.58	$7.91
Lease payments	40,000	40,000
Tax rate	0.4	0.4

13 - 6

Why are ratios useful?

- Standardize numbers; facilitate comparisons
- Used to highlight weaknesses and strengths

13 - 7

What are the five major categories of ratios, and what questions do they answer?

- Liquidity: Can we make required payments as they fall due?
- Asset management: Do we have the right amount of assets for the level of sales?

(More...)

13 - 8

- Debt management: Do we have the right mix of debt and equity?
- Profitability: Do sales prices exceed unit costs, and are sales high enough as reflected in PM, ROE, and ROA?
- Market value: Do investors like what they see as reflected in P/E and M/B ratios?

13 - 9

Calculate the firm's forecasted current and quick ratios for 2005.

$$CR_{05} = \frac{CA}{CL} = \frac{\$2,680}{\$1,040} = 2.58x.$$

$$QR_{05} = \frac{CA - Inv.}{CL}$$

$$= \frac{\$2,680 - \$1,716}{\$1,040} = 0.93x.$$

13 - 10

Comments on CR and QR

	2005E	2004	2003	Ind.
CR	2.58x	1.46x	2.3x	2.7x
QR	0.93x	0.5x	0.8x	1.0x

- Expected to improve but still below the industry average.
- Liquidity position is weak.

13 - 11

What is the inventory turnover ratio as compared to the industry average?

$$\text{Inv. turnover} = \frac{\text{Sales}}{\text{Inventories}} = \frac{\$7{,}036}{\$1{,}716} = 4.10\text{x}.$$

	2005E	2004	2003	Ind.
Inv. T.	4.1x	4.5x	4.8x	6.1x

13 - 12

Comments on Inventory Turnover

- Inventory turnover is below industry average.
- Firm might have old inventory, or its control might be poor.
- No improvement is currently forecasted.

13 - 13

DSO is the average number of days after making a sale before receiving cash.

$$\text{DSO} = \frac{\text{Receivables}}{\text{Average sales per day}}$$

$$= \frac{\text{Receivables}}{\text{Sales/365}} = \frac{\$878}{\$7,036/365}$$

= 45.5 days.

13 - 14

Appraisal of DSO

	2005	2004	2003	Ind.
DSO	45.5	39.5	37.4	32.0

- Firm collects too slowly, and situation is getting worse.
- Poor credit policy.

13 - 15

Fixed Assets and Total Assets Turnover Ratios

$$\text{Fixed assets turnover} = \frac{\text{Sales}}{\text{Net fixed assets}}$$

$$= \frac{\$7,036}{\$837} = 8.41\text{x}.$$

$$\text{Total assets turnover} = \frac{\text{Sales}}{\text{Total assets}}$$

$$= \frac{\$7,036}{\$3,517} = 2.00\text{x}.$$

(More...)

13 - 16

	2005E	2004	2003	Ind.
FA TO	8.4x	6.2x	10.0x	7.0x
TA TO	2.0x	2.0x	2.3x	2.5x

- FA turnover is expected to exceed industry average. Good.
- TA turnover not up to industry average. Caused by excessive current assets (A/R and inventory).

13 - 17

Calculate the debt, TIE, and EBITDA coverage ratios.

$$\text{Debt ratio} = \frac{\text{Total liabilities}}{\text{Total assets}} = \frac{\$1,040 + \$500}{\$3,517} = 43.8\%.$$

$$\text{TIE} = \frac{\text{EBIT}}{\text{Int. expense}} = \frac{\$502.6}{\$80} = 6.3\text{x}.$$

(More...)

13 - 18

$$\text{EBITDA coverage} = \text{EC}$$

$$\frac{\text{EBIT + Depr. \& Amort. + Lease payments}}{\text{Interest expense} + \text{Lease pmt.} + \text{Loan pmt.}}$$

$$= \frac{\$502.6 + \$120 + \$40}{\$80 + \$40 + \$0} = 5.5\text{x}.$$

All three ratios reflect use of debt, but focus on different aspects.

13 - 19

How do the debt management ratios compare with industry averages?

	2005E	2004	2003	Ind.
D/A	43.8%	80.7%	54.8%	50.0%
TIE	6.3x	0.1x	3.3x	6.2x
EC	5.5x	0.8x	2.6x	8.0x

Recapitalization improved situation, but lease payments drag down EC.

13 - 20

Profit Margin (PM)

$$PM = \frac{NI}{Sales} = \frac{\$253.6}{\$7,036} = 3.6\%.$$

	2005E	2004	2003	Ind.
PM	3.6%	-1.6%	2.6%	3.6%

Very bad in 2004, but projected to meet industry average in 2005. Looking good.

13 - 21

Basic Earning Power (BEP)

$$BEP = \frac{EBIT}{Total\ assets}$$

$$= \frac{\$502.6}{\$3,517} = 14.3\%.$$

(More...)

13 - 22

	2005E	2004	2003	Ind.
BEP	14.3%	0.6%	14.2%	17.8%

- BEP removes effect of taxes and financial leverage. Useful for comparison.
- Projected to be below average.
- Room for improvement.

13 - 23

Return on Assets (ROA) and Return on Equity (ROE)

$$ROA = \frac{\text{Net income}}{\text{Total assets}}$$

$$= \frac{\$253.6}{\$3,517} = 7.2\%.$$

(More...)

13 - 24

$$ROE = \frac{\text{Net income}}{\text{Common equity}}$$

$$= \frac{\$253.6}{\$1,977} = 12.8\%.$$

	2005E	2004	2003	Ind.
ROA	7.2%	-3.3%	6.0%	9.0%
ROE	12.8%	-17.1%	13.3%	18.0%

Both below average but improving.

13 - 25

Effects of Debt on ROA and ROE

- ROA is lowered by debt--interest expense lowers net income, which also lowers ROA.
- However, the use of debt lowers equity, and if equity is lowered more than net income, ROE would increase.

13 - 26

Calculate and appraise the P/E, P/CF, and M/B ratios.

Price = $12.17.

$$EPS = \frac{NI}{\text{Shares out.}} = \frac{\$253.6}{250} = \$1.01.$$

$$P/E = \frac{\text{Price per share}}{EPS} = \frac{\$12.17}{\$1.01} = 12x.$$

13 - 27

Industry P/E Ratios

Industry	Ticker*	P/E
Banking	STI	17.6
Software	MSFT	33.0
Drug	PFE	31.7
Electric Utilities	DUK	13.7
Semiconductors	INTC	57.5
Steel	NUE	28.1
Tobacco	MO	12.3
Water Utilities	CFT	21.8
S&P 500		30.4

*Ticker is for typical firm in industry, but P/E ratio is for the industry, not the individual firm.

13 - 28

$$\text{CF per share} = \frac{\text{NI + Depr.}}{\text{Shares out.}}$$

$$= \frac{\$253.6 + \$120.0}{250} = \$1.49.$$

$$\text{P/CF} = \frac{\text{Price per share}}{\text{Cash flow per share}}$$

$$= \frac{\$12.17}{\$1.49} = 8.2\text{x}.$$

13 - 29

$$\text{BVPS} = \frac{\text{Com. equity}}{\text{Shares out.}}$$

$$= \frac{\$1{,}977}{250} = \$7.91.$$

$$\text{M/B} = \frac{\text{Mkt. price per share}}{\text{Book value per share}}$$

$$= \frac{\$12.17}{\$7.91} = 1.54\text{x}.$$

13 - 30

	2005E	2004	2003	Ind.
P/E	12.0x	-6.3x	9.7x	14.2x
P/CF	8.2x	27.5x	8.0x	7.6x
M/B	1.5x	1.1x	1.3x	2.9x

- P/E: How much investors will pay for $1 of earnings. High is good.
- M/B: How much paid for $1 of book value. Higher is good.
- P/E and M/B are high if ROE is high, risk is low.

13 - 31

Common Size Balance Sheets: Divide all items by Total Assets

Assets	2003	2004	2005E	Ind.
Cash	0.6%	0.3%	0.4%	0.3%
ST Invest.	3.3%	0.7%	2.0%	0.3%
AR	23.9%	21.9%	25.0%	22.4%
Invent.	48.7%	44.6%	48.8%	41.2%
Total CA	76.5%	67.4%	76.2%	64.1%
Net FA	23.5%	32.6%	23.8%	35.9%
TA	100.0%	100.0%	100.0%	100.0%

13 - 32

Divide all items by Total Liabilities & Equity

	2003	2004	2005E	Ind.
AP	9.9%	11.2%	10.2%	11.9%
Notes pay.	13.6%	24.9%	8.5%	2.4%
Accruals	9.3%	9.9%	10.8%	9.5%
Total CL	32.8%	46.0%	29.6%	23.7%
LT Debt	22.0%	34.6%	14.2%	26.3%
Total eq.	45.2%	19.3%	56.2%	50.0%
Total L&E	100.0%	100.0%	100.0%	100.0%

13 - 33

Analysis of Common Size Balance Sheets

- Computron has higher proportion of inventory and current assets than Industry.
- Computron now has more equity (which means LESS debt) than Industry.
- Computron has more short-term debt than industry, but less long-term debt than industry.

13 - 34

Common Size Income Statement: Divide all items by Sales

	2003	2004	2005E	Ind.
Sales	100.0%	100.0%	100.0%	100.0%
COGS	83.4%	85.4%	82.4%	84.5%
Other exp.	9.9%	12.3%	8.7%	4.4%
Depr.	0.6%	2.0%	1.7%	4.0%
EBIT	6.1%	0.3%	7.1%	7.1%
Int. Exp.	1.8%	3.0%	1.1%	1.1%
EBT	4.3%	-2.7%	6.0%	5.9%
Taxes	1.7%	-1.1%	2.4%	2.4%
NI	2.6%	-1.6%	3.6%	3.6%

13 - 35

Analysis of Common Size Income Statements

- Computron has lower COGS (86.7) than industry (84.5), but higher other expenses. Result is that Computron has similar EBIT (7.1) as industry.

13 - 36

Percentage Change Analysis: Find Percentage Change from First Year (2003)

Income St.	2003	2004	2005E
Sales	0.0%	70.0%	105.0%
COGS	0.0%	73.9%	102.5%
Other exp.	0.0%	111.8%	80.3%
Depr.	0.0%	518.8%	534.9%
EBIT	0.0%	-91.7%	140.4%
Int. Exp.	0.0%	181.6%	28.0%
EBT	0.0%	-208.2%	188.3%
Taxes	0.0%	-208.2%	188.3%
NI	0.0%	-208.2%	188.3%

13 - 37

Analysis of Percent Change Income Statement

- We see that 2005 sales grew 105% from 2003, and that NI grew 188% from 2003.
- So Computron has become more profitable.

13 - 38

Percentage Change Balance Sheets

Assets	2003	2004	2005E
Cash	0.0%	-19.1%	55.6%
ST Invest.	0.0%	-58.8%	47.4%
AR	0.0%	80.0%	150.0%
Invent.	0.0%	80.0%	140.0%
Total CA	0.0%	73.2%	138.4%
Net FA	0.0%	172.6%	142.7%
TA	0.0%	96.5%	139.4%

13 - 39

Liab. & Eq.	2003	2004	2005E
AP	0.0%	122.5%	147.1%
Notes pay.	0.0%	260.0%	50.0%
Accruals	0.0%	109.5%	179.4%
Total CL	0.0%	175.9%	115.9%
LT Debt	0.0%	209.2%	54.6%
Total eq.	0.0%	-16.0%	197.9%
Total L&E	0.0%	96.5%	139.4%

Analysis of Percent Change Balance Sheets

- We see that total assets grew at a rate of 139%, while sales grew at a rate of only 105%. So asset utilization remains a problem.

Explain the Du Pont System

- The Du Pont system focuses on:
  - Expense control (PM)
  - Asset utilization (TATO)
  - Debt utilization (EM)
- It shows how these factors combine to determine the ROE.

The Du Pont System

$$\left(\begin{array}{c}\text{Profit}\\\text{margin}\end{array}\right)\left(\begin{array}{c}\text{TA}\\\text{turnover}\end{array}\right)\left(\begin{array}{c}\text{Equity}\\\text{multiplier}\end{array}\right) = \text{ROE}$$

$$\frac{\text{NI}}{\text{Sales}} \times \frac{\text{Sales}}{\text{TA}} \times \frac{\text{TA}}{\text{CE}} = \text{ROE}.$$

2003	2.6%	x	2.3	x	2.2 =		13.2%
2004	-1.6%	x	2.0	x	5.2 =		-16.6%
2005	3.6%	x	2.0	x	1.8 =		13.0%
Ind.	3.6%	x	2.5	x	2.0 =		18.0%

13 - 43

What are some potential problems and limitations of financial ratio analysis?

- Comparison with industry averages is difficult if the firm operates many different divisions.
- "Average" performance is not necessarily good.
- Seasonal factors can distort ratios.

(More...)

13 - 44

- Window dressing techniques can make statements and ratios look better.
- Different accounting and operating practices can distort comparisons.
- Sometimes it is difficult to tell if a ratio value is "good" or "bad."
- Often, different ratios give different signals, so it is difficult to tell, on balance, whether a company is in a strong or weak financial condition.

13 - 45

What are some qualitative factors analysts should consider when evaluating a company's likely future financial performance?

- Are the company's revenues tied to a single customer?
- To what extent are the company's revenues tied to a single product?
- To what extent does the company rely on a single supplier?

(More...)

13 - 46

- What percentage of the company's business is generated overseas?
- What is the competitive situation?
- What does the future have in store?
- What is the company's legal and regulatory environment?

14 - 1

CHAPTER 14
Financial Planning and Forecasting Pro Forma Financial Statements

- Financial planning
- Additional Funds Needed (AFN) formula
- Pro forma financial statements
  - Sales forecasts
  - Percent of sales method

14 - 2

Financial Planning and Pro Forma Statements

- Three important uses:
  - Forecast the amount of external financing that will be required
  - Evaluate the impact that changes in the operating plan have on the value of the firm
  - Set appropriate targets for compensation plans

14 - 3

Steps in Financial Forecasting

- Forecast sales
- Project the assets needed to support sales
- Project internally generated funds
- Project outside funds needed
- Decide how to raise funds
- See effects of plan on ratios and stock price

14 - 4

2004 Balance Sheet (Millions of $)

Cash & sec.	$ 20	Accts. pay. & accruals	$ 100
Accounts rec.	240	Notes payable	100
Inventories	240	Total CL	$ 200
Total CA	$ 500	L-T debt	100
		Common stk	500
Net fixed assets	500	Retained earnings	200
Total assets	$1,000	Total claims	$1,000

14 - 5

2004 Income Statement (Millions of $)

Sales	$2,000.00
Less: COGS (60%)	1,200.00
SGA costs	700.00
EBIT	$ 100.00
Interest	10.00
EBT	$ 90.00
Taxes (40%)	36.00
Net income	$ 54.00
Dividends (40%)	$21.60
Add'n to RE	$32.40

14 - 6

AFN (Additional Funds Needed): Key Assumptions

- Operating at full capacity in 2004.
- Each type of asset grows proportionally with sales.
- Payables and accruals grow proportionally with sales.
- 2004 profit margin ($54/$2,000 = 2.70%) and payout (40%) will be maintained.
- Sales are expected to increase by $500 million.

14 - 7

Definitions of Variables in AFN

- A^*/S_0: assets required to support sales; called capital intensity ratio.
- ΔS: increase in sales.
- L^*/S_0: spontaneous liabilities ratio
- M: profit margin (Net income/sales)
- RR: retention ratio; percent of net income not paid as dividend.

14 - 8

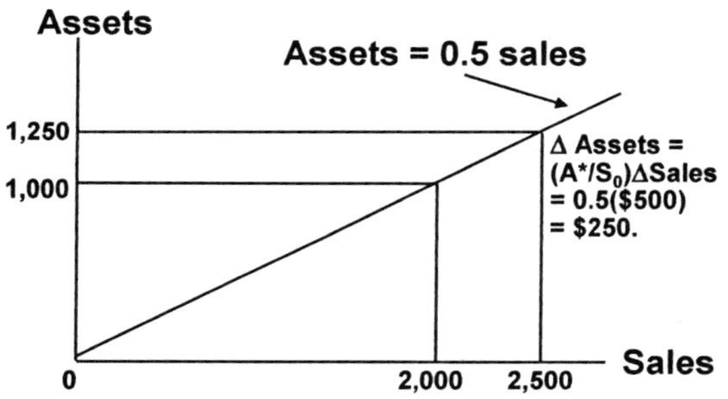

A^*/S_0 = \$1,000/\$2,000 = 0.5 = \$1,250/\$2,500.

14 - 9

Assets must increase by \$250 million. What is the AFN, based on the AFN equation?

$$\begin{aligned} \text{AFN} &= (A^*/S_0)\Delta S - (L^*/S_0)\Delta S - M(S_1)(RR) \\ &= (\$1{,}000/\$2{,}000)(\$500) \\ &\quad - (\$100/\$2{,}000)(\$500) \\ &\quad - 0.0270(\$2{,}500)(1 - 0.4) \\ &= \$184.5 \text{ million.} \end{aligned}$$

14 - 10

How would increases in these items affect the AFN?

- Higher sales:
  - Increases asset requirements, increases AFN.
- Higher dividend payout ratio:
  - Reduces funds available internally, increases AFN.

(More...)

14 - 11

- Higher profit margin:
  - Increases funds available internally, decreases AFN.
- Higher capital intensity ratio, A^*/S_0:
  - Increases asset requirements, increases AFN.
- Pay suppliers sooner:
  - Decreases spontaneous liabilities, increases AFN.

14 - 12

Projecting Pro Forma Statements with the Percent of Sales Method

- Project sales based on forecasted growth rate in sales
- Forecast some items as a percent of the forecasted sales
  - Costs
  - Cash
  - Accounts receivable

(More...)

14 - 13

- Items as percent of sales (Continued...)
  - Inventories
  - Net fixed assets
  - Accounts payable and accruals
- Choose other items
  - Debt
  - Dividend policy (which determines retained earnings)
  - Common stock

14 - 14

Sources of Financing Needed to Support Asset Requirements

- Given the previous assumptions and choices, we can estimate:
  - Required assets to support sales
  - Specified sources of financing
- Additional funds needed (AFN) is:
  - Required assets minus specified sources of financing

14 - 15

Implications of AFN

- If AFN is positive, then you must secure additional financing.
- If AFN is negative, then you have more financing than is needed.
  - Pay off debt.
  - Buy back stock.
  - Buy short-term investments.

14 - 16

How to Forecast Interest Expense

- Interest expense is actually based on the daily balance of debt during the year.
- There are three ways to approximate interest expense. Base it on:
  - Debt at end of year
  - Debt at beginning of year
  - Average of beginning and ending debt

More...

14 - 17

Basing Interest Expense on Debt at End of Year

- Will over-estimate interest expense if debt is added throughout the year instead of all on January 1.
- Causes circularity called financial feedback: more debt causes more interest, which reduces net income, which reduces retained earnings, which causes more debt, etc.

More...

14 - 18

Basing Interest Expense on Debt at Beginning of Year

- Will under-estimate interest expense if debt is added throughout the year instead of all on December 31.
- But doesn't cause problem of circularity.

More...

14 - 19

Basing Interest Expense on Average of Beginning and Ending Debt

- Will accurately estimate the interest payments if debt is added smoothly throughout the year.
- But has problem of circularity.

More...

14 - 20

A Solution that Balances Accuracy and Complexity

- Base interest expense on beginning debt, but use a slightly higher interest rate.
  - Easy to implement
  - Reasonably accurate
- See *Ch 14 Mini Case Feedback.xls* for an example basing interest expense on average debt.

14 - 21

Percent of Sales: Inputs

	2004 Actual	2005 Proj.
COGS/Sales	60%	60%
SGA/Sales	35%	35%
Cash/Sales	1%	1%
Acct. rec./Sales	12%	12%
Inv./Sales	12%	12%
Net FA/Sales	25%	25%
AP & accr./Sales	5%	5%

14 - 22

Other Inputs

Percent growth in sales	25%
Growth factor in sales (g)	1.25
Interest rate on debt	10%
Tax rate	40%
Dividend payout rate	40%

14 - 23

2005 Forecasted Income Statement

	2004	Factor	2005 1st Pass
Sales	$2,000	g=1.25	$2,500.0
Less: COGS		Pct=60%	1,500.0
SGA		Pct=35%	875.0
EBIT			$125.0
Interest		0.1(Debt$_{04}$)	20.0
EBT			$105.0
Taxes (40%)			42.0
Net. income			$63.0
Div. (40%)			$25.2
Add. to RE			$37.8

14 - 24

2005 Balance Sheet (Assets)

Forecasted assets are a percent of forecasted sales.

2005 Sales = $2,500

	Factor	2005
Cash	Pct= 1%	$25.0
Accts. rec.	Pct=12%	300.0
Inventories	Pct=12%	300.0
Total CA		$625.0
Net FA	Pct=25%	625.0
Total assets		$1,250.0

14 - 25

2005 Preliminary Balance Sheet (Claims)

2005 Sales = $2,500

	2004	Factor	2005 Without AFN
AP/accruals		Pct=5%	$125.0
Notes payable	100	→	100.0
Total CL			$225.0
L-T debt	100	→	100.0
Common stk.	500	→	500.0
Ret. earnings	200	+37.8*	237.8
Total claims			$1,062.8

*From forecasted income statement.

14 - 26

What are the additional funds needed (AFN)?

- Required assets = $1,250.0
- Specified sources of fin. = $1,062.8
- Forecast AFN = $ 187.2

NWC must have the assets to make forecasted sales, and so it needs an equal amount of financing. So, we must secure another $187.2 of financing.

14 - 27

Assumptions about How AFN Will Be Raised

- No new common stock will be issued.
- Any external funds needed will be raised as debt, 50% notes payable, and 50% L-T debt.

14 - 28

How will the AFN be financed?

Additional notes payable =
0.5 ($187.2) = $93.6.

Additional L-T debt =
0.5 ($187.2) = $93.6.

14 - 29

2005 Balance Sheet (Claims)

	w/o AFN	AFN	With AFN
AP/accruals	$ 125.0		$ 125.0
Notes payable	100.0	+93.6	193.6
Total CL	$ 225.0		$ 318.6
L-T debt	100.0	+93.6	193.6
Common stk.	500.0		500.0
Ret. earnings	237.8		237.8
Total claims	$1,071.0		$1,250.0

14 - 30

Equation AFN = $184.5 vs. Pro Forma AFN = $187.2. Why are they different?

- Equation method assumes a constant profit margin.
- Pro forma method is more flexible. More important, it allows different items to grow at different rates.

14 - 31

Forecasted Ratios

	2004	2005(E)	Industry
Profit Margin	2.70%	2.52%	4.00%
ROE	7.71%	8.54%	15.60%
DSO (days)	43.80	43.80	32.00
Inv. turnover	8.33x	8.33x	11.00x
FA turnover	4.00x	4.00x	5.00x
Debt ratio	30.00%	40.98%	36.00%
TIE	10.00x	6.25x	9.40x
Current ratio	2.50x	1.96x	3.00x

14 - 32

What are the forecasted free cash flow and ROIC?

	2004	2005(E)
Net operating WC (CA - AP & accruals)	$400	$500
Total operating capital (Net op. WC + net FA)	$900	$1,125
NOPAT (EBITx(1-T))	$60	$75
Less Inv. in op. capital		$225
Free cash flow		-$150
ROIC (NOPAT/Capital)		6.7%

14 - 33

Proposed Improvements

	Before	After
DSO (days)	43.80	32.00
Accts. rec./Sales	12.00%	8.77%
Inventory turnover	8.33x	11.00x
Inventory/Sales	12.00%	9.09%
SGA/Sales	35.00%	33.00%

14 - 34

Impact of Improvements (see *Ch 14 Mini Case.xls* for details)

	Before	After
AFN	$187.2	$15.7
Free cash flow	-$150.0	$33.5
ROIC (NOPAT/Capital)	6.7%	10.8%
ROE	7.7%	12.3%

14 - 35

Suppose in 2004 fixed assets had been operated at only 75% of capacity.

$$\text{Capacity sales} = \frac{\text{Actual sales}}{\text{\% of capacity}}$$

$$= \frac{\$2,000}{0.75} = \$2,667.$$

With the existing fixed assets, sales could be $2,667. Since sales are forecasted at only $2,500, no new fixed assets are needed.

14 - 36

How would the excess capacity situation affect the 2005 AFN?

- The previously projected increase in fixed assets was $125.
- Since no new fixed assets will be needed, AFN will fall by $125, to

  $187.2 - $125 = $62.2.

14 - 37

Economies of Scale

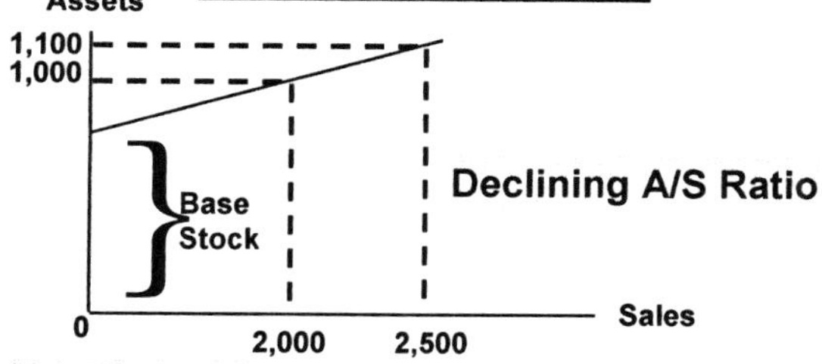

$1,000/$2,000 = 0.5; $1,100/$2,500 = 0.44. Declining ratio shows economies of scale. Going from S = $0 to S = $2,000 requires $1,000 of assets. Next $500 of sales requires only $100 of assets.

14 - 38

Lumpy Assets

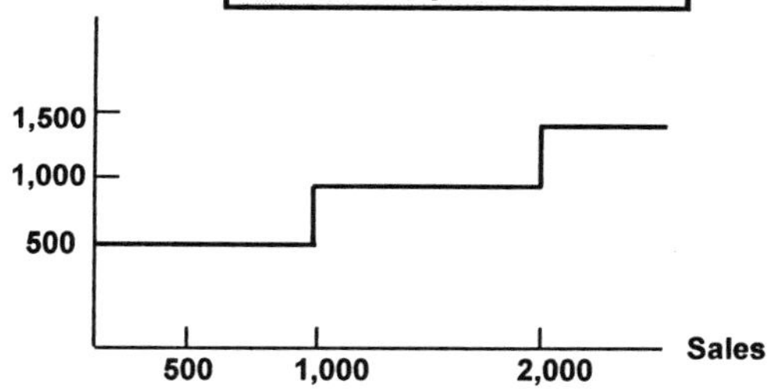

A/S changes if assets are lumpy. Generally will have excess capacity, but eventually a small ΔS leads to a large ΔA.

14 - 39

Summary: How different factors affect the AFN forecast.

- Excess capacity: lowers AFN.
- Economies of scale: leads to less-than-proportional asset increases.
- Lumpy assets: leads to large periodic AFN requirements, recurring excess capacity.

15 - 1

CHAPTER 15
Corporate Valuation, Value-Based Management, and Corporate Governance

- Corporate Valuation
- Value-Based Management
- Corporate Governance

15 - 2

Corporate Valuation: List the two types of assets that a company owns.

- Assets-in-place
- Financial, or nonoperating, assets

15 - 3

Assets-in-Place

- Assets-in-place are tangible, such as buildings, machines, inventory.
- Usually they are expected to grow.
- They generate free cash flows.
- The PV of their expected future free cash flows, discounted at the WACC, is the value of operations.

15 - 4

Value of Operations

$$V_{Op} = \sum_{t=1}^{\infty} \frac{FCF_t}{(1+WACC)^t}$$

15 - 5

Nonoperating Assets

- Marketable securities
- Ownership of non-controlling interest in another company
- Value of nonoperating assets usually is very close to figure that is reported on balance sheets.

determined by the market

15 - 6

Total Corporate Value

- Total corporate value is sum of:
  - Value of operations
  - Value of nonoperating assets

15 - 7

Claims on Corporate Value

- Debtholders have first claim.
- Preferred stockholders have the next claim.
- Any remaining value belongs to stockholders.

15 - 8

Applying the Corporate Valuation Model

- Forecast the financial statements, as shown in Chapter 14.
- Calculate the projected free cash flows.
- Model can be applied to a company that does not pay dividends, a privately held company, or a division of a company, since FCF can be calculated for each of these situations.

15 - 9

Data for Valuation

- FCF_0 = $20 million
- WACC = 10% (cost of capital)
- g = 5%
- Marketable securities = $100 million
- Debt = $200 million
- Preferred stock = $50 million
- Book value of equity = $210 million

15 - 10

Value of Operations: Constant Growth

Suppose FCF grows at constant rate g.

$$V_{Op} = \sum_{t=1}^{\infty} \frac{FCF_t}{(1+WACC)^t}$$

$$= \sum_{t=1}^{\infty} \frac{FCF_0 (1+g)^t}{(1+WACC)^t}$$

15 - 11

Constant Growth Formula

- Notice that the term in parentheses is less than one and gets smaller as t gets larger. As t gets very large, term approaches zero.

$$V_{Op} = \sum_{t=1}^{\infty} FCF_0 \left(\frac{1+g}{1+WACC} \right)^t$$

15 - 12

Constant Growth Formula (Cont.)

- The summation can be replaced by a single formula:

$$V_{Op} = \frac{FCF_1}{(WACC-g)}$$

$$= \frac{FCF_0 (1+g)}{(WACC-g)}$$

When dealing with a constant growth company

15 - 13

Find Value of Operations

$$V_{Op} = \frac{FCF_0(1+g)}{(WACC-g)}$$

$$V_{Op} = \frac{20(1+0.05)}{(0.10-0.05)} = 420$$

15 - 14

Value of Equity

- Sources of Corporate Value
  - Value of operations = $420
  - Value of non-operating assets = $100 or marketable securities
- Claims on Corporate Value
  - Value of Debt = $200
  - Value of Preferred Stock = $50
  - Value of Equity = ?

15 - 15

Value of Equity

Total corporate value = V_{Op} + Mkt. Sec.
= $420 + $100
= $520 million

Value of equity = Total - Debt - Pref.
= $520 - $200 - $50
= $270 million

15 - 16

Market Value Added (MVA)

- MVA = Total corporate value of firm minus total book value of firm
- Total book value of firm = book value of equity + book value of debt + book value of preferred stock
- MVA = \$520 - (\$210 + \$200 + \$50)

  = \$60 million

15 - 17

Breakdown of Corporate Value

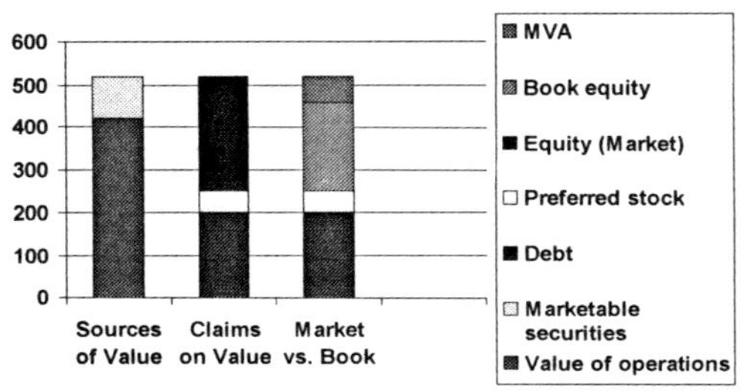

15 - 18

Expansion Plan: Nonconstant Growth

- Finance expansion by borrowing \$40 million and halting dividends.
- Projected free cash flows (FCF):
  - Year 1 FCF = -\$5 million.
  - Year 2 FCF = \$10 million.
  - Year 3 FCF = \$20 million
  - FCF grows at constant rate of 6% after year 3.

(More...)

15 - 19

- The weighted average cost of capital, r_c, is 10%.
- The company has 10 million shares of stock.

15 - 20

Horizon Value

- Free cash flows are forecast for three years in this example, so the forecast horizon is three years.
- Growth in free cash flows is not constant during the forecast,so we can't use the constant growth formula to find the value of operations at time 0.

15 - 21

Horizon Value (Cont.)

- Growth is constant after the horizon (3 years), so we can modify the constant growth formula to find the value of all free cash flows beyond the horizon, discounted back to the horizon.

also known as Terminal or continual value

15 - 22

Horizon Value Formula

$$HV = V_{Op\ at\ time\ t} = \frac{FCF_t(1+g)}{(WACC - g)}$$

- Horizon value is also called terminal value, or continuing value.

15 - 23

Find the value of operations by discounting the free cash flows at the cost of capital.

Timeline: 0, 1, 2, 3, 4; r_c=10% (from 0 to 1); g = 6% (from 3 to 4)

FCF= -5.00 (year 1), 10.00 (year 2), 20.00 (year 3), 21.2 (year 4)

-4.545 ← -5.00

8.264 ← 10.00

15.026 ← 20.00

398.197 ← $V_{op\ at\ 3} = \frac{\$21.2}{0.10 - 0.06} = \$530.$

416.942 = V_{op}

15 - 24

Find the price per share of common stock.

Value of equity = Value of operations
- Value of debt
= \$416.94 - \$40
= \$376.94 million.

Price per share = \$376.94 /10 = \$37.69.

15 - 25

Value-Based Management (VBM)

- VBM is the systematic application of the corporate valuation model to all corporate decisions and strategic initiatives.
- The objective of VBM is to increase Market Value Added (MVA)

15 - 26

MVA and the Four Value Drivers

- MVA is determined by four drivers:
  - Sales growth
  - Operating profitability (OP=NOPAT/Sales)
  - Capital requirements (CR=Operating capital / Sales)
  - Weighted average cost of capital

15 - 27

MVA for a Constant Growth Firm

$$MVA_t =$$

$$\left[\frac{\text{Sales}_t(1+g)}{WACC-g}\right]\left[OP - WACC\left(\frac{CR}{(1+g)}\right)\right]$$

15 - 28

Insights from the Constant Growth Model

- The first bracket is the MVA of a firm that gets to keep all of its sales revenues (i.e., its operating profit margin is 100%) and that never has to make additional investments in operating capital.

$$\left[\frac{Sales_t(1+g)}{WACC-g}\right]$$

15 - 29

Insights (Cont.)

- The second bracket is the operating profit (as a %) the firm gets to keep, less the return that investors require for having tied up their capital in the firm.

$$\left[OP - WACC\left(\frac{CR}{(1+g)}\right)\right]$$

15 - 30

Improvements in MVA due to the Value Drivers

- MVA will improve if:
  - WACC is reduced
  - operating profitability (OP) increases
  - the capital requirement (CR) decreases

15 - 31

The Impact of Growth

- The second term in brackets can be either positive or negative, depending on the relative size of profitability, capital requirements, and required return by investors.

$$\left[\text{OP} - \text{WACC}\left(\frac{\text{CR}}{(1+g)}\right)\right]$$

15 - 32

The Impact of Growth (Cont.)

- If the second term in brackets is negative, then growth decreases MVA. In other words, profits are not enough to offset the return on capital required by investors.
- If the second term in brackets is positive, then growth increases MVA.

15 - 33

Expected Return on Invested Capital (EROIC)

- The expected return on invested capital is the NOPAT expected next period divided by the amount of capital that is currently invested:

$$\text{EROIC}_t = \frac{\text{NOPAT}_{t+1}}{\text{Capital}_t}$$

15 - 34

MVA in Terms of Expected ROIC

$$MVA_t = \frac{Capital_t [EROIC_t - WACC]}{WACC - g}$$

If the spread between the expected return, $EROIC_t$, and the required return, WACC, is positive, then MVA is positive and growth makes MVA larger. The opposite is true if the spread is negative.

15 - 35

The Impact of Growth on MVA

- A company has two divisions. Both have current sales of $1,000, current expected growth of 5%, and a WACC of 10%.
- Division A has high profitability (OP=6%) but high capital requirements (CR=78%).
- Division B has low profitability (OP=4%) but low capital requirements (CR=27%).

15 - 36

What is the impact on MVA if growth goes from 5% to 6%?

	Division A		Division B	
OP	6%	6%	4%	4%
CR	78%	78%	27%	27%
Growth	5%	6%	5%	6%
MVA	(300.0)	(360.0)	300.0	385.0

Note: MVA is calculated using the formula on slide 15-27.

15 - 37

Expected ROIC and MVA

	Division A		Division B	
$Capital_0$	$780	$780	$270	$270
Growth	5%	6%	5%	6%
$Sales_1$	$1,050	$1,060	$1,050	$1,060
$NOPAT_1$	$63	$63.6	$42	$42.4
$EROIC_0$	8.1%	8.2%	15.6%	15.7%
MVA	(300.0)	(360.0)	300.0	385.0

15 - 38

Analysis of Growth Strategies

- The expected ROIC of Division A is less than the WACC, so the division should postpone growth efforts until it improves EROIC by reducing capital requirements (e.g., reducing inventory) and/or improving profitability.
- The expected ROIC of Division B is greater than the WACC, so the division should continue with its growth plans.

15 - 39

Two Primary Mechanisms of Corporate Governance

- "Stick"
    - Provisions in the charter that affect takeovers.
    - Composition of the board of directors.
- "Carrot: Compensation plans.

15 - 40

Entrenched Management

- Occurs when there is little chance that poorly performing managers will be replaced.
- Two causes:
  - Anti-takeover provisions in the charter
  - Weak board of directors

15 - 41

How are entrenched managers harmful to shareholders?

- Management consumes perks:
  - Lavish offices and corporate jets
  - Excessively large staffs
  - Memberships at country clubs
- Management accepts projects (or acquisitions) to make firm larger, even if MVA goes down.

15 - 42

Anti-Takeover Provisions

- Targeted share repurchases (i.e., greenmail)
- Shareholder rights provisions (i.e., poison pills)
- Restricted voting rights plans

15 - 43

Board of Directors

- Weak boards have many insiders (i.e., those who also have another position in the company) compared with outsiders.
- Interlocking boards are weaker (CEO of company A sits on board of company B, CEO of B sits on board of A).

15 - 44

Stock Options in Compensation Plans

- Gives owner of option the right to buy a share of the company's stock at a specified price (called the exercise price) even if the actual stock price is higher.
- Usually can't exercise the option for several years (called the vesting period).

15 - 45

Stock Options (Cont.)

- Can't exercise the option after a certain number of years (called the expiration, or maturity, date).

16 - 1

Chapter 16: Capital Structure Decisions: The Basics

- Overview and preview of capital structure effects
- Business versus financial risk
- The impact of debt on returns
- Capital structure theory
- Example: Choosing the optimal structure
- Setting the capital structure in practice

16 - 2

Basic Definitions

- V = value of firm
- FCF = free cash flow
- WACC = weighted average cost of capital
- r_s and r_d are costs of stock and debt
- r_e and w_d are percentages of the firm that are financed with stock and debt.

16 - 3

How can capital structure affect value?

$$V = \sum_{t=1}^{\infty} \frac{FCF_t}{(1+WACC)^t}$$

WACC = w_d (1-T) r_d + w_e r_s

(Continued...)

16 - 4

A Preview of Capital Structure Effects

- The impact of capital structure on value depends upon the effect of debt on:
  - WACC
  - FCF

(Continued...)

16 - 5

The Effect of Additional Debt on WACC

- Debtholders have a prior claim on cash flows relative to stockholders.
  - Debtholders' "fixed" claim increases risk of stockholders' "residual" claim.
  - Cost of stock, r_s, goes up.
- Firm's can deduct interest expenses.
  - Reduces the taxes paid
  - Frees up more cash for payments to investors
  - Reduces after-tax cost of debt

(Continued...)

16 - 6

The Effect on WACC (Continued)

- Debt increases risk of bankruptcy
  - Causes pre-tax cost of debt, r_d, to increase
- Adding debt increase percent of firm financed with low-cost debt (w_d) and decreases percent financed with high-cost equity (w_e)
- Net effect on WACC = uncertain.

(Continued...)

16 - 7

The Effect of Additional Debt on FCF

- **Additional debt increases the probability of bankruptcy.**
  - **Direct costs: Legal fees, "fire" sales, etc.**
  - **Indirect costs: Lost customers, reduction in productivity of managers and line workers, reduction in credit (i.e., accounts payable) offered by suppliers**

(Continued…)

Northwest Bankrupcy

16 - 8

- **Impact of indirect costs**
  - **NOPAT goes down due to lost customers and drop in productivity**
  - **Investment in capital goes up due to increase in net operating working capital (accounts payable goes up as suppliers tighten credit).**

(Continued…)

16 - 9

- **Additional debt can affect the behavior of managers.**
  - **Reductions in agency costs: debt "pre-commits," or "bonds," free cash flow for use in making interest payments. Thus, managers are less likely to waste FCF on perquisites or non-value adding acquisitions.**
  - **Increases in agency costs: debt can make managers too risk-averse, causing "underinvestment" in risky but positive NPV projects.**

(Continued…)

16 - 10

Asymmetric Information and Signaling

- Managers know the firm's future prospects better than investors.
- Managers would not issue additional equity if they thought the current stock price was less than the true value of the stock (given their inside information).
- Hence, investors often perceive an additional issuance of stock as a negative signal, and the stock price falls.

16 - 11

What is business risk?

- Uncertainty about future pre-tax operating income (EBIT).

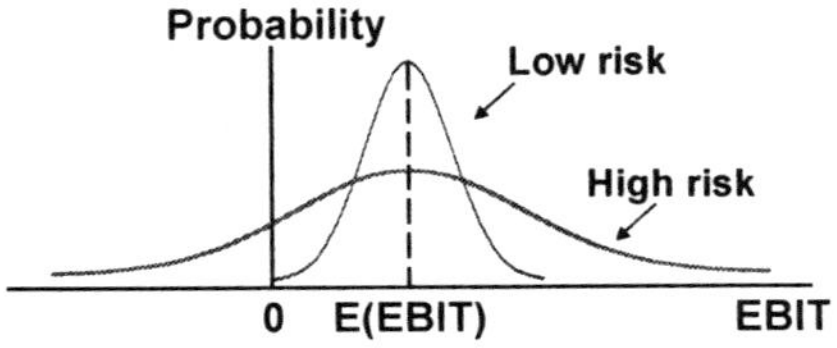

- Note that business risk focuses on operating income, so it ignores financing effects.

16 - 12

Factors That Influence Business Risk

- Uncertainty about demand (unit sales).
- Uncertainty about output prices.
- Uncertainty about input costs.
- Product and other types of liability.
- Degree of operating leverage (DOL).

High Fixed Cost will increase % of a firms Riskyness

16 - 13

What is operating leverage, and how does it affect a firm's business risk?

- Operating leverage is the change in EBIT caused by a change in quantity sold.
- The higher the proportion of fixed costs within a firm's overall cost structure, the greater the operating leverage.

(More...)

16 - 14

- Higher operating leverage leads to more business risk, because a small sales decline causes a larger EBIT decline.

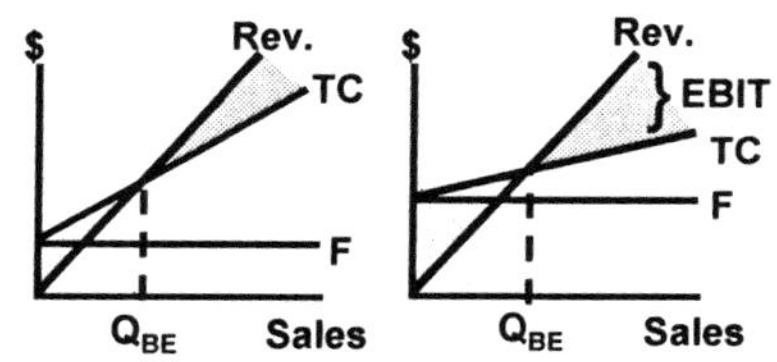

(More...)

16 - 15

Operating Breakeven

- Q is quantity sold, F is fixed cost, V is variable cost, TC is total cost, and P is price per unit.
- Operating breakeven = Q_{BE}

$$Q_{BE} = F / (P - V)$$

- Example: F=\$200, P=\$15, and V=\$10:

$$Q_{BE} = \$200 / (\$15 - \$10) = 40.$$

(More...)

Breakeven Quantity

16 - 16

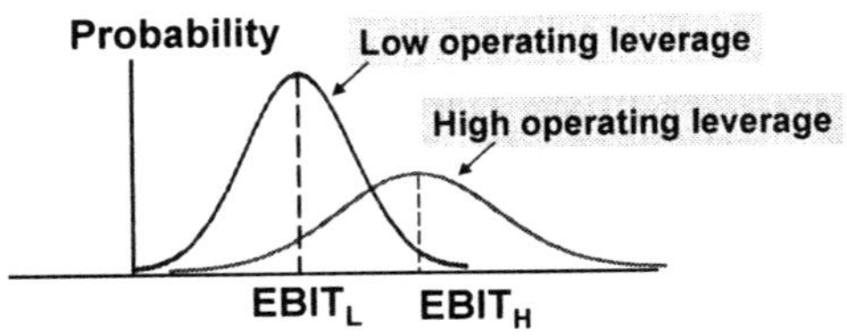

- In the typical situation, higher operating leverage leads to higher expected EBIT, but also increases risk.

16 - 17

Business Risk versus Financial Risk

- Business risk:
  - Uncertainty in future EBIT.
  - Depends on business factors such as competition, operating leverage, etc.
- Financial risk:
  - Additional business risk concentrated on common stockholders when financial leverage is used.
  - Depends on the amount of debt and preferred stock financing.

16 - 18

Consider Two Hypothetical Firms

Firm U	Firm L
No debt	\$10,000 of 12% debt
\$20,000 in assets	\$20,000 in assets
40% tax rate	40% tax rate

Both firms have same operating leverage, business risk, and EBIT of \$3,000. They differ only with respect to use of debt.

16 - 19

Impact of Leverage on Returns

unleveraged   leveraged

	Firm U	Firm L
EBIT	$3,000	$3,000
Interest	0	1,200
EBT	$3,000	$1,800
Taxes (40%)	1,200	720
NI	$1,800	$1,080
ROE	9.0%	10.8%

16 - 20

Why does leveraging increase return?

- More EBIT goes to investors in Firm L.
  - Total dollars paid to investors:
    - U: NI = $1,800.
    - L: NI + Int = $1,080 + $1,200 = $2,280.
  - Taxes paid:
    - U: $1,200; L: $720.
- Equity $ proportionally lower than NI.

More dollars goes to investors

16 - 21

Now consider the fact that EBIT is not known with certainty. What is the impact of uncertainty on stockholder profitability and risk for Firm U and Firm L?

Continued...

16 - 22

Firm U: Unleveraged

	Economy		
	Bad	Avg.	Good
Prob.	0.25	0.50	0.25
EBIT	$2,000	$3,000	$4,000
Interest	0	0	0
EBT	$2,000	$3,000	$4,000
Taxes (40%)	800	1,200	1,600
NI	$1,200	$1,800	$2,400

16 - 23

Firm L: Leveraged

	Economy		
	Bad	Avg.	Good
Prob.*	0.25	0.50	0.25
EBIT*	$2,000	$3,000	$4,000
Interest	1,200	1,200	1,200
EBT	$ 800	$1,800	$2,800
Taxes (40%)	320	720	1,120
NI	$ 480	$1,080	$1,680

*Same as for Firm U.

16 - 24

Basic Earning Power

Firm U	Bad	Avg.	Good
BEP	10.0%	15.0%	20.0%
ROIC	6.0%	9.0%	12.0%
ROE	6.0%	9.0%	12.0%
TIE	n.a.	n.a.	n.a.
Firm L	**Bad**	**Avg.**	**Good**
BEP	10.0%	15.0%	20.0%
ROIC	6.0%	9.0%	12.0%
ROE	4.8%	10.8%	16.8%
TIE	1.7x	2.5x	3.3x

16 - 25

Profitability Measures:

	U	L
E(BEP)	15.0%	15.0%
E(ROIC)	9.0%	9.0%
E(ROE)	9.0%	10.8%

Risk Measures:

σ_{ROIC}	2.12%	2.12%
σ_{ROE}	2.12%	4.24%

16 - 26

Conclusions

- Basic earning power (EBIT/TA) and ROIC (NOPAT/Capital = EBIT(1-T)/TA) are unaffected by financial leverage.
- L has higher expected ROE: tax savings and smaller equity base.
- L has much wider ROE swings because of fixed interest charges. Higher expected return is accompanied by higher risk.

(More...)

16 - 27

- In a stand-alone risk sense, Firm L's stockholders see much more risk than Firm U's.
  - U and L: σ_{ROIC} = 2.12%.
  - U: σ_{ROE} = 2.12%.
  - L: σ_{ROE} = 4.24%.
- L's financial risk is $\sigma_{ROE} - \sigma_{ROIC}$ = 4.24% - 2.12% = 2.12%. (U's is zero.)

(More...)

16 - 28

- For leverage to be positive (increase expected ROE), BEP must be > r_d.
- If r_d > BEP, the cost of leveraging will be higher than the inherent profitability of the assets, so the use of financial leverage will depress net income and ROE.
- In the example, E(BEP) = 15% while interest rate = 12%, so leveraging "works."

16 - 29

Capital Structure Theory

- MM theory
  - Zero taxes
  - Corporate taxes
  - Corporate and personal taxes
- Trade-off theory
- Signaling theory
- Debt financing as a managerial constraint

16 - 30

MM Theory: Zero Taxes

- MM prove, under a very restrictive set of assumptions, that a firm's value is unaffected by its financing mix:
  - $V_L = V_U$.
- Therefore, capital structure is irrelevant.
- Any increase in ROE resulting from financial leverage is exactly offset by the increase in risk (i.e., r_s), so WACC is constant.

16 - 31

MM Theory: Corporate Taxes

- Corporate tax laws favor debt financing over equity financing.
- With corporate taxes, the benefits of financial leverage exceed the risks: More EBIT goes to investors and less to taxes when leverage is used.
- MM show that: $V_L = V_U + TD$. → Total Debt
- If T=40%, then every dollar of debt adds 40 cents of extra value to firm.

16 - 32

MM relationship between value and debt when corporate taxes are considered.

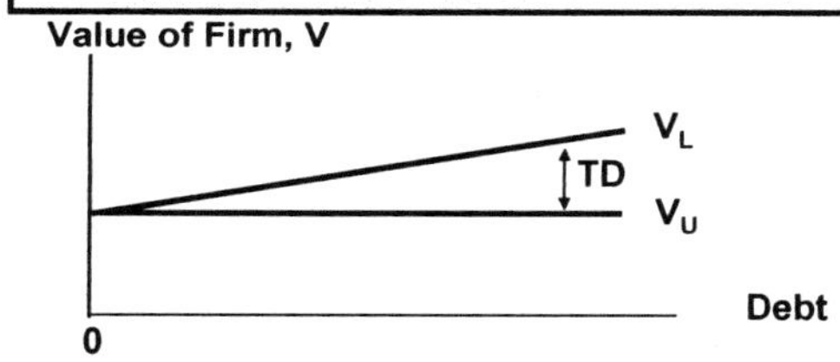

Under MM with corporate taxes, the firm's value increases continuously as more and more debt is used.

16 - 33

MM relationship between capital costs and leverage when corporate taxes are considered.

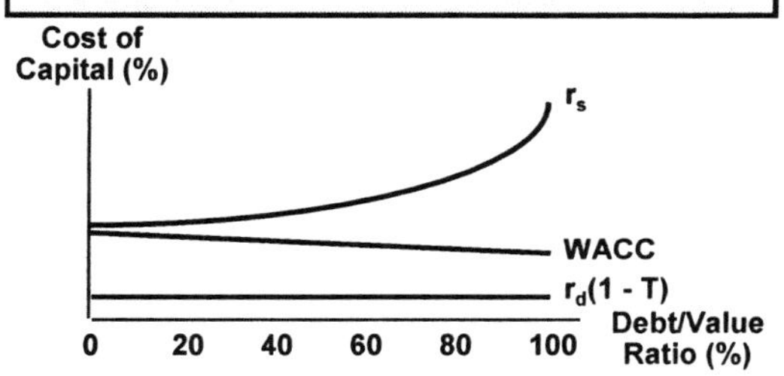

16 - 34

Miller's Theory: Corporate and Personal Taxes

- **Personal taxes lessen the advantage of corporate debt:**
  - **Corporate taxes favor debt financing since corporations can deduct interest expenses.**
  - **Personal taxes favor equity financing, since no gain is reported until stock is sold, and long-term gains are taxed at a lower rate.**

16 - 35

Miller's Model with Corporate and Personal Taxes

$$V_L = V_U + \left[1 - \frac{(1 - T_c)(1 - T_s)}{(1 - T_d)}\right]D.$$

T_c = corporate tax rate.
T_d = personal tax rate on debt income.
T_s = personal tax rate on stock income.

16 - 36

T_c = 40%, T_d = 30%, and T_s = 12%.

$$V_L = V_U + \left[1 - \frac{(1 - 0.40)(1 - 0.12)}{(1 - 0.30)}\right]D$$

$$= V_U + (1 - 0.75)D$$

$$= V_U + 0.25D.$$

Value rises with debt; each \$1 increase in debt raises L's value by \$0.25.

16 - 37

Conclusions with Personal Taxes

- Use of debt financing remains advantageous, but benefits are less than under only corporate taxes.
- Firms should still use 100% debt.
- Note: However, Miller argued that in equilibrium, the tax rates of marginal investors would adjust until there was no advantage to debt.

16 - 38

Trade-off Theory

- MM theory ignores bankruptcy (financial distress) costs, which increase as more leverage is used.
- At low leverage levels, tax benefits outweigh bankruptcy costs.
- At high levels, bankruptcy costs outweigh tax benefits.
- An optimal capital structure exists that balances these costs and benefits.

Tax Benefits + bankruptcy cost

16 - 39

Signaling Theory

- MM assumed that investors and managers have the same information.
- But, managers often have better information. Thus, they would:
  - Sell stock if stock is overvalued.
  - Sell bonds if stock is undervalued.
- Investors understand this, so view new stock sales as a negative signal.
- Implications for managers?

16 - 40

Debt Financing and Agency Costs

- One agency problem is that managers can use corporate funds for non-value maximizing purposes.
- The use of financial leverage:
  - Bonds "free cash flow."
  - Forces discipline on managers to avoid perks and non-value adding acquisitions.

(More...)

16 - 41

- A second agency problem is the potential for "underinvestment".
  - Debt increases risk of financial distress.
  - Therefore, managers may avoid risky projects even if they have positive NPVs.

16 - 42

Choosing the Optimal Capital Structure: Example

Currently is all-equity financed.

Expected EBIT = $500,000.

Firm expects zero growth.

100,000 shares outstanding; r_s = 12%;

P_0 = $25; T = 40%; b = 1.0; r_{RF} = 6%;

RP_M = 6%.

16 - 43

Estimates of Cost of Debt

Percent financed with debt, w_d	r_d
0%	-
20%	8.0%
30%	8.5%
40%	10.0%
50%	12.0%

If company recapitalizes, debt would be issued to repurchase stock.

Picked numbers @ Random

16 - 44

The Cost of Equity at Different Levels of Debt: Hamada's Equation

- **MM theory implies that beta changes with leverage.**
- **b_U is the beta of a firm when it has no debt (the unlevered beta)**
- **$b_L = b_U [1 + (1 - T)(D/S)]$**

16 - 45

The Cost of Equity for w_d = 20%

- **Use Hamada's equation to find beta:**

$$b_L = b_U [1 + (1 - T)(D/S)]$$
$$= 1.0 [1 + (1-0.4) (20\% / 80\%)]$$
$$= 1.15$$

- **Use CAPM to find the cost of equity:**

$$r_s = r_{RF} + b_L (RP_M)$$
$$= 6\% + 1.15 (6\%) = 12.9\%$$

16 - 46

Cost of Equity vs. Leverage

w_d	D/S	b_L	r_s
0%	0.00	1.000	12.00%
20%	0.25	1.150	12.90%
30%	0.43	1.257	13.54%
40%	0.67	1.400	14.40%
50%	1.00	1.600	15.60%

16 - 47

The WACC for w_d = 20%

- WACC = w_d (1-T) r_d + w_e r_s
- WACC = 0.2 (1 – 0.4) (8%) + 0.8 (12.9%)
- WACC = 11.28%
- Repeat this for all capital structures under consideration.

16 - 48

WACC vs. Leverage

w_d	r_d	r_s	WACC	
0%	0.0%	12.00%	12.00%	
20%	8.0%	12.90%	11.28%	
30%	8.5%	13.54%	11.01%	←
40%	10.0%	14.40%	11.04%	
50%	12.0%	15.60%	11.40%	

16 - 49

Corporate Value for w_d = 20%

- V = FCF / (WACC-g)
- g=0, so investment in capital is zero; so FCF = NOPAT = EBIT (1-T).
- NOPAT = ($500,000)(1-0.40) = $300,000.
- V = $300,000 / 0.1128 = $2,659,574.

16 - 50

Corporate Value vs. Leverage

w_d	WACC	Corp. Value
0%	12.00%	$2,500,000
20%	11.28%	$2,659,574
30%	11.01%	$2,724,796 ←
40%	11.04%	$2,717,391
50%	11.40%	$2,631,579

16 - 51

Debt and Equity for w_d = 20%

- The dollar value of debt is:

  D = w_d V = 0.2 ($2,659,574) = $531,915.
- S = V – D

  S = $2,659,574 - $531,915 = $2,127,659.

Dollar value of debt @ 20%

16 - 52

Debt and Stock Value vs. Leverage

w_d	Debt, D	Stock Value, S
0%	$0	$2,500,000
20%	$531,915	$2,127,660
30%	$817,439	$1,907,357
40%	$1,086,957	$1,630,435
50%	$1,315,789	$1,315,789

Note: these are rounded; see Ch 16 Mini Case.xls for full calculations.

16 - 53

Wealth of Shareholders

- **Value of the equity declines as more debt is issued, because debt is used to repurchase stock.**
- **But total wealth of shareholders is value of stock after the recap plus the cash received in repurchase, and this total goes up (It is equal to Corporate Value on earlier slide).**

16 - 54

Stock Price for w_d = 20%

- **The firm issues debt, which changes its WACC, which changes value.**
- **The firm then uses debt proceeds to repurchase stock.**
- **Stock price changes after debt is issued, but does not change during actual repurchase (or arbitrage is possible).**

(More...)

16 - 55

Stock Price for w_d = 20% (Continued)

- The stock price after debt is issued but before stock is repurchased reflects shareholder wealth:
  - S, value of stock
  - Cash paid in repurchase.

(More...)

16 - 56

Stock Price for w_d = 20% (Continued)

- D_0 and n_0 are debt and outstanding shares before recap.
- $D - D_0$ is equal to cash that will be used to repurchase stock.
- $S + (D - D_0)$ is wealth of shareholders' after the debt is issued but immediately before the repurchase.

(More...)

16 - 57

Stock Price for w_d = 20% (Continued)

- $$P = \frac{S + (D - D_0)}{n_0}$$

$$P = \frac{\$2,127,660 + (\$531,915 - 0)}{100,000}$$

P = $26.596 per share.

Cost to share

16 - 58

Number of Shares Repurchased

- # Repurchased = $(D - D_0) / P$

  # Rep. = ($531,915 – 0) / $26.596

  = 20,000.

- # Remaining = n = S / P

  n = $2,127,660 / $26.596

  = 80,000.

16 - 59

Price per Share vs. Leverage

w_d	P	# shares Repurch.	# shares Remaining
0%	$25.00	0	100,000
20%	$26.60	20,000	80,000
30%	$27.25	30,000	70,000 ←
40%	$27.17	40,000	60,000
50%	$26.32	50,000	50,000

16 - 60

Optimal Capital Structure

- w_d = 30% gives:
  - Highest corporate value
  - Lowest WACC
  - Highest stock price per share
- But w_d = 40% is close. Optimal range is pretty flat.

16 - 61

What other factors would managers consider when setting the target capital structure?

- Debt ratios of other firms in the industry.
- Pro forma coverage ratios at different capital structures under different economic scenarios.
- Lender and rating agency attitudes (impact on bond ratings).

16 - 62

- Reserve borrowing capacity.
- Effects on control.
- Type of assets: Are they tangible, and hence suitable as collateral?
- Tax rates.

17 - 1

CHAPTER 17
Capital Structure Decisions: Extensions

- MM and Miller models
- Hamada's equation
- Financial distress and agency costs
- Trade-off models
- Asymmetric information theory

17 - 2

Who are Modigliani and Miller (MM)?

- They published theoretical papers that changed the way people thought about financial leverage.
- They won Nobel prizes in economics because of their work.
- MM's papers were published in 1958 and 1963. Miller had a separate paper in 1977. The papers differed in their assumptions about taxes.

17 - 3

What assumptions underlie the MM and Miller models?

- Firms can be grouped into homogeneous classes based on business risk.
- Investors have identical expectations about firms' future earnings.
- There are no transactions costs.

(More...)

17 - 4

- All debt is riskless, and both individuals and corporations can borrow unlimited amounts of money at the risk-free rate.
- All cash flows are perpetuities. This implies perpetual debt is issued, firms have zero growth, and expected EBIT is constant over time.

(More...)

17 - 5

- MM's first paper (1958) assumed zero taxes. Later papers added taxes.
- No agency or financial distress costs.
- These assumptions were necessary for MM to prove their propositions on the basis of investor arbitrage.

17 - 6

MM with Zero Taxes (1958)

Proposition I:

$$V_L = V_U.$$

Proposition II:

$$r_{sL} = r_{sU} + (r_{sU} - r_d)(D/S).$$

17 - 7

Given the following data, find V, S, r_s, and WACC for Firms U and L.

Firms U and L are in same risk class.

$EBIT_{U,L}$ = $500,000.

Firm U has no debt; r_{sU} = 14%.

Firm L has $1,000,000 debt at r_d = 8%.

The basic MM assumptions hold.

There are no corporate or personal taxes.

17 - 8

1. Find V_U and V_L.

$$V_U = \frac{EBIT}{r_{sU}} = \frac{\$500,000}{0.14} = \$3,571,429.$$

$V_L = V_U$ = $3,571,429.

17 - 9

2. Find the market value of Firm L's debt and equity.

$$V_L = D + S = \$3,571,429$$

$$\$3,571,429 = \$1,000,000 + S$$

$$S = \$2,571,429.$$

17 - 10

3. Find r_{sL}.

$$r_{sL} = r_{sU} + (r_{sU} - r_d)(D/S)$$
$$= 14.0\% + (14.0\% - 8.0\%)\left(\frac{\$1,000,000}{\$2,571,429}\right)$$
$$= 14.0\% + 2.33\% = 16.33\%.$$

17 - 11

4. Proposition I implies WACC = r_{sU}. Verify for L using WACC formula.

$$\text{WACC} = w_d r_d + w_{ce} r_s = (D/V)r_d + (S/V)r_s$$
$$= \left(\frac{\$1,000,000}{\$3,571,429}\right)(8.0\%)$$
$$+ \left(\frac{\$2,571,429}{\$3,571,429}\right)(16.33\%)$$
$$= 2.24\% + 11.76\% = 14.00\%.$$

17 - 12

Graph the MM relationships between capital costs and leverage as measured by D/V.

Without taxes

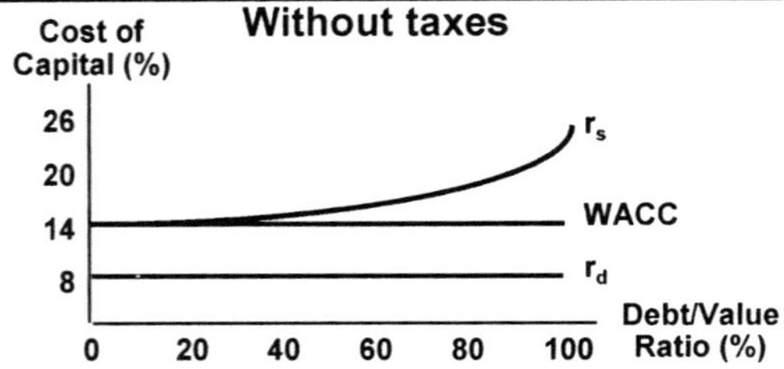

17 - 13

- The more debt the firm adds to its capital structure, the riskier the equity becomes and thus the higher its cost.
- Although r_d remains constant, r_s increases with leverage. The increase in r_s is exactly sufficient to keep the WACC constant.

17 - 14

Graph value versus leverage.

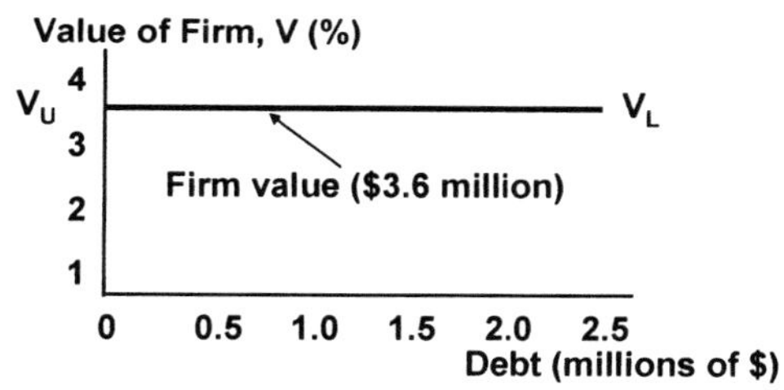

With zero taxes, MM argue that value is unaffected by leverage.

17 - 15

Find V, S, r_s, and WACC for Firms U and L assuming a 40% corporate tax rate.

With corporate taxes added, the MM propositions become:

Proposition I:

$$V_L = V_U + TD.$$

Proposition II:

$$r_{sL} = r_{sU} + (r_{sU} - r_d)(1 - T)(D/S).$$

17 - 16

Notes About the New Propositions

1. When corporate taxes are added, $V_L \neq V_U$. V_L increases as debt is added to the capital structure, and the greater the debt usage, the higher the value of the firm.
2. r_{sL} increases with leverage at a slower rate when corporate taxes are considered.

17 - 17

1. Find V_U and V_L.

$$V_U = \frac{EBIT(1 - T)}{r_{sU}} = \frac{\$500{,}000(0.6)}{0.14} = \$2{,}142{,}857.$$

Note: Represents a 40% decline from the no taxes situation.

$$\begin{aligned} V_L = V_U + TD &= \$2{,}142{,}857 + 0.4(\$1{,}000{,}000) \\ &= \$2{,}142{,}857 + \$400{,}000 \\ &= \$2{,}542{,}857. \end{aligned}$$

17 - 18

2. Find market value of Firm L's debt and equity.

$$V_L = D + S = \$2{,}542{,}857$$

$$\$2{,}542{,}857 = \$1{,}000{,}000 + S$$

$$S = \$1{,}542{,}857.$$

17 - 19

3. Find r_{sL}.

$$r_{sL} = r_{sU} + (r_{sU} - r_d)(1 - T)(D/S)$$

$$= 14.0\% + (14.0\% - 8.0\%)(0.6)\left(\frac{\$1{,}000{,}000}{\$1{,}542{,}857}\right)$$

$$= 14.0\% + 2.33\% = 16.33\%.$$

17 - 20

4. Find Firm L's WACC.

$$WACC_L = (D/V)r_d(1 - T) + (S/V)r_s$$

$$= \left(\frac{\$1{,}000{,}000}{\$2{,}542{,}857}\right)(8.0\%)(0.6)$$

$$+ \left(\frac{\$1{,}542{,}857}{\$2{,}542{,}857}\right)(16.33\%)$$

$$= 1.89\% + 9.91\% = 11.80\%.$$

When corporate taxes are considered, the WACC is lower for L than for U.

17 - 21

MM relationship between capital costs and leverage when corporate taxes are considered.

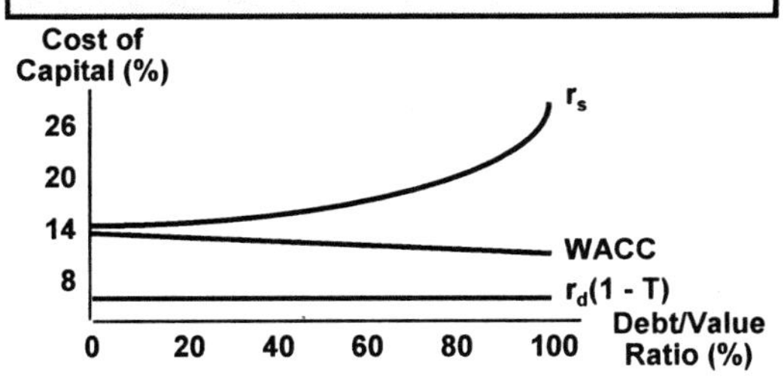

17 - 22

MM relationship between value and debt when corporate taxes are considered.

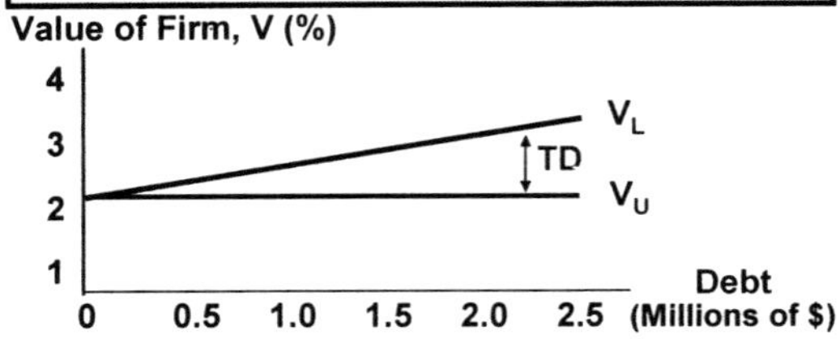

Under MM with corporate taxes, the firm's value increases continuously as more and more debt is used.

17 - 23

Assume investors have the following tax rates: T_d = 30% and T_s = 12%. What is the gain from leverage according to the Miller model?

Miller's Proposition I:

$$V_L = V_U + \left[1 - \frac{(1 - T_c)(1 - T_s)}{(1 - T_d)}\right]D.$$

T_c = corporate tax rate.
T_d = personal tax rate on debt income.
T_s = personal tax rate on stock income.

17 - 24

T_c = 40%, T_d = 30%, and T_s = 12%.

$$V_L = V_U + \left[1 - \frac{(1 - 0.40)(1 - 0.12)}{(1 - 0.30)}\right]D$$

$$= V_U + (1 - 0.75)D$$

$$= V_U + 0.25D.$$

Value rises with debt; each $100 increase in debt raises L's value by $25.

17 - 25

How does this gain compare to the gain in the MM model with corporate taxes?

If only corporate taxes, then

$$V_L = V_U + T_cD = V_U + 0.40D.$$

Here $100 of debt raises value by $40. Thus, personal taxes lowers the gain from leverage, but the net effect depends on tax rates.

(More...)

17 - 26

- If T_s declines, while T_c and T_d remain constant, the slope coefficient (which shows the benefit of debt) is decreased.
- A company with a low payout ratio gets lower benefits under the Miller model than a company with a high payout, because a low payout decreases T_s.

17 - 27

When Miller brought in personal taxes, the value enhancement of debt was lowered. Why?

1. Corporate tax laws favor debt over equity financing because interest expense is tax deductible while dividends are not.

(More...)

17 - 28

2. However, personal tax laws favor equity over debt because stocks provide both tax deferral and a lower capital gains tax rate.
3. This lowers the relative cost of equity vis-a-vis MM's no-personal-tax world and decreases the spread between debt and equity costs.
4. Thus, some of the advantage of debt financing is lost, so debt financing is less valuable to firms.

17 - 29

What does capital structure theory prescribe for corporate managers?

1. MM, No Taxes: Capital structure is irrelevant--no impact on value or WACC.
2. MM, Corporate Taxes: Value increases, so firms should use (almost) 100% debt financing.
3. Miller, Personal Taxes: Value increases, but less than under MM, so again firms should use (almost) 100% debt financing.

17 - 30

Do firms follow the recommendations of capital structure theory?

1. Firms don't follow MM/Miller to 100% debt. Debt ratios average about 40%.
2. However, debt ratios did increase after MM. Many think debt ratios were too low, and MM led to changes in financial policies.

17 - 31

How is all of this analysis different if firms U and L are growing?

- Under MM (with taxes and no growth)
  - $V_L = V_U + TD$
  - This assumes the tax shield is discounted at the cost of debt.
- Assume the growth rate is 7%
- The debt tax shield will be larger if the firms grow:

17 - 32

7% growth, TS discount rate of r_{TS}

Value of (growing) tax shield =

$$V_{TS} = r_d TD/(r_{TS} - g)$$

So value of levered firm =

$$V_L = V_U + r_d TD/(r_{TS} - g)$$

17 - 33

What should r_{TS} be?

- The smaller is r_{TS}, the larger the value of the tax shield. If $r_{TS} < r_{sU}$, then with rapid growth the tax shield becomes unrealistically large—r_{TS} must be equal to r_U to give reasonable results when there is growth. So we assume $r_{TS} = r_{sU}$.

17 - 34

Levered cost of equity

- In this case, the levered cost of equity is $r_{sL} = r_{sU} + (r_{sU} - r_d)(D/S)$
- This looks just like MM *without taxes* even though we allow taxes and allow for growth. The reason is if $r_{TS} = r_{sU}$, then larger values of the tax shield don't change the risk of the equity.

17 - 35

Levered beta

If there is growth and $r_{TS} = r_{sU}$ then the equation that is equivalent to the Hamada equation is

$$\beta_L = \beta_U + (\beta_U - \beta_D)(D/S)$$

Notice: This looks like Hamada *without taxes*. Again, this is because in this case the tax shield doesn't change the risk of the equity.

17 - 36

Relevant information for valuation

- EBIT = \$500,000
- T = 40%
- $r_U = 14\% = r_{TS}$
- $r_d = 8\%$
- Required reinvestment in net operating assets = 10% of EBIT = \$50,000.
- Debt = \$1,000,000

17 - 37

Calculating V_U

NOPAT = EBIT(1-T)
= \$500,000 (.60) = \$300,000
Investment in net op. assets
= EBIT (0.10) = \$50,000
FCF = NOPAT – Inv. in net op. assets
= \$300,000 - \$50,000
= \$250,000 (this is expected FCF next year)

17 - 38

Value of unlevered firm, V_U

Value of unlevered firm =

$V_U = FCF/(r_{sU} - g)$
= \$250,000/(0.14 – 0.07)
= \$3,571,429

17 - 39

Value of tax shield, V_{TS} and V_L

$V_{TS} = r_d TD/(r_{sU} - g)$
= 0.08(0.40)\$1,000,000/(0.14-0.07)
= \$457,143

$V_L = V_U + V_{TS}$
= \$3,571,429 + \$457,143
= \$4,028,571

17 - 40

Cost of equity and WACC

- Just like with MM with taxes, the cost of equity increases with D/V, and the WACC declines.
- But since r_{sL} doesn't have the (1-T) factor in it, for a given D/V, r_{sL} is *greater* than MM would predict, and WACC is *greater* than MM would predict.

17 - 41

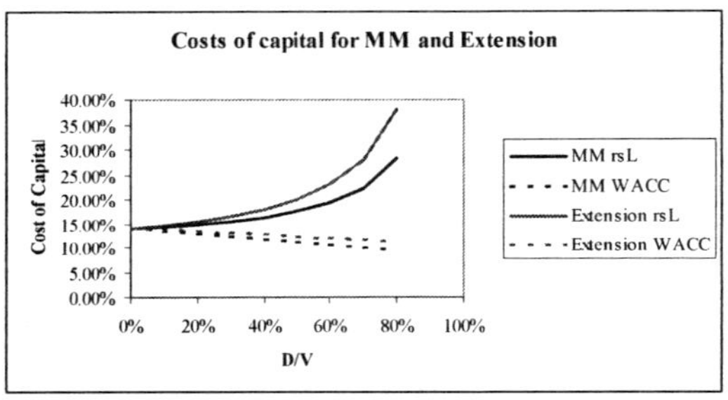

17 - 42

What if L's debt is risky?

If L's debt is risky then, by definition, management might default on it. The decision to make a payment on the debt or to default looks very much like the decision whether to exercise a call option. So the equity looks like an option.

17 - 43

Equity as an option

Suppose the firm has $2 million face value of 1-year zero coupon debt, and the current value of the firm (debt plus equity) is $4 million.

If the firm pays off the debt when it matures, the equity holders get to keep the firm. If not, they get nothing because the debtholders foreclose.

17 - 44

Equity as an option

The equity holder's position looks like a call option with

P = underlying value of firm = $4 million

X = exercise price = $2 million

t = time to maturity = 1 year

Suppose r_{RF} = 6%

σ = volatility of debt + equity = 0.60

17 - 45

Use Black-Scholes to price this option

$$V = P[N(d_1)] - Xe^{-r_{RF}t}[N(d_2)].$$

$$d_1 = \frac{\ln(P/X) + [r_{RF} + (\sigma^2/2)]t}{\sigma\sqrt{t}}.$$

$$d_2 = d_1 - \sigma\sqrt{t}.$$

17 - 46

Black-Scholes Solution

$V = \$4[N(d_1)] - \$2e^{-(0.06)(1.0)}[N(d_2)].$

$$d_1 = \frac{\ln(\$4/\$2) + [(0.06 + 0.36/2)](1.0)}{(0.60)(1.0)}$$

$= 1.5552.$

$d_2 = d_1 - (0.60)(1.0) = d_1 - 0.60$

$= 1.5552 - 0.6000 = 0.9552.$

17 - 47

$N(d_1) = N(1.5552) = 0.9401$

$N(d_2) = N(0.9552) = 0.8383$

Note: Values obtained from Excel using NORMSDIST function.

$V = \$4(0.9401) - \$2e^{-0.06}(0.8303)$

$= \$3.7604 - \$2(0.9418)(0.8303)$

$= \$2.196$ Million = Value of Equity

17 - 48

Value of Debt

The value of debt must be what is left over:

Value of debt = Total Value – Equity

= \$4 million – 2.196 million

= \$1.804 million

17 - 49

This value of debt gives us a yield

Debt yield for 1-year zero coupon debt
= (face value / price) – 1
= ($2 million/ 1.804 million) – 1
= 10.9%

17 - 50

How does σ affect an option's value?

Higher volatility σ means higher option value.

17 - 51

Managerial Incentives

When an investor buys a stock option, the riskiness of the stock (σ) is already determined. But a manager can change a firm's σ by changing the assets the firm invests in. That means changing σ can change the value of the equity, even if it doesn't change the expected cash flows:

17 - 52

Managerial Incentives

So changing σ can transfer wealth from bondholders to stockholders by making the option value of the stock worth more, which makes what is left, the debt value, worth less.

17 - 53

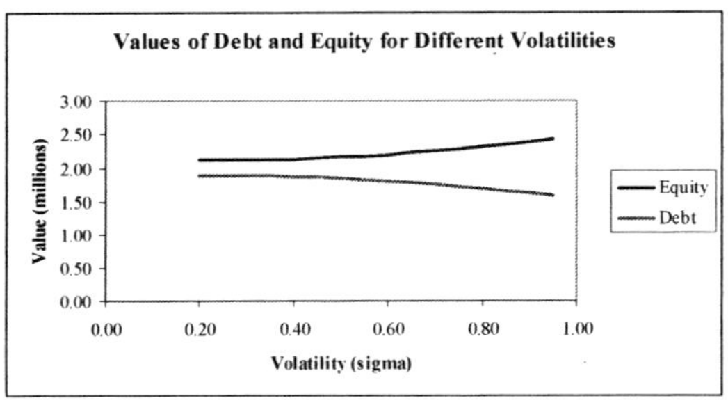

17 - 54

Bait and Switch

Managers who know this might tell debtholders they are going to invest in one kind of asset, and, instead, invest in riskier assets. This is called *bait and switch* and bondholders will require higher interest rates for firms that do this, or refuse to do business with them.

17 - 55

If the debt is risky coupon debt

If the risky debt has coupons, then with each coupon payment management has an option on an option—if it makes the interest payment then it purchases the right to later make the principal payment and keep the firm. This is called *a compound option.*

18 - 1

CHAPTER 18
Distributions to Shareholders: Dividends and Repurchases

- Theories of investor preferences
- Signaling effects
- Residual model
- Stock repurchases
- Stock dividends and stock splits
- Dividend reinvestment plans

18 - 2

What is "distribution policy"?

- The distribution policy defines:
  - The level of cash distributions to shareholders
  - The form of the distribution (dividend vs. stock repurchase)
  - The stability of the distribution

18 - 3

Dividend Yields for Selected Industries

Industry	Div. Yield %
Airline	0.2
Software & Programming	0.3
Biotechnology & Drugs	0.3
Restaurants	1.0
Chemical Manufacturing	2.2
Paper & Paper Products	2.7
Electric Utilities	4.4
Tobacco	5.6

Source: Yahoo Industry Data

18 - 4

Do investors prefer high or low payouts? There are three theories:

- Dividends are irrelevant: Investors don't care about payout.
- Bird-in-the-hand: Investors prefer a high payout.
- Tax preference: Investors prefer a low payout, hence growth.

18 - 5

Dividend Irrelevance Theory

- Investors are indifferent between dividends and retention-generated capital gains. If they want cash, they can sell stock. If they don't want cash, they can use dividends to buy stock.
- Modigliani-Miller support irrelevance.
- Theory is based on unrealistic assumptions (no taxes or brokerage costs), hence may not be true. Need empirical test.

18 - 6

Bird-in-the-Hand Theory

- Investors think dividends are less risky than potential future capital gains, hence they like dividends.
- If so, investors would value high payout firms more highly, i.e., a high payout would result in a high P_0.

18 - 7

Tax Preference Theory

- Low payouts mean higher capital gains. Capital gains taxes are deferred.
- This could cause investors to prefer firms with low payouts, i.e., a high payout results in a low P_0.

18 - 8

Implications of 3 Theories for Managers

Theory	Implication
Irrelevance	Any payout OK
Bird-in-the-hand	Set high payout
Tax preference	Set low payout

18 - 9

Which theory is most correct?

- Empirical testing has not been able to determine which theory, if any, is correct.
- Thus, managers use judgment when setting policy.
- Analysis is used, but it must be applied with judgment.

18 - 10

What's the "clientele effect"?

- Different groups of investors, or clienteles, prefer different dividend policies.
- Firm's past dividend policy determines its current clientele of investors.
- Clientele effects impede changing dividend policy. Taxes & brokerage costs hurt investors who have to switch companies due to a change in payout policy.

18 - 11

What's the "information content," or "signaling," hypothesis?

- Investors view dividend changes as *signals* of management's view of the future. Managers hate to cut dividends, so won't raise dividends unless they think raise is sustainable.
- Therefore, a stock price increase at time of a dividend increase could reflect higher expectations for future EPS, not a desire for dividends.

18 - 12

What's the "residual distribution model"?

- Find the reinvested earnings needed for the capital budget.
- Pay out any leftover earnings (the residual) as either dividends or stock repurchases.
- This policy minimizes flotation and equity signaling costs, hence minimizes the WACC.

18 - 13

Using the Residual Model to Calculate Distributions Paid

$$\text{Distr.} = \text{Net income} - \left[\left(\begin{array}{c}\text{Target}\\\text{equity}\\\text{ratio}\end{array}\right)\left(\begin{array}{c}\text{Total}\\\text{capital}\\\text{budget}\end{array}\right)\right].$$

18 - 14

Data for SSC

- Capital budget: $800,000. Given.
- Target capital structure: 40% debt, 60% equity. Want to maintain.
- Forecasted net income: $600,000.
- If all distributions are in the form of dividends, how much of the $600,000 should we pay out as dividends?

18 - 15

Of the $800,000 capital budget, 0.6($800,000) = $480,000 must be equity to keep at target capital structure. [0.4($800,000) = $320,000 will be debt.]

With $600,000 of net income, the residual is $600,000 - $480,000 = $120,000 = dividends paid.

Payout ratio = $120,000/$600,000
= 0.20 = 20%.

18 - 16

How would a drop in NI to $400,000 affect the dividend? A rise to $800,000?

- NI = $400,000: Need $480,000 of equity, so should retain the whole $400,000. Dividends = 0.
- NI = $800,000: Dividends = $800,000 - $480,000 = $320,000. Payout = $320,000/$800,000 = 40%.

18 - 17

How would a change in investment opportunities affect dividend under the residual policy?

- Fewer good investments would lead to smaller capital budget, hence to a higher dividend payout.
- More good investments would lead to a lower dividend payout.

18 - 18

Advantages and Disadvantages of the Residual Dividend Policy

- Advantages: Minimizes new stock issues and flotation costs.
- Disadvantages: Results in variable dividends, sends conflicting signals, increases risk, and doesn't appeal to any specific clientele.
- Conclusion: Consider residual policy when setting target payout, but don't follow it rigidly.

18 - 19

Stock Repurchases

Repurchases: Buying own stock back from stockholders.

Reasons for repurchases:

- **As an alternative to distributing cash as dividends.**
- **To dispose of one-time cash from an asset sale.**
- **To make a large capital structure change.**

18 - 20

Advantages of Repurchases

- **Stockholders can tender or not.**
- **Helps avoid setting a high dividend that cannot be maintained.**
- **Repurchased stock can be used in takeovers or resold to raise cash as needed.**
- **Income received is capital gains rather than higher-taxed dividends.**
- **Stockholders may take as a positive signal--management thinks stock is undervalued.**

18 - 21

Disadvantages of Repurchases

- **May be viewed as a negative signal (firm has poor investment opportunities).**
- **IRS could impose penalties if repurchases were primarily to avoid taxes on dividends.**
- **Selling stockholders may not be well informed, hence be treated unfairly.**
- **Firm may have to bid up price to complete purchase, thus paying too much for its own stock.**

18 - 22

Setting Dividend Policy

- Forecast capital needs over a planning horizon, often 5 years.
- Set a target capital structure.
- Estimate annual equity needs.
- Set target payout based on the residual model.
- Generally, some dividend growth rate emerges. Maintain target growth rate if possible, varying capital structure somewhat if necessary.

18 - 23

Stock Dividends vs. Stock Splits

- Stock dividend: Firm issues new shares in lieu of paying a cash dividend. If 10%, get 10 shares for each 100 shares owned.
- Stock split: Firm increases the number of shares outstanding, say 2:1. Sends shareholders more shares.

18 - 24

Both stock dividends and stock splits increase the number of shares outstanding, so "the pie is divided into smaller pieces."

Unless the stock dividend or split conveys information, or is accompanied by another event like higher dividends, *the stock price falls so as to keep each investor's wealth unchanged.*

But splits/stock dividends may get us to an "optimal price range."

18 - 25

When should a firm consider splitting its stock?

- There's a widespread belief that the *optimal price range* for stocks is $20 to $80.
- Stock splits can be used to keep the price in the optimal range.
- Stock splits generally occur when management is confident, so are interpreted as *positive signals*.

18 - 26

What's a "dividend reinvestment plan (DRIP)"?

- Shareholders can automatically reinvest their dividends in shares of the company's common stock. Get more stock than cash.
- There are two types of plans:
  - Open market
  - New stock

18 - 27

Open Market Purchase Plan

- Dollars to be reinvested are turned over to trustee, who buys shares on the open market.
- Brokerage costs are reduced by volume purchases.
- Convenient, easy way to invest, thus useful for investors.

18 - 28

New Stock Plan

- Firm issues new stock to DRIP enrollees, keeps money and uses it to buy assets.
- No fees are charged, plus sells stock at discount of 5% from market price, which is about equal to flotation costs of underwritten stock offering.

18 - 29

Optional investments sometimes possible, up to $150,000 or so.

Firms that need new equity capital use new stock plans.

Firms with no need for new equity capital use open market purchase plans.

Most NYSE listed companies have a DRIP. Useful for investors.

19 - 1

CHAPTER 19
Initial Public Offerings, Investment Banking, and Financial Restructuring

- Initial Public Offerings
- Investment Banking and Regulation
- The Maturity Structure of Debt
- Refunding Operations
- The Risk Structure of Debt

19 - 2

What agencies regulate securities markets?

- The Securities and Exchange Commission (SEC) regulates:
  - Interstate public offerings.
  - National stock exchanges.
  - Trading by corporate insiders.
  - The corporate proxy process.
- The Federal Reserve Board controls margin requirements. (More...)

19 - 3

- States control the issuance of securities within their boundaries.
- The securities industry, through the exchanges and the National Association of Securities Dealers (NASD), takes actions to ensure the integrity and credibility of the trading system.
- Why is it important that securities markets be tightly regulated?

19 - 4

How are start-up firms usually financed?

- Founder's resources
- Angels
- Venture capital funds
  - Most capital in fund is provided by institutional investors
  - Managers of fund are called venture capitalists
  - Venture capitalists (VCs) sit on boards of companies they fund

19 - 5

Differentiate between a private placement and a public offering.

- In a private placement, such as to angels or VCs, securities are sold to a few investors rather than to the public at large.
- In a public offering, securities are offered to the public and must be registered with SEC.

(More...)

19 - 6

- Privately placed stock is not registered, so sales must be to "accredited" (high net worth) investors.
  - Send out "offering memorandum" with 20-30 pages of data and information, prepared by securities lawyers.
  - Buyers certify that they meet net worth/income requirements and they will not sell to unqualified investors.

19 - 7

Why would a company consider going public?

- **Advantages of going public**
  - **Current stockholders can diversify.**
  - **Liquidity is increased.**
  - **Easier to raise capital in the future.**
  - **Going public establishes firm value.**
  - **Makes it more feasible to use stock as employee incentives.**
  - **Increases customer recognition.**

(More...)

19 - 8

- **Disadvantages of Going Public**
  - **Must file numerous reports.**
  - **Operating data must be disclosed.**
  - **Officers must disclose holdings.**
  - **Special "deals" to insiders will be more difficult to undertake.**
  - **A small new issue may not be actively traded, so market-determined price may not reflect true value.**
  - **Managing investor relations is time-consuming.**

19 - 9

What are the steps of an IPO?

- **Select investment banker**
- **File registration document (S-1) with SEC**
- **Choose price range for preliminary (or "red herring") prospectus**
- **Go on roadshow**
- **Set final offer price in final prospectus**

19 - 10

What criteria are important in choosing an investment banker?

- Reputation and experience in this industry
- Existing mix of institutional and retail (i.e., individual) clients
- Support in the post-IPO secondary market
  - Reputation of analyst covering the stock

19 - 11

Would companies going public use a negotiated deal or a competitive bid?

- A negotiated deal.
  - The competitive bid process is only feasible for large issues by major firms. Even here, the use of bids is rare for equity issues.
  - It would cost investment bankers too much to learn enough about the company to make an intelligent bid.

19 - 12

Would the sale be on an underwritten or best efforts basis?

- Most offerings are underwritten.
- In very small, risky deals, the investment banker may insist on a best efforts basis.
- On an underwritten deal, the price is not set until
  - Investor interest is assessed.
  - Oral commitments are obtained.

19 - 13

Describe how an IPO would be priced.

- Since the firm is going public, there is no established price.
- Banker and company project the company's future earnings and free cash flows
- The banker would examine market data on similar companies.

(More...)

19 - 14

- Price set to place the firm's P/E and M/B ratios in line with publicly traded firms in the same industry having similar risk and growth prospects.
- On the basis of all relevant factors, the investment banker would determine a ballpark price, and specify a range (such as $10 to $12) in the preliminary prospectus.

(More...)

19 - 15

What is a roadshow?

- Senior management team, investment banker, and lawyer visit potential institutional investors
- Usually travel to ten to twenty cities in a two-week period, making three to five presentations each day.
- Management can't say anything that is not in prospectus, because company is in "quiet period."

19 - 16

What is "book building?"

- Investment banker asks investors to indicate how many shares they plan to buy, and records this in a "book".
- Investment banker hopes for oversubscribed issue.
- Based on demand, investment banker sets final offer price on evening before IPO.

19 - 17

What are typical first-day returns?

- For 75% of IPOs, price goes up on first day.
- Average first-day return is 14.1%.
- About 10% of IPOs have first-day returns greater than 30%.
- For some companies, the first-day return is well over 100%.

19 - 18

- There is an inherent conflict of interest, because the banker has an incentive to set a low price:
  - to make brokerage customers happy.
  - to make it easy to sell the issue.
- Firm would like price to be high.
- Note that original owners generally sell only a small part of their stock, so if price increases, they benefit.
- Later offerings easier if first goes well.

19 - 19

What are the long-term returns to investors in IPOs?

- Two-year return following IPO is lower than for comparable non-IPO firms.
- On average, the IPO offer price is too low, and the first-day run-up is too high.

19 - 20

What are the direct costs of an IPO?

- Underwriter usually charges a 7% spread between offer price and proceeds to issuer.
- Direct costs to lawyers, printers, accountants, etc. can be over $400,000.

19 - 21

What are the indirect costs of an IPO?

- Money left on the table
  - (End of price on first day - Offer price) x Number of shares
- Typical IPO raises about $70 million, and leaves $9 million on table.
- Preparing for IPO consumes most of management's attention during the pre-IPO months.

19 - 22

If firm issues 7 million shares at $10, what are net proceeds if spread is 7%?

Gross proceeds = 7 x $10 million
= $70 million

Underwriting fee = 7% x $70 million
= $4.9 million

Net proceeds = $70 - $4.9
= $65.1 million

19 - 23

What are equity carve-outs?

- A special IPO in which a parent company creates a new public company by selling stock in a subsidiary to outside investors.
- Parent usually retains controlling interest in new public company.

19 - 24

How are investment banks involved in non-IPO issuances?

- Shelf registration (SEC Rule 415), in which issues are registered but the entire issue is not sold at once, but partial sales occur over a period of time.
- Public and private debt issues
- Seasoned equity offerings (public and private placements)

19 - 25

What is a rights offering?

- A rights offering occurs when current shareholders get the first right to buy new shares.
- Shareholders can either exercise the right and buy new shares, or sell the right to someone else.
- Wealth of shareholders doesn't change whether they exercise right or sell it.

19 - 26

What is meant by going private?

- Going private is the reverse of going public.
- Typically, the firm's managers team up with a small group of outside investors and purchase all of the publicly held shares of the firm.
- The new equity holders usually use a large amount of debt financing, so such transactions are called leveraged buyouts (LBOs).

19 - 27

Advantages of Going Private

- Gives managers greater incentives and more flexibility in running the company.
- Removes pressure to report high earnings in the short run.
- After several years as a private firm, owners typically go public again. Firm is presumably operating more efficiently and sells for more.

19 - 28

Disadvantages of Going Private

- Firms that have recently gone private are normally leveraged to the hilt, so it's difficult to raise new capital.
- A difficult period that normally could be weathered might bankrupt the company.

19 - 29

How do companies manage the maturity structure of their debt?

- Maturity matching
  - Match maturity of assets and debt
- Information asymmetries
  - Firms with strong future prospects will issue short-term debt

19 - 30

Under what conditions would a firm exercise a bond call provision?

- If interest rates have fallen since the bond was issued, the firm can replace the current issue with a new, lower coupon rate bond.
- However, there are costs involved in refunding a bond issue. For example,
  - The call premium.
  - Flotation costs on the new issue.

(More...)

19 - 31

- The NPV of refunding compares the interest savings benefit with the costs of the refunding. A positive NPV indicates that refunding today would increase the value of the firm.
- However, it interest rates are expected to fall further, it may be better to delay refunding until some time in the future.

19 - 32

Managing Debt Risk with Project Financing

- Project financings are used to finance a specific large capital project.
- Sponsors provide the equity capital, while the rest of the project's capital is supplied by lenders and/or lessors.
- Interest is paid from project's cash flows, and borrowers don't have recourse.

19 - 33

Managing Debt Risk with Securitization

- Securitization is the process whereby financial instruments that were previously illiquid are converted to a form that creates greater liquidity.
- Examples are bonds backed by mortgages, auto loans, credit card loans (asset-backed), and so on.

20 - 1

CHAPTER 20
Lease Financing

- Types of leases
- Tax treatment of leases
- Effects on financial statements
- Lessee's analysis
- Lessor's analysis
- Other issues in lease analysis

20 - 2

Who are the two parties to a lease transaction?

- The lessee, who uses the asset and makes the lease, or rental, payments.
- The lessor, who owns the asset and receives the rental payments.
- Note that the lease decision is a financing decision for the lessee and an investment decision for the lessor.

20 - 3

What are the five primary lease types?

- Operating lease
  - Short-term and normally cancelable
  - Maintenance usually included
- Financial lease
  - Long-term and normally noncancelable
  - Maintenance usually not included
- Sale and leaseback
- Combination lease
- "Synthetic" lease

20 - 4

How are leases treated for tax purposes?

- Leases are classified by the IRS as either guideline or nonguideline.
- For a guideline lease, the entire lease payment is deductible to the lessee.
- For a nonguideline lease, only the imputed interest payment is deductible.
- Why should the IRS be concerned about lease provisions?

20 - 5

How does leasing affect a firm's balance sheet?

- For accounting purposes, leases are classified as either capital or operating.
- Capital leases must be shown directly on the lessee's balance sheet.
- Operating leases, sometimes referred to as off-balance sheet financing, must be disclosed in the footnotes.
- Why are these rules in place?

20 - 6

What impact does leasing have on a firm's capital structure?

- Leasing is a substitute for debt.
- As such, leasing uses up a firm's debt capacity.
- Assume a firm has a 50/50 target capital structure. Half of its assets are leased. How should the remaining assets be financed?

20 - 7

Assume that Lewis Securities plans to acquire some new equipment having a 6-year useful life.

- **If the equipment is leased:**
  - **Firm could obtain a 4-year lease which includes maintenance.**
  - **Lease meets IRS guidelines to expense lease payments.**
  - **Rental payment would be $260,000 at the beginning of each year.**

20 - 8

- **Other information:**
  - **Equipment cost: $1,000,000.**
  - **Loan rate on equipment = 10%.**
  - **Marginal tax rate = 40%.**
  - **3-year MACRS life.**
  - **If company borrows and buys, 4 year maintenance contract costs $20,000 at beginning of each year.**
  - **Residual value at t = 4: $200,000.**

20 - 9

Time Line: After-Tax Cost of Owning (In Thousands)

	0	1	2	3	4
AT loan pmt		-60	-60	-60	-1,060
Dep shld		132	180	60	28
Maint	-20	-20	-20	-20	
Tax sav	8	8	8	8	
RV					200
Tax					-80
NCF	-12	60	108	-12	-912

20 - 10

- Note the depreciation shield in each year equals the depreciation expense times the lessee's tax rate. For Year 1, the depreciation shield is

  $330,000(0.40) = $132,000.

- The present value of the cost of owning cash flows, when discounted at 6%, is -$591,741.

20 - 11

Why use 6% as the discount rate?

- Leasing is similar to debt financing.
  - The cash flows have relatively low risk; most are fixed by contract.
  - Therefore, the firm's 10% cost of debt is a good candidate.
- The tax shield of interest payments must be recognized, so the discount rate is

  10%(1 - T) = 10%(1 - 0.4) = 6.0%.

20 - 12

Time Line: After-Tax Cost of Leasing (In Thousands)

	0	1	2	3	4
Lease pmt	-260	- 260	- 260	- 260	
Tax sav	104	104	104	104	
NCF	-156	- 156	- 156	- 156	

PV cost of leasing @ 6% = -$572,990.

20 - 13

What is the net advantage to leasing (NAL)?

- NAL = PV cost of leasing - PV cost of owning
  = - $572,990 - (-$591,741)
  = $18,751.
- Should the firm lease or buy the equipment? Why?

20 - 14

- Note that we have assumed the company will not continue to use the asset after the lease expires; that is, project life is the same as the term of the lease.
- What changes to the analysis would be required if the lessee planned to continue using the equipment after the lease expired?

20 - 15

Assume the RV could be $0 or $400,000, with an expected value of $200,000. How could this risk be reflected?

- The discount rate applied to the residual value inflow (a positive CF) should be increased to account for the increased risk.
- All other cash flows should be discounted at the original 6% rate.

(More...)

20 - 16

- If the residual value were included as an outflow (a *negative* CF) in the cost of leasing cash flows, the increased risk would be reflected by applying a lower discount rate to the residual value cash flow.
- Again, all other cash flows have relatively low risk, and hence would be discounted at the 6% rate.

20 - 17

What effect would increased uncertainty about the residual value have on the lessee's decision?

- The lessor owns the equipment when the lease expires.
- Therefore, residual value risk is passed from the lessee to the lessor.
- Increased residual value risk makes the lease more attractive to the lessee.

20 - 18

How should the lessor analyze the lease transaction?

- To the lessor, writing the lease is an investment.
- Therefore, the lessor must compare the return on the lease investment with the return available on alternative investments of similar risk.

20 - 19

Assume the following data for Consolidated Leasing, the lessor:

- $280,000 rental payment instead of $260,000.
- All other data are the same as for the lessee.

20 - 20

Time Line: Lessor's Analysis (In Thousands)

	0	1	2	3	4
Cost	-1,000				
Dep shld		132	180	60	28
Maint	-20	-20	-20	-20	
Tax sav	8	8	8	8	
Lse pmt	280	280	280	280	
Tax	-112	- 112	- 112	- 112	
RV					200
RV tax					-80
NCF	-844	288	336	216	148

20 - 21

- The NPV of the net cash flows, when discounted at 6%, is $25,325.
- The IRR is 7.46%.
- Should the lessor write the lease? Why?

20 - 22

Find the lessor's NPV if the lease payment were $260,000.

- With lease payments of $260,000, the lessor's cash flows would be equal, but opposite in sign, to the lessee's NAL.
- Thus, lessor's NPV = -$18,751.
- If all inputs are symmetrical, leasing is a zero-sum game.
- What are the implications?

20 - 23

What impact would a cancellation clause have on the lease's riskiness from the lessee's standpoint? From the lessor's standpoint?

- A cancellation clause would lower the risk of the lease to the lessee but raise the lessor's risk.
- To account for this, the lessor would increase the annual lease payment or else impose a penalty for early cancellation.

20 - 24

Other Issues in Lease Analysis

- Do higher residual values make leasing less attractive to the lessee?
- Is lease financing more available or "better" than debt financing?
- Is the lease analysis presented here applicable to real estate leases? To auto leases?

(More...)

20 - 25

- Would spreadsheet models be useful in lease analyses?
- What impact do tax laws have on the attractiveness of leasing? Consider the following provisions:
  - Investment tax credit (when available)
  - Tax rate differentials between the lessee and the lessor
  - Alternative minimum tax (AMT)

20 - 26

Numerical analyses often indicate that owning is less costly than leasing. Why, then, is leasing so popular?

- Provision of maintenance services.
- Risk reduction for the lessee.
  - Project life
  - Residual value
  - Operating risk
- Portfolio risk reduction enables lessor to better bear these risks.

21 - 1

CHAPTER 21
Hybrid Financing: Preferred Stock, Warrants, and Convertibles

- Types of hybrid securities
  - Preferred stock
  - Warrants
  - Convertibles
- Features and risk
- Cost of capital to issuers

21 - 2

How does preferred stock differ from common stock and debt?

- Preferred dividends are specified by contract, but they may be omitted without placing the firm in default.
- Most preferred stocks prohibit the firm from paying common dividends when the preferred is in arrears.
- Usually cumulative up to a limit.

(More...)

21 - 3

- Some preferred stock is perpetual, but most new issues have sinking fund or call provisions which limit maturities.
- Preferred stock has no voting rights, but may require companies to place preferred stockholders on the board (sometimes a majority) if the dividend is passed.
- Is preferred stock closer to debt or common stock? What is its risk to investors? To issuers?

21 - 4

What are the advantages and disadvantages of preferred stock financing?

- Advantages
  - Dividend obligation not contractual
  - Avoids dilution of common stock
  - Avoids large repayment of principal
- Disadvantages
  - Preferred dividends not tax deductible, so typically costs more than debt
  - Increases financial leverage, and hence the firm's cost of common equity

21 - 5

What is floating rate preferred?

- Dividends are indexed to the rate on treasury securities instead of being fixed.
- Excellent S-T corporate investment:
  - Only 30% of dividends are taxable to corporations.
  - The floating rate generally keeps issue trading near par.

21 - 6

- However, if the issuer is risky, the floating rate preferred stock may have too much price instability for the liquid asset portfolios of many corporate investors.

21 - 7

How can a knowledge of call options help one understand warrants and convertibles?

- A warrant is a long-term call option.
- A convertible consists of a fixed rate bond (or preferred stock)plus a long-term call option.

21 - 8

Given the following facts, what coupon rate must be set on a bond with warrants if the total package is to sell for $1,000?

- P_0 = $20.
- r_d of 20-year annual payment bond without warrants = 12%.
- 50 warrants with an exercise price of $25 each are attached to bond.
- Each warrant's value is estimated to be $3.

21 - 9

Step 1: Calculate V_{Bond}

$$V_{Package} = V_{Bond} + V_{Warrants} = \$1,000.$$

$$V_{Warrants} = 50(\$3) = \$150.$$

$$V_{Bond} + \$150 = \$1,000$$

$$V_{Bond} = \$850.$$

21 - 10

Step 2: Find Coupon Payment and Rate

20	12	-850		1000
N	I/YR	PV	PMT	FV

Solve for payment = 100

Therefore, the required coupon rate is \$100/\$1,000 = 10%.

21 - 11

If after issue the warrants immediately sell for \$5 each, what would this imply about the value of the package?

- At issue, the package was actually worth

  $V_{Package}$ = \$850 + 50(\$5) = \$1,100,

  which is \$100 more than the selling price.

(More...)

21 - 12

- The firm could have set lower interest payments whose PV would be smaller by \$100 per bond, or it could have offered fewer warrants and/or set a higher exercise price.
- Under the original assumptions, current stockholders would be losing value to the bond/warrant purchasers.

21 - 13

Assume that the warrants expire 10 years after issue. When would you expect them to be exercised?

- Generally, a warrant will sell in the open market at a premium above its value if exercised (it can't sell for less).
- Therefore, warrants tend not to be exercised until just before expiration.

(More...)

21 - 14

- In a stepped-up exercise price, the exercise price increases in steps over the warrant's life. Because the value of the warrant falls when the exercise price is increased, step-up provisions encourage in-the-money warrant holders to exercise just prior to the step-up.
- Since no dividends are earned on the warrant , holders will tend to exercise voluntarily if a stock's payout ratio rises enough.

21 - 15

Will the warrants bring in additional capital when exercised?

- When exercised, each warrant will bring in the exercise price, $25.
- This is equity capital and holders will receive one share of common stock per warrant.
- The exercise price is typically set some 20% to 30% above the current stock price when the warrants are issued.

21 - 16

Because warrants lower the cost of the accompanying debt issue, should all debt be issued with warrants?

No. As we shall see, the warrants have a cost which must be added to the coupon interest cost.

21 - 17

What is the expected return to the bond-with-warrant holders (and cost to the issuer) if the warrants are expected to be exercised in 5 years when P = $36.75?

- The company will exchange stock worth $36.75 for one warrant plus $25. The opportunity cost to the company is $36.75 - $25.00 = $11.75 per warrant.
- Bond has 50 warrants, so the opportunity cost per bond = 50($11.75) = $587.50.

(More...)

21 - 18

- Here are the cash flows on a time line:

0	1	4	5	6	19	20
+1,000	-100	-100	-100	-100	-100	-100
			-587.50			-1,000
			-687.50			-1,100

Input the cash flows into a calculator to find IRR = 14.7%. This is the pre-tax cost of the bond and warrant package.

(More...)

21 - 19

- The cost of the bond with warrants package is higher than the 12% cost of straight debt because part of the expected return is from capital gains, which are riskier than interest income.
- The cost is lower than the cost of equity because part of the return is fixed by contract.

(More...)

21 - 20

- When the warrants are exercised, there is a wealth transfer from existing stockholders to exercising warrant holders.
- But, bondholders previously transferred wealth to existing stockholders, in the form of a low coupon rate, when the bond was issued.

21 - 21

- At the time of exercise, either more or less wealth than expected may be transferred from the existing shareholders to the warrant holders, depending upon the stock price.
- At the time of issue, on a risk-adjusted basis, the expected cost of a bond-with-warrants issue is the same as the cost of a straight-debt issue.

21 - 22

Assume the following convertible bond data:

- 20-year, 10.5% annual coupon, callable convertible bond will sell at its $1,000 par value; straight debt issue would require a 12% coupon.
- Call protection = 5 years and call price = $1,100. Call the bonds when conversion value > $1,200, but the call must occur on the issue date anniversary.
- P_0 = $20; D_0 = $1.48; g = 8%.
- Conversion ratio = CR = 40 shares.

21 - 23

What conversion price (P_c) is built into the bond?

$$P_c = \frac{\text{Par value}}{\text{\# Shares received}}$$

$$= \frac{\$1,000}{40} = \$25.$$

Like with warrants, the conversion price is typically set 20%-30% above the stock price on the issue date.

21 - 24

Examples of real convertible bonds issued by Internet companies

Issuer	Size of issue	Cvt Price	Price at issue
Amazon.com	$1,250 mil	$156.05	$122
Beyond.com	55 mil	18.34	16
CNET	173 mil	74.81	84
DoubleClick	250 mil	165	134
Mindspring	180 mil	62.5	60
NetBank	100 mil	35.67	32
PSINet	400 mil	62.36	55
SportsLine.com	150 mil	65.12	52

21 - 25

What is (1) the convertible's straight debt value and (2) the implied value of the convertibility feature?

Straight debt value:

20	12		105	1000
N	I/YR	PV	PMT	FV

Solution: -887.96

21 - 26

Implied Convertibility Value

- Because the convertibles will sell for \$1,000, the implied value of the convertibility feature is

  \$1,000 - \$887.96 = \$112.04.

- The convertibility value corresponds to the warrant value in the previous example.

21 - 27

What is the formula for the bond's expected conversion value in any year?

Conversion value = $CV_t = CR(P_0)(1 + g)^t$.

t = 0

$CV_0 = 40(\$20)(1.08)^0 = \$800.$

t = 10

$CV_{10} = 40(\$20)(1.08)^{10}$
$= \$1,727.14.$

21 - 28

What is meant by the floor value of a convertible? What is the floor value at t = 0? At t = 10?

- The floor value is the higher of the straight debt value and the conversion value.
- Straight debt value$_0$ = \$887.96.
- CV_0 = \$800.

Floor value at Year 0 = \$887.96.

21 - 29

- Straight debt value$_{10}$ = \$915.25.
- CV_{10} = \$1,727.14.

Floor value$_{10}$ = \$1,727.14.

- A convertible will generally sell above its floor value prior to maturity because convertibility constitutes a call option that has value.

21 - 30

If the firm intends to force conversion on the first anniversary date after CV > \$1,200, when is the issue expected to be called?

N	I/YR	PV	PMT	FV
	8	-800	0	1200

Solution: n = 5.27

Bond would be called at t = 6 since call must occur on anniversary date.

21 - 31

What is the convertible's expected cost of capital to the firm?

0	1	2	3	4	5	6
1,000	-105	-105	-105	-105	-105	-105
						-1,269.50
						-1,374.50

$CV_6 = 40(\$20)(1.08)^6 = \$1,269.50.$

Input the cash flows in the calculator and solve for IRR = 13.7%.

21 - 32

Does the cost of the convertible appear to be consistent with the costs of debt and equity?

- For consistency, need $r_d < r_c < r_s$.
- Why?

(More...)

21 - 33

- Check the values:

r_d = 12% and r_c = 13.7%.

$$r_s = \frac{D_0(1 + g)}{P_0} + g = \frac{\$1.48(1.08)}{\$20} + 0.08$$

$$= 16.0\%.$$

Since r_c is between r_d and r_s, the costs are consistent with the risks.

21 - 34

WACC Effects

Assume the firm's tax rate is 40% and its debt ratio is 50%. Now suppose the firm is considering either:

(1) issuing convertibles, or

(2) issuing bonds with warrants.

Its new target capital structure will have 40% straight debt, 40% common equity and 20% convertibles or bonds with warrants. What effect will the two financing alternatives have on the firm's WACC?

21 - 35

Convertibles Step 1: Find the after-tax cost of the convertibles.

0	1	2	3	4	5	6
1,000	-63	-63	-63	-63	-63	-63
						-1,269.50
						-1,332.50

INT(1 - T) = \$105(0.6) = \$63.

With a calculator, find:

r_c (AT) = IRR = 9.81%.

21 - 36

Convertibles Step 2: Find the after-tax cost of straight debt.

r_d (AT) = 12%(0.06) = 7.2%.

21 - 37

Convertibles Step 3: Calculate the WACC.

WACC (with convertibles) = 0.4(7.2%) + 0.2(9.81%) + 0.4(16%)

= 11.24%.

WACC (without convertibles) = 0.5(7.2%) + 0.5(16%)

= 11.60%.

21 - 38

- Some notes:
  - We have assumed that r_s is not affected by the addition of convertible debt.
  - In practice, most convertibles are subordinated to the other debt, which muddies our assumption of r_d = 12% when convertibles are used.
  - When the convertible is converted, the debt ratio would decrease and the firm's financial risk would decline.

21 - 39

Warrants Step 1: Find the after-tax cost of the bond with warrants.

0	1 ...	4	5	6 ...	19	20
+1,000	-60	-60	-60	-60	-60	-60
			-587.50			-1,000
			-647.50			-1,060

INT(1 - T) = $100(0.60) = $60.

Warrants(Opportunity loss per warrant)
= 50($11.75) = $587.50.

Solve for: r_w (AT) = 10.32%.

21 - 40

Warrants Step 2: Calculate the WACC if the firm uses warrants.

WACC (with warrants) = 0.4(7.2%) + 0.2(10.32%) + 0.4(16%) = 11.34%.

WACC (without warrants) = 0.5(7.2%) + 0.5(16%) = 11.60%.

21 - 41

Besides cost, what other factors should be considered?

- The firm's future needs for equity capital:
  - Exercise of warrants brings in new equity capital.
  - Convertible conversion brings in no new funds.
  - In either case, new lower debt ratio can support more financial leverage.

(More...)

21 - 42

- Does the firm want to commit to 20 years of debt?
  - Convertible conversion removes debt, while the exercise of warrants does not.
  - If stock price does not rise over time, then neither warrants nor convertibles would be exercised. Debt would remain outstanding.

21 - 43

Recap the differences between warrants and convertibles.

- Warrants bring in new capital, while convertibles do not.
- Most convertibles are callable, while warrants are not.
- Warrants typically have shorter maturities than convertibles, and expire before the accompanying debt.

(More...)

21 - 44

- Warrants usually provide for fewer common shares than do convertibles.
- Bonds with warrants typically have much higher flotation costs than do convertible issues.
- Bonds with warrants are often used by small start-up firms. Why?

21 - 45

How do convertibles help minimize agency costs?

- Agency costs due to conflicts between shareholders and bondholders
  - Asset substitution (or bait-and-switch). Firm issues low cost straight debt, then invests in risky projects
  - Bondholders suspect this, so they charge high interest rates
  - Convertible debt allows bondholders to share in upside potential, so it has low rate.

21 - 46

Agency Costs Between Current Shareholders and New Shareholders

- Information asymmetry: company knows its future prospects better than outside investors
  - Outside investors think company will issue new stock only if future prospects are not as good as market anticipates
  - Issuing new stock send negative signal to market, causing stock price to fall

21 - 47

- Company with good future prospects can issue stock "through the back door" by issuing convertible bonds
  - Avoids negative signal of issuing stock directly
  - Since prospects are good, bonds will likely be converted into equity, which is what the company wants to issue

22 - 1

CHAPTER 22
Working Capital Management

- Alternative working capital policies
- Cash, inventory, and A/R management
- Accounts payable management
- Short-term financing policies
- Bank debt and commercial paper

22 - 2

Basic Definitions

- Gross working capital:
  Total current assets.
- Net working capital:
  Current assets - Current liabilities.
- Net operating working capital (NOWC):
  Operating CA – Operating CL =
  (Cash + Inv. + A/R) – (Accruals + A/P)

(More...)

22 - 3

- Working capital management:
  Includes both establishing working capital policy and then the day-to-day control of cash, inventories, receivables, accruals, and accounts payable.
- Working capital policy:
  - The level of each current asset.
  - How current assets are financed.

22 - 4

Selected Ratios for SKI

	SKI	Industry
Current	1.75x	2.25x
Quick	0.83x	1.20x
Debt/Assets	58.76%	50.00%
Turnover of cash	16.67x	22.22x
DSO (365-day basis)	45.63	32.00
Inv. turnover	4.82x	7.00x
F. A. turnover	11.35x	12.00x
T. A. turnover	2.08x	3.00x
Profit margin	2.07%	3.50%
ROE	10.45%	21.00%
Payables deferral	30.00	33.00

22 - 5

How does SKI's working capital policy compare with the industry?

- Working capital policy is reflected in a firm's current ratio, quick ratio, turnover of cash and securities, inventory turnover, and DSO.
- These ratios indicate SKI has large amounts of working capital relative to its level of sales. Thus, SKI is following a relaxed policy.

22 - 6

Is SKI inefficient or just conservative?

- A relaxed policy may be appropriate if it reduces risk more than profitability.
- However, SKI is much less profitable than the average firm in the industry. This suggests that the company probably has excessive working capital.

22 - 7

Cash Conversion Cycle

The cash conversion cycle focuses on the time between payments made for materials and labor and payments received from sales:

$$\text{Cash conversion cycle} = \text{Inventory conversion period} + \text{Receivables collection period} - \text{Payables deferral period}.$$

22 - 8

Cash Conversion Cycle (Cont.)

$$CCC = \frac{\text{Days per year}}{\text{Inv. turnover}} + \text{Days sales outstanding} - \text{Payables deferral period}$$

$$CCC = \frac{365}{4.82} + 45.6 - 30$$

$$CCC = 75.7 + 45.6 - 30$$

$$CCC = 91.3 \text{ days.}$$

22 - 9

Cash Management: Cash doesn't earn interest, so why hold it?

- **Transactions:** Must have some cash to pay current bills.
- **Precaution:** "Safety stock." But lessened by credit line and marketable securities.
- **Compensating balances:** For loans and/or services provided.
- **Speculation:** To take advantage of bargains, to take discounts, and so on. Reduced by credit line, marketable securities.

22 - 10

What's the goal of cash management?

- To have sufficient cash on hand to meet the needs listed on the previous slide.
- However, since cash is a non-earning asset, to have not one dollar more.

22 - 11

Ways to Minimize Cash Holdings

- Use lockboxes.
- Insist on wire transfers from customers.
- Synchronize inflows and outflows.
- Use a remote disbursement account.

(More…)

22 - 12

- Increase forecast accuracy to reduce the need for a cash "safety stock."
- Hold marketable securities instead of a cash "safety stock."
- Negotiate a line of credit (also reduces need for a "safety stock").

22 - 13

Cash Budget: The Primary Cash Management Tool

- Purpose: Uses forecasts of cash inflows, outflows, and ending cash balances to predict loan needs and funds available for temporary investment.
- Timing: Daily, weekly, or monthly, depending upon budget's purpose. Monthly for annual planning, daily for actual cash management.

22 - 14

Data Required for Cash Budget

1. Sales forecast.
2. Information on collections delay.
3. Forecast of purchases and payment terms.
4. Forecast of cash expenses: wages, taxes, utilities, and so on.
5. Initial cash on hand.
6. Target cash balance.

22 - 15

SKI's Cash Budget for January and February

	Net Cash Inflows	
	January	February
Collections	$67,651.95	$62,755.40
Purchases	44,603.75	36,472.65
Wages	6,690.56	5,470.90
Rent	2,500.00	2,500.00
Total payments	$53,794.31	$44,443.55
Net CF	$13,857.64	$18,311.85

22 - 16

Cash Budget (Continued)

	January	February
Cash at start if no borrowing	$ 3,000.00	$16,857.64
Net CF (slide 13)	13,857.64	18,311.85
Cumulative cash	$16,857.64	$35,169.49
Less: target cash	1,500.00	1,500.00
Surplus	$15,357.64	$33,669.49

22 - 17

Should depreciation be explicitly included in the cash budget?

- No. Depreciation is a noncash charge. Only cash payments and receipts appear on cash budget.
- However, depreciation does affect taxes, which do appear in the cash budget.

22 - 18

What are some other potential cash inflows besides collections?

- Proceeds from fixed asset sales.
- Proceeds from stock and bond sales.
- Interest earned.
- Court settlements.

22 - 19

How can interest earned or paid on short-term securities or loans be incorporated in the cash budget?

- Interest earned: Add line in the collections section.
- Interest paid: Add line in the payments section.
- Found as interest rate x surplus/loan line of cash budget for preceding month.
- Note: Interest on any other debt would need to be incorporated as well.

22 - 20

How could bad debts be worked into the cash budget?

- Collections would be reduced by the amount of bad debt losses.
- For example, if the firm had 3% bad debt losses, collections would total only 97% of sales.
- Lower collections would lead to lower surpluses and higher borrowing requirements.

22 - 21

SKI's forecasted cash budget indicates that the company's cash holdings will exceed the targeted cash balance every month, except for October and November.

- Cash budget indicates the company probably is holding too much cash.
- SKI could improve its EVA by either investing its excess cash in more productive assets or by paying it out to the firm's shareholders.

22 - 22

What reasons might SKI have for maintaining a relatively high amount of cash?

- If sales turn out to be considerably less than expected, SKI could face a cash shortfall.
- A company may choose to hold large amounts of cash if it does not have much faith in its sales forecast, or if it is very conservative.
- The cash may be there, in part, to fund a planned fixed asset acquisition.

22 - 23

Inventory Management: Categories of Inventory Costs

- Carrying Costs: Storage and handling costs, insurance, property taxes, depreciation, and obsolescence.
- Ordering Costs: Cost of placing orders, shipping, and handling costs.
- Costs of Running Short: Loss of sales, loss of customer goodwill, and the disruption of production schedules.

22 - 24

Is SKI holding too much inventory?

- SKI's inventory turnover (4.82) is considerably lower than the industry average (7.00). The firm is carrying a lot of inventory per dollar of sales.
- By holding excessive inventory, the firm is increasing its operating costs which reduces its NOPAT. Moreover, the excess inventory must be financed, so EVA is further lowered.

22 - 25

If SKI reduces its inventory, without adversely affecting sales, what effect will this have on its cash position?

- Short run: Cash will increase as inventory purchases decline.
- Long run: Company is likely to then take steps to reduce its cash holdings.

22 - 26

Accounts Receivable Management: Do SKI's customers pay more or less promptly than those of its competitors?

- SKI's days' sales outstanding (DSO) of 45.6 days is well above the industry average (32 days).
- SKI's customers are paying less promptly.
- SKI should consider tightening its credit policy to reduce its DSO.

22 - 27

Elements of Credit Policy

- Cash Discounts: Lowers price. Attracts new customers and reduces DSO.
- Credit Period: How long to pay? Shorter period reduces DSO and average A/R, but it may discourage sales.

(More...)

22 - 28

- Credit Standards: Tighter standards reduce bad debt losses, but may reduce sales. Fewer bad debts reduces DSO.
- Collection Policy: Tougher policy will reduce DSO, but may damage customer relationships.

22 - 29

Does SKI face any risk if it tightens its credit policy?

YES! A tighter credit policy may discourage sales. Some customers may choose to go elsewhere if they are pressured to pay their bills sooner.

22 - 30

If SKI succeeds in reducing DSO without adversely affecting sales, what effect would this have on its cash position?

- Short run: If customers pay sooner, this increases cash holdings.
- Long run: Over time, the company would hopefully invest the cash in more productive assets, or pay it out to shareholders. Both of these actions would increase EVA.

22 - 31

Is there a cost to accruals? Do firms have much control over amount of accruals?

- Accruals are free in that no explicit interest is charged.
- Firms have little control over the level of accruals. Levels are influenced more by industry custom, economic factors, and tax laws.

22 - 32

What is trade credit?

- Trade credit is credit furnished by a firm's suppliers.
- Trade credit is often the largest source of short-term credit, especially for small firms.
- Spontaneous, easy to get, but cost can be high.

22 - 33

SKI buys $506,985 net, on terms of 1/10, net 30, and pays on Day 40. How much free and costly trade credit, and what's the cost of costly trade credit?

Net daily purchases = $506,985/365

= $1,389.

Annual gross purch. = $506,985/(1-0.01)

=$512,106

22 - 34

Gross/Net Breakdown

- Company buys goods worth $506,985. That's the cash price.
- They must pay $5,121 more if they don't take discounts.
- Think of the extra $5,121 as a financing cost similar to the interest on a loan.
- Want to compare that cost with the cost of a bank loan.

22 - 35

Payables level if take discount:
Payables = $1,389(10) = $13,890.

Payables level if don't take discount:
Payables = $1,389(40) = $55,560.

Credit Breakdown:

Total trade credit	=	$55,560
Free trade credit	=	13,890
Costly trade credit	=	$41,670

22 - 36

Nominal Cost of Costly Trade Credit

Firm loses 0.01($512,106) = $5,121 of discounts to obtain $41,670 in extra trade credit, so

$$r_{Nom} = \frac{\$5,121}{\$41,670} = 0.1229 = 12.29\%.$$

But the $5,121 is paid all *during* the year, not at year-end, so EAR rate is higher.

22 - 37

Nominal Cost Formula, 1/10, net 40

$$r_{Nom} = \frac{\text{Discount } \%}{1-\text{Discount } \%} \times \frac{365 \text{ days}}{\text{Days taken} - \text{Discount period}}$$

$$= \frac{1}{99} \times \frac{365}{30} = 0.0101 \times 12.1667$$

$$= 0.1229 = 12.29\%.$$

Pays 1.01% 12.167 times per year.

22 - 38

Effective Annual Rate, 1/10, net 40

Periodic rate = 0.01/0.99 = 1.01%.

Periods/year = 365/(40 – 10) = 12.1667.

EAR = (1 + Periodic rate)^n – 1.0
= (1.0101)$^{12.1667}$ – 1.0 = 13.01%.

22 - 39

Working Capital Financing Policies

- **Moderate: Match the maturity of the assets with the maturity of the financing.**
- **Aggressive: Use short-term financing to finance permanent assets.**
- **Conservative: Use permanent capital for permanent assets and temporary assets.**

22 - 40

Moderate Financing Policy

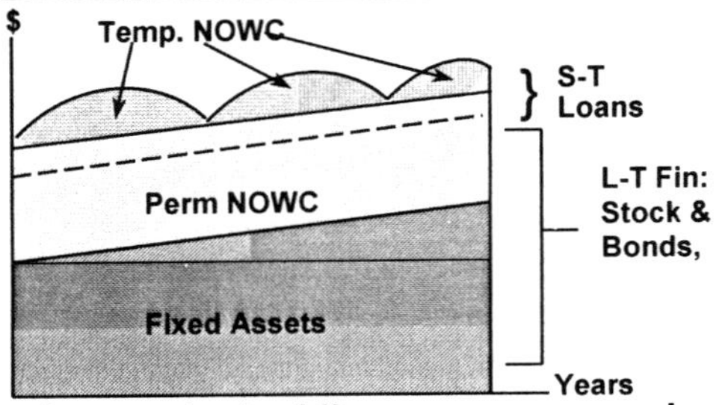

Lower dashed line, more aggressive.

22 - 41

Conservative Financing Policy

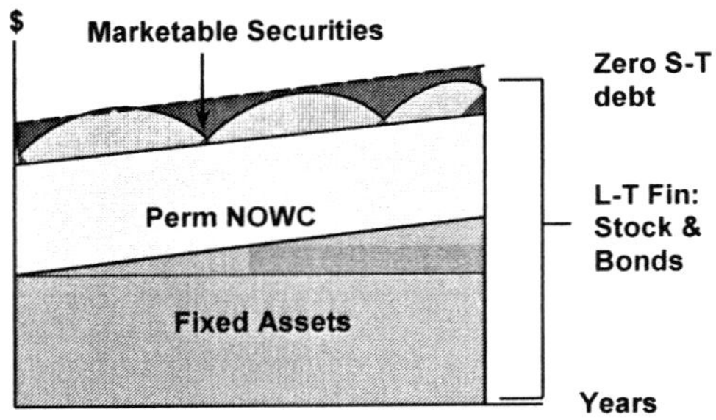

22 - 42

What are the advantages of short-term debt vs. long-term debt?

- Low cost-- yield curve usually slopes upward.
- Can get funds relatively quickly.
- Can repay without penalty.

22 - 43

What are the disadvantages of short-term debt vs. long-term debt?

- Higher risk. The required repayment comes quicker, and the company may have trouble rolling over loans.

22 - 44

Commercial Paper (CP)

- Short term notes issued by large, strong companies. SKI couldn't issue CP--it's too small.
- CP trades in the market at rates just above T-bill rate.
- CP is bought with surplus cash by banks and other companies, then held as a marketable security for liquidity purposes.

23 - 1

CHAPTER 23
Derivatives and Risk Management

- Risk management and stock value maximization.
- Derivative securities.
- Fundamentals of risk management.
- Using derivatives to reduce interest rate risk.

23 - 2

Do stockholders care about volatile cash flows?

- If volatility in cash flows is not caused by systematic risk, then stockholders can eliminate the risk of volatile cash flows by diversifying their portfolios.
- Stockholders might be able to reduce impact of volatile cash flows by using risk management techniques in their own portfolios.

23 - 3

How can risk management increase the value of a corporation?

Risk management allows firms to:

- Have greater debt capacity, which has a larger tax shield of interest payments.
- Implement the optimal capital budget without having to raise external equity in years that would have had low cash flow due to volatility. (More...)

23 - 4

Risk management allows firms to:

- Avoid costs of financial distress.
  - Weakened relationships with suppliers.
  - Loss of potential customers.
  - Distractions to managers.
- Utilize comparative advantage in hedging relative to hedging ability of investors.

(More...)

23 - 5

Risk management allows firms to:

- Reduce borrowing costs by using interest rate swaps.

  Example: Two firms with different credit ratings, Hi and Lo:

  Hi can borrow fixed at 11% and floating at LIBOR + 1%.

  Lo can borrow fixed at 11.4% and floating at LIBOR + 1.5%.

(More...)

23 - 6

Hi wants fixed rate, but it will issue floating and "swap" with Lo. Lo wants floating rate, but it will issue fixed and swap with Hi. Lo also makes "side payment" of 0.45% to Hi.

	Hi	Lo
CF to lender	-(LIBOR+1%)	-11.40%
CF Hi to Lo	-11.40%	+11.40%
CF Lo to Hi	+(LIBOR+1%)	-(LIBOR+1%)
CF Lo to Hi	+0.45%	-0.45%
Net CF	-10.95%	-(LIBOR+1.45%)

(More...)

23 - 7

Risk management allows firms to:

- Minimize negative tax effects due to convexity in tax code.

  Example: EBT of $50K in Years 1 and 2, total EBT of $100K,

  Tax = $7.5K each year, total tax of $15.

  EBT of $0K in Year 1 and $100K in Year 2,

  Tax = $0K in Year 1 and $22.5K in Year 2.

23 - 8

What is corporate risk management?

Corporate risk management is the management of unpredictable events that would have adverse consequences for the firm.

23 - 9

Definitions of Different Types of Risk

- **Speculative risks:** Those that offer the chance of a gain as well as a loss.
- **Pure risks:** Those that offer only the prospect of a loss.
- **Demand risks:** Those associated with the demand for a firm's products or services.
- **Input risks:** Those associated with a firm's input costs.

(More...)

23 - 10

- **Financial risks:** Those that result from financial transactions.
- **Property risks:** Those associated with loss of a firm's productive assets.
- **Personnel risk:** Risks that result from human actions.
- **Environmental risk:** Risk associated with polluting the environment.
- **Liability risks:** Connected with product, service, or employee liability.
- **Insurable risks:** Those which typically can be covered by insurance.

23 - 11

What are the three steps of corporate risk management?

Step 1. Identify the risks faced by the firm.

Step 2. Measure the potential impact of the identified risks.

Step 3. Decide how each relevant risk should be dealt with.

23 - 12

What are some actions that companies can take to minimize or reduce risk exposures?

- Transfer risk to an insurance company by paying periodic premiums.
- Transfer functions which produce risk to third parties.
- Purchase derivatives contracts to reduce input and financial risks.

(More...)

23 - 13

- Take actions to reduce the probability of occurrence of adverse events.
- Take actions to reduce the magnitude of the loss associated with adverse events.
- Avoid the activities that give rise to risk.

23 - 14

What is a financial risk exposure?

- Financial risk exposure refers to the risk inherent in the financial markets due to price fluctuations.
- Example: A firm holds a portfolio of bonds, interest rates rise, and the value of the bonds falls.

23 - 15

Financial Risk Management Concepts

- **Derivative:** Security whose value stems or is derived from the value of other assets. Swaps, options, and futures are used to manage financial risk exposures.
- **Futures:** Contracts which call for the purchase or sale of a financial (or real) asset at some future date, but at a price determined today. Futures (and other derivatives) can be used either as highly leveraged speculations or to hedge and thus reduce risk.

(More...)

23 - 16

■ **Hedging:** Generally conducted where a price change could negatively affect a firm's profits.

- **Long hedge:** Involves the purchase of a futures contract to guard against a price increase.
- **Short hedge:** Involves the sale of a futures contract to protect against a price decline in commodities or financial securities.

(More...)

23 - 17

■ **Swaps:** Involve the exchange of cash payment obligations between two parties, usually because each party prefers the terms of the other's debt contract. Swaps can reduce each party's financial risk.

23 - 18

How can commodity futures markets be used to reduce input price risk?

The purchase of a commodity futures contract will allow a firm to make a future purchase of the input at today's price, even if the market price on the item has risen substantially in the interim.

23 - 19

Chapter 23 Extension: Insurance and Bond Portfolio Risk Management

- Risk identification and measurement
- Property loss, liability loss, and financial loss exposures
- Bond portfolio risk management

23 - 20

How are risk exposures identified and measured?

- Large corporations have risk management personnel which have the responsibility to identify and measure risks facing the firm.
- Checklists are used to identify risks.
- Small firms can obtain risk management services from insurance companies or risk management consulting firms.

23 - 21

Describe (1) "property" loss and (2) "liability" loss exposures.

- Property loss exposures: Result from various perils which threaten a firm's real and personal properties.
  - Physical perils: Natural events
  - Social perils: Related to human actions
  - Economic perils: Stem from external economic events

23 - 22

- Liability loss exposures: Result from penalties imposed when responsibilities are not met.
  - Bailee exposure: Risks associated with having temporary possession of another's property while some service is being performed. (Cleaners ruin your new suit.)
  - Ownership exposure: Risks inherent in the ownership of property. (Customer is injured from fall in store.)

23 - 23

- Business operation exposure: Risks arising from business practices or operations. (Airline sued following crash.)
- Professional liability exposure: Stems from the risks inherent in professions requiring advanced training and licensing. (Doctor sued when patient dies, or accounting firm sued for not detecting overstated profits.)

23 - 24

What actions can companies take to reduce property and liability exposures?

- Both property and liability exposures can be accommodated by either self-insurance or passing the risk on to an insurance company.
- The more risk passed on to an insurer, the higher the cost of the policy. Insurers like high deductibles, both to lower their losses and to reduce moral hazard.

23 - 25

How can diversification reduce business risk?

- By appropriately spreading business risk over several activities or operations, the firm can significantly reduce the impact of a single random event on corporate performance.
- Examples: Geographic and product diversification.

23 - 26

What is a financial risk exposure?

- Financial risk exposure refers to the risk inherent in the financial markets due to price fluctuations.
- Example: A firm holds a portfolio of bonds, interest rates rise, and the value of the bonds falls.

23 - 27

Financial risk management concepts:

- **Duration:** Average time to bondholders' receipt of cash flows, including interest and principal repayment. Duration is used to help assess interest rate and reinvestment rate risks.
- **Immunization:** Process of selecting durations for bonds in a portfolio such that gains or losses from reinvestment exactly match gains or losses from price changes.

24 - 1

CHAPTER 24
Bankruptcy, Reorganization, and Liquidation

- Financial distress process
- Federal bankruptcy law
- Reorganization
- Liquidation

24 - 2

What are the major causes of business failure?

- Economic factors
  - industry weakness
  - poor location/product
- Financial factors
  - too much debt
  - insufficient capital

Most failures occur because a number of factors combine to make the business unsustainable.

24 - 3

Do business failures occur evenly over time?

- A large number of businesses fail each year, but the number in any one year has never been a large percentage of the total business population.
- The failure rate of businesses has tended to fluctuate with the state of the economy.

24 - 4

What size firm, large or small, is more prone to business failure?

- Bankruptcy is more frequent among smaller firms.
- Large firms tend to get more help from external sources to avoid bankruptcy, given their greater impact on the economy.

24 - 5

What key issues must managers face in the financial distress process?

- Is it a temporary problem (technical insolvency) or a permanent problem caused by asset values below debt obligations (insolvency in bankruptcy)?
- Who should bear the losses?
- Would the firm be more valuable if it continued to operate or if it were liquidated?

(More...)

24 - 6

- Should the firm file for bankruptcy, or should it try to use informal procedures?
- Who would control the firm during liquidation or reorganization?

24 - 7

What informal remedies are available to firms in financial distress?

- Informal reorganization
- Informal liquidation
- Why might informal remedies be preferable to formal bankruptcy?
- What types of companies are most suitable for informal remedies?

24 - 8

Informal Bankruptcy Terminology

- Workout: Voluntary informal reorganization plan.
- Restructuring: Current debt terms are revised to facilitate the firm's ability to pay.
    - Extension: Creditors postpone the dates of required interest or principal payments, or both. Creditors prefer extension because they are promised eventual payment in full. (More...)

24 - 9

- Composition: Creditors voluntarily reduce their fixed claims on the debtor by either accepting a lower principal amount or accepting equity in lieu of debt repayment.
- Assignment: An informal procedure for liquidating a firm's assets. Title to the debtor's assets is transferred to a third party, called a trustee or assignee, and then the assets are sold off.

24 - 10

Describe the following terms related to U.S. bankruptcy law:

- Chapter 11: Business reorganization guidelines.
- Chapter 7: Liquidation procedures.
- Trustee:
  - Appointed to control the company when current management is incompetent or fraud is suspected.
  - Used only in unusual circumstances.

(More...)

24 - 11

- Voluntary bankruptcy: A bankruptcy petition filed in federal court by the distressed firm's management.
- Involuntary bankruptcy: A bankruptcy petition filed in federal court by the distressed firm's creditors.

24 - 12

What are the major differences between an informal reorganization and reorganization in bankruptcy?

- Informal Reorganization:
  - Less costly
  - Relatively simple to create
  - Typically allows creditors to recover more money and sooner.

(More...)

24 - 13

- Reorganization in Bankruptcy
  - Avoids holdout problems.
  - Due to automatic stay provision, avoids common pool problem.
  - Interest and principal payments may be delayed without penalty until reorganization plan is approved.

(More...)

24 - 14

- Permits the firm to issue debtor in possession (DIP) financing.
- Gives debtor exclusive right to submit a proposed reorganization plan for agreement from the parties involved.
- Reduces fraudulent conveyance problem.
- Cramdown if majority in each creditor class approve plan.

24 - 15

What is a prepackaged bankruptcy?

- New type of reorganization
  - Combines the advantages of both formal and informal reorganizations.
  - Avoids holdout problems
  - Preserves creditors' claims
  - Favorable tax treatment.
- Agreement to plan obtained from creditors prior to filing for bankruptcy.
- Plan filed with bankruptcy petition.

24 - 16

List the priority of claims in a Chapter 7 liquidation.

- Secured creditors.
- Trustee's administrative costs.
- Expenses incurred after involuntary case begun but before trustee appointed.
- Wages due workers within 3 months prior to filing.

(More...)

24 - 17

- Unpaid contributions to employee benefit plans that should have been paid within 6 months prior to filing.
- Unsecured claims for customer deposits.
- Taxes due.
- Unfunded pension plan liabilities.
- General (unsecured) creditors.
- Preferred stockholders.
- Common stockholders.

24 - 18

Liquidation Illustration Data (millions of $)

Creditor Claims:	
Accounts payable	$10.0
Notes payable	5.0
Accrued wages	0.3
Federal taxes	0.5
State and local taxes	0.2
First mortgage	3.0
Second mortgage	0.5
Subordinated debentures*	4.0
	$23.5

*Subordinated to notes payable.

(More...)

24 - 19

Proceeds from liquidation:

From current assets	$14.0
From fixed assets*	2.5
Total receipts	$16.5

* All fixed assets pledged as collateral to mortgage holders.

24 - 20

Priority Distribution (millions of $)

Creditor	Claim	Distribution	Unsatisfied
Accrued wages	$0.3	$0.3	$0.0
Federal taxes	0.5	0.5	0.0
Other taxes	0.2	0.2	0.0
First mortgage	3.0	2.5	0.5
Second mortgage	0.5	0.0	0.5
	$4.5	$3.5	$1.0

Notes: (1) First mortgage receives entire proceeds from sale of fixed assets, leaving $0 for the second mortgage.
(2) $16.5 - $3.5 = $13.0 remains for distribution to general creditors.

24 - 21

General Creditor Distribution (millions of $)

Creditor	Remaining GC Claim	Initial Distrib.[a]	Final Amount[b]	Percent Received
Accounts payable	$10.0	$6.500	$6.500	65.0%
Notes payable	5.0	3.250	5.000	100.0
Accrued wages	0.0		0.300	100.0
Federal taxes	0.0		0.500	100.0
Other taxes	0.0		0.200	100.0
First mortgage	0.5	0.325	2.825	94.2
Second mortgage	0.5	0.325	0.325	65.0
Sub. deb.	4.0	2.600	0.850	21.2
	$20.0	$13.000	$16.500	

[a] Pro rata amount = $13/$20 = 0.65.
[b] Includes priority distribution and $1.75 transfer from subordinated debentures.

24 - 22

Other Motivations for Bankruptcy

- Normally, bankruptcy is motivated by serious current financial problems.
- However, some companies have used bankruptcy proceedings for other purposes:
  - To break union contracts
  - To hasten liability settlements

24 - 23

Some Criticisms of Bankruptcy Laws

- Critics contend that current (1978) bankruptcy laws are flawed.
- Too much value is siphoned off by lawyers, managers, and trustees.
- Companies that have no hope remain alive too long, leaving little for creditors when liquidation does occur.
- Companies in bankruptcy can hurt other companies in industry.

24 - 24

Chapter 24 Extension

- MDA to predict bankruptcy
- Recent business failures

24 - 25

What is MDA, and how can it be used to predict bankruptcy?

- Multiple discriminant analysis (MDA) is a statistical technique similar to multiple regression.
- It identifies the characteristics of firms that went bankrupt in the past.
- Then, data from any firm can be entered into the model to assess the likelihood of future bankruptcy.

24 - 26

MDA Illustration

- Assume you have the following 2003 data for 12 companies:
  - Current ratio
  - Debt ratio
- Six of the companies (marked by Xs) went bankrupt in 2004 while six (marked by dots) remained solvent.

(More...)

24 - 27

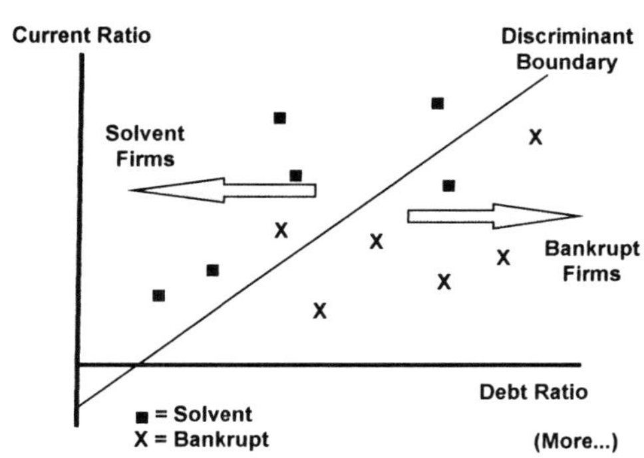

(More...)

24 - 28

- The discriminant boundary, or Z line, statistically separates the bankrupt and solvent companies.
- Note that two companies have been misclassified by the MDA program: One bankrupt company falls on the solvent (left) side and one solvent company falls on the bankrupt (right) side.

(More...)

24 - 29

- Assume the equation for the boundary line is

  Z = -2 + 1.5(Current ratio) - 5.0(Debt ratio).

- Furthermore, if Z = -1 to +1, the future of the company is uncertain. If Z > 1, bankruptcy is unlikely; if Z < -1, bankruptcy is likely to occur.

24 - 30

Using MDA To Predict Bankruptcy

- Suppose Firm S has CR = 4.0 and DR = 0.40. Then,

  Z = -2 + 1.5(4.0) - 5.0(0.40) = +2.0,

  and firm is unlikely to go bankrupt.
- Suppose Firm B has CR = 1.5 and DR = 0.75. Then,

  Z = -2 + 1.5(1.5) - 5.0(0.75) = -3.5,

  and firm is likely to go bankrupt.

24 - 31

Some Final Points

- The most well-known bankruptcy prediction model is Edward Altman's five factor model.
- Such models tend to work relatively well, but only for the near term.
- The more similar the historical sample to the firm being evaluated, the better the prediction.

25 - 1

CHAPTER 25
Mergers, LBOs, Divestitures, and Holding Companies

- Types of mergers
- Merger analysis
- Role of investment bankers
- LBOs, divestitures, and holding companies

25 - 2

What are some valid economic justifications for mergers?

- Synergy: Value of the whole exceeds sum of the parts. Could arise from:
  - Operating economies
  - Financial economies
  - Differential management efficiency
  - Taxes (use accumulated losses)

(More...)

25 - 3

- Break-up value: Assets would be more valuable if broken up and sold to other companies.

25 - 4

What are some questionable reasons for mergers?

- Diversification
- Purchase of assets at below replacement cost
- Acquire other firms to increase size, thus making it more difficult to be acquired

25 - 5

Five Largest Completed Mergers (as of January 2003)

BUYER	TARGET	VALUE (Billion)
Vodafone AirTouch	Mannesman	$161
Pfizer	Warner-Lambert	116
America Online	Time Warner	106
Exxon	Mobil	81
Glaxo Wellcome	SmithKline Beecham	74

25 - 6

Differentiate between hostile and friendly mergers

- Friendly merger:
  - The merger is supported by the managements of both firms.

(More...)

25 - 7

- Hostile merger:
  - Target firm's management resists the merger.
  - Acquirer must go directly to the target firm's stockholders, try to get 51% to tender their shares.
  - Often, mergers that start out hostile end up as friendly, when offer price is raised.

25 - 8

Reasons why alliances can make more sense than acquisitions

- Access to new markets and technologies
- Multiple parties share risks and expenses
- Rivals can often work together harmoniously
- Antitrust laws can shelter cooperative R&D activities

25 - 9

Reason for APV

- Often in a merger the capital structure changes rapidly over the first several years.
- This causes the WACC to change from year to year.
- It is hard to incorporate year-to-year changes in WACC in the corporate valuation model.

25 - 10

The APV Model

Value of firm if it had no debt
+ Value of tax savings due to debt
= Value of operations

First term is called the *unlevered value of the firm*. The second term is called the value of the *interest tax shield.*

(More...)

25 - 11

APV Model

Unlevered value of firm = PV of FCFs discounted at unlevered cost of equity, r_{sU}.

Value of interest tax shield = PV of interest tax savings at unlevered cost of equity. Interest tax savings = Interest(tax rate) = TS_t .

25 - 12

Note to APV

- APV is the best model to use when the capital structure is changing.
- The Corporate Valuation model is easier than APV to use when the capital structure is constant—such as at the horizon.

25 - 13

Steps in APV Valuation

1. Project FCF_t, TS_t, horizon growth rate, and horizon capital structure.
2. Calculate the unlevered cost of equity, r_{sU}.
3. Calculate WACC at horizon.
4. Calculate horizon value using constant growth corporate valuation model.
5. Calculate V_{ops} as PV of FCF_t, TS_t and horizon value, all discounted at r_{sU}.

25 - 14

APV Valuation Analysis (In Millions)

Free Cash Flows after Merger Occurs

	2005	2006	2007	2008
Net sales	$60.0	$90.0	$112.5	$127.5
Cost of goods sold (60%)	36.0	54.0	67.5	76.5
Selling/admin. expenses	4.5	6.0	7.5	9.0
EBIT	19.5	30.0	37.5	42.0
Taxes on EBIT (40%)	7.8	12.0	15.0	16.8
NOPAT	11.7	18.0	22.5	25.2
Net Retentions	0.0	7.5	6.0	4.5
Free Cash Flow	11.7	10.5	16.5	20.7

25 - 15

Interest Tax Savings after Merger

	2005	2006	2007	2008
Interest expense	5.0	6.5	6.5	7.0
Interest tax savings	2.0	2.6	2.6	2.8

Interest tax savings are calculated as interest(T). T = 40%

25 - 16

What are the net retentions?

- Recall that firms must reinvest in order to replace worn out assets and grow.
- Net retentions = gross retentions – depreciation.

25 - 17

Conceptually, what is the appropriate discount rate to apply to the target's cash flows?

- After acquisition, the free cash flows belong to the remaining debtholders in the target and the various investors in the acquiring firm: their debtholders, stockholders, and others such as preferred stockholders.
- These cash flows can be redeployed within the acquiring firm.

(More...)

25 - 18

- Free cash flow is the cash flow that would occur if the firm had no debt, so it should be discounted at the unlevered cost of equity.
- The interest tax shields are also discounted at the unlevered cost of equity.

25 - 19

Note: Comparison of APV with Corporate Valuation Model

- APV discounts FCF at r_{sU} and adds in present value of the tax shields—the value of the tax savings are incorporated explicitly.
- Corp. Val. Model discounts FCF at WACC, which has a (1-T) factor to account for the value of the tax shield.
- Both models give same answer IF carefully done. BUT it is difficult to apply the Corp. Val. Model when WACC is changing from year-to-year.

25 - 20

Discount rate for Horizon Value

- At the horizon the capital structure is constant, so the corporate valuation model can be used, so discount FCFs at WACC.

25 - 21

Discount Rate Calculations

$r_{sL} = r_{RF} + (r_M - r_{RF})b_{Target}$

$= 7\% + (4\%)1.3 = 12.2\%$

$r_{sU} = w_d r_d + w_s r_{sL}$

$= 0.20(9\%) + 0.80(12.2\%) = 11.56\%$

$WACC = w_d(1\text{-}T)r_d + w_s r_{sL}$

$=0.20(0.60)9\% + 0.80(12.2\%)$

$= 10.84\%$

25 - 22

Horizon, or Continuing, Value

$$\text{Horizon value} = \frac{(FCF_{2008})(1+g)}{WACC - g}$$

$$= \frac{\$20.7(1.06)}{0.1084 - 0.06}$$

= $453.3 million.

What Is the value of the Target Firm's operations to the Acquiring Firm? (In Millions)

	2005	2006	2007	2008
Free Cash Flow	$11.7	$10.5	$16.5	$ 20.7
Horizon value				453.3
Interest tax shield	2.0	2.6	2.6	2.8
Total	$13.7	$13.1	$19.1	$476.8

$$V_{Ops} = \frac{\$13.7}{(1.1156)^1} + \frac{\$13.1}{(1.1156)^2} + \frac{\$19.1}{(1.1156)^3} + \frac{\$476.8}{(1.1156)^4}$$

= $344.4 million.

25 - 24

What is the value of the Target's equity?

- The Target has $55 million in debt.
- Vops – debt = equity
- 344.4 million – 55 million = $289.4 million = equity value of target to the acquirer.

25 - 25

Would another potential acquirer obtain the same value?

- **No. The cash flow estimates would be different, both due to forecasting inaccuracies and to differential synergies.**
- **Further, a different beta estimate, financing mix, or tax rate would change the discount rate.**

25 - 26

Assume the target company has 20 million shares outstanding. The stock last traded at $11 per share, which reflects the target's value on a stand-alone basis. How much should the acquiring firm offer?

25 - 27

Estimate of target's value	=	**$289.4 million**
Target's current value	=	**$220.0million**
Merger premium	=	**$ 69.4 million**

Presumably, the target's value is increased by $69.4 million due to merger synergies, although realizing such synergies has been problematic in many mergers.

(More...)

25 - 28

- The offer could range from $11 to $289.4/20 = $14.47 per share.
- At $11, all merger benefits would go to the acquiring firm's shareholders.
- At $14.47, all value added would go to the target firm's shareholders.
- The graph on the next slide summarizes the situation.

25 - 29

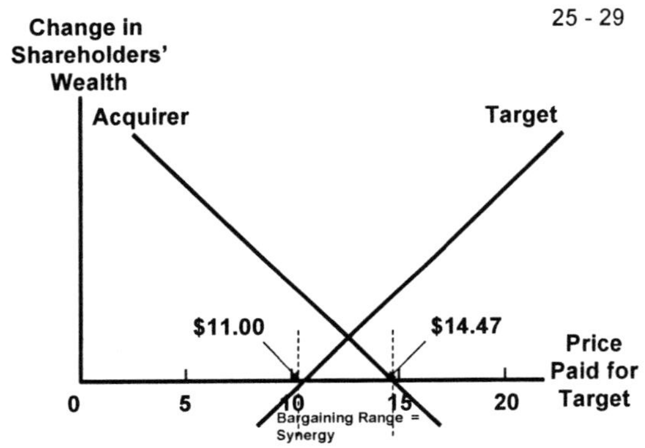

25 - 30

Points About Graph

- Nothing magic about crossover price.
- Actual price would be determined by bargaining. Higher if target is in better bargaining position, lower if acquirer is.
- If target is good fit for many acquirers, other firms will come in, price will be bid up. If not, could be close to $11.

(More...)

25 - 31

- Acquirer might want to make high "preemptive" bid to ward off other bidders, or low bid and then plan to go up. Strategy is important.
- Do target's managers have 51% of stock and want to remain in control?
- What kind of personal deal will target's managers get?

25 - 32

What if the Acquirer intended to increase the debt level in the Target to 40% with an interest rate of 10%?

- Free cash flows wouldn't change
- Assume interest payments in short term won't change (if they did, it is easy to incorporate that difference)
- Long term r_{sL} will change, so horizon WACC will change, so horizon value will change.

25 - 33

New WACC Calculation

New $r_{sL} = r_{sU} + (r_{sU} - r_d)(D/S)$
$= 11.56\% + (11.56\% - 10\%)(0.4/0.6)$
$= 12.60\%$

New WACC $= w_d r_d(1\text{-}T) + w_s r_{sL}$
$= 0.4(10\%)(1\text{-}0.4) + 0.6(12.6\%)$
$= 9.96\%$

25 - 34

New Horizon Value Calculation

$$\text{Horizon value} = \frac{(FCF_{2008})(1+g)}{WACC - g}$$

$$= \frac{\$20.7(1.06)}{0.1084 - 0.06}$$

= $554.1 million.

25 - 35

New V_{ops} and V_{equity}

	2005	2006	2007	2008
Free Cash Flow	$11.7	$10.5	$16.5	$ 20.7
Horizon value				554.1
Interest tax shield	2.0	2.6	2.6	2.8
Total	$13.7	$13.1	$19.1	$577.6

$$V_{Ops} = \frac{\$13.7}{(1.1156)^1} + \frac{\$13.1}{(1.1156)^2} + \frac{\$19.1}{(1.1156)^3} + \frac{\$577.6}{(1.1156)^4}$$

= $409.5 million.

25 - 36

New Equity Value

- $409.5 million - 55 million = $354.5 million
- This is $65 million, or $3.25 per share more than if the horizon capital structure is 20% debt.
- The added value is the value of the additional tax shield from the increased debt.

25 - 37

Do mergers really create value?

- According to empirical evidence, acquisitions do create value as a result of economies of scale, other synergies, and/or better management.
- Shareholders of target firms reap most of the benefits, that is, the final price is close to full value.
  - Target management can always say no.
  - Competing bidders often push up prices.

25 - 38

What method is used to account for for mergers?

- Pooling of interests is GONE. Only purchase accounting may be used now.

(More...)

25 - 39

- Purchase:
  - The assets of the acquired firm are "written up" to reflect purchase price if it is greater than the net asset value.
  - Goodwill is often created, which appears as an asset on the balance sheet.
  - Common equity account is increased to balance assets and claims.

25 - 40

Goodwill Amortization

- Goodwill is NO LONGER amortized over time for shareholder reporting.
- Goodwill is subject to an annual "impairment test." If its fair market value has declined, then goodwill is reduced. Otherwise it is not.
- Goodwill is still amortized for Federal Tax purposes.

25 - 41

What are some merger-related activities of investment bankers?

- Identifying targets
- Arranging mergers
- Developing defensive tactics
- Establishing a fair value
- Financing mergers
- Arbitrage operations

25 - 42

What is a leveraged buyout (LB0)?

- In an LBO, a small group of investors, normally including management, buys all of the publicly held stock, and hence takes the firm private.
- Purchase often financed with debt.
- After operating privately for a number of years, investors take the firm public to "cash out."

25 - 43

What are are the advantages and disadvantages of going private?

- Advantages:
  - Administrative cost savings
  - Increased managerial incentives
  - Increased managerial flexibility
  - Increased shareholder participation
- Disadvantages:
  - Limited access to equity capital
  - No way to capture return on investment

25 - 44

What are the major types of divestitures?

- Sale of an entire subsidiary to another firm.
- Spinning off a corporate subsidiary by giving the stock to existing shareholders.
- Carving out a corporate subsidiary by selling a minority interest.
- Outright liquidation of assets.

25 - 45

What motivates firms to divest assets?

- Subsidiary worth more to buyer than when operated by current owner.
- To settle antitrust issues.
- Subsidiary's value increased if it operates independently.
- To change strategic direction.
- To shed money losers.
- To get needed cash when distressed.

25 - 46

What are holding companies?

- A holding company is a corporation formed for the sole purpose of owning the stocks of other companies.
- In a typical holding company, the subsidiary companies issue their own debt, but their equity is held by the holding company, which, in turn, sells stock to individual investors.

25 - 47

What are the advantages and disadvantages of holding companies?

- Advantages:
  - Control with fractional ownership.
  - Isolation of risks.
- Disadvantages:
  - Partial multiple taxation.
  - Ease of enforced dissolution.

26 - 1

CHAPTER 26
Multinational Financial Management

- Factors that make multinational financial management different
- Exchange rates and trading
- International monetary system
- International financial markets
- Specific features of multinational financial management

26 - 2

What is a multinational corporation?

- A multinational corporation is one that operates in two or more countries.
- At one time, most multinationals produced and sold in just a few countries.
- Today, many multinationals have world-wide production and sales.

26 - 3

Why do firms expand into other countries?

- To seek new markets.
- To seek new supplies of raw materials.
- To gain new technologies.
- To gain production efficiencies.
- To avoid political and regulatory obstacles.
- To reduce risk by diversification.

26 - 4

What are the major factors that distinguish multinational from domestic financial management?

- Currency differences
- Economic and legal differences
- Language differences
- Cultural differences
- Government roles
- Political risk

26 - 5

Consider the following exchange rates:

	U.S. $ to buy 1 Unit
Euro	0.8000
Swedish krona	0.1000

Are these currency prices direct or indirect quotations?

Since they are prices of foreign currencies expressed in U.S. dollars, they are direct quotations (dollars per currency).

26 - 6

What is an indirect quotation?

- An indirect quotation gives the amount of a foreign currency required to buy one U.S. dollar (currency per dollar).
- Note than an indirect quotation is the reciprocal of a direct quotation.
- Euros and British pounds are normally quoted as direct quotations. All other currencies are quoted as indirect.

26 - 7

Calculate the indirect quotations for euros and kronas.

	# of Units of Foreign Currency per U.S. $
Euro	1.25
Swedish krona	10.00

Euro: 1 / 0.8000 = 1.25.
Krona: 1 / 0.1000 = 10.00.

26 - 8

What is a cross rate?

- A cross rate is the exchange rate between any two currencies not involving U.S. dollars.
- In practice, cross rates are usually calculated from direct or indirect rates. That is, on the basis of U.S. dollar exchange rates.

26 - 9

Calculate the two cross rates between euros and kronas.

- Cross rate $= \frac{\text{Euros}}{\text{Dollar}} \times \frac{\text{Dollars}}{\text{Krona}}$
  = 1.25 x 0.1000
  = 0.125 euros/krona.
- Cross rate $= \frac{\text{Kronas}}{\text{Dollar}} \times \frac{\text{Dollars}}{\text{Euros}}$
  = 10.00 x 0.8000
  = 8.00 kronas/euro.

26 - 10

Note:

- The two cross rates are reciprocals of one another.
- They can be calculated by dividing either the direct or indirect quotations.

26 - 11

Assume the firm can produce a liter of orange juice in the U.S. and ship it to Spain for $1.75. If the firm wants a 50% markup on the product, what should the juice sell for in Spain?

Target price = ($1.75)(1.50)=$2.625

Spanish price = ($2.625)(1.25 euros/$)

= € 3.28.

26 - 12

Now the firm begins producing the orange juice in Spain. The product costs 2.0 euros to produce and ship to Sweden, where it can be sold for 20 kronas. What is the dollar profit on the sale?

2.0 euros (8.0 kronas/euro) = 16 kronas.

20 - 16 = 4.0 kronas profit.

Dollar profit = 4.0 kronas(0.1000 dollars per krona) = $0.40.

26 - 13

What is exchange rate risk?

Exchange rate risk is the risk that the value of a cash flow in one currency translated from another currency will decline due to a change in exchange rates.

26 - 14

Currency Appreciation and Depreciation

- Suppose the exchange rate goes from 10 kronas per dollar to 15 kronas per dollar.
- A dollar now buys more kronas, so the dollar is appreciating, or strengthening.
- The krona is depreciating, or weakening.

26 - 15

Affect of Dollar Appreciation

- Suppose the profit in kronas remains unchanged at 4.0 kronas, but the dollar appreciates, so the exchange rate is now 15 kronas/dollar.
- Dollar profit = 4.0 kronas / (15 kronas per dollar) = $0.267.
- Strengthening dollar hurts profits from international sales.

26 - 16

Describe the current and former international monetary systems.

- The current system is a floating rate system.
- Prior to 1971, a fixed exchange rate system was in effect.
  - The U.S. dollar was tied to gold.
  - Other currencies were tied to the dollar.

26 - 17

The European Monetary Union

In 2002, the full implementation of the "euro" was completed (those still holding former currencies have 10 years to exchange them at a bank). The newly formed European Central Bank now controls the monetary policy of the EMU.

26 - 18

The 12 Member Nations of the European Monetary Union

Austria	Germany	Netherlands
Belgium	Ireland	Portugal
Finland	Italy	Spain
France	Luxembourg	Greece

26 - 19

What is a convertible currency?

- A currency is convertible when the issuing country promises to redeem the currency at current market rates.
- Convertible currencies are traded in world currency markets.

26 - 20

What problems arise when a firm operates in a country whose currency is not convertible?

- It becomes very difficult for multi-national companies to conduct business because there is no easy way to take profits out of the country.
- Often, firms will barter for goods to export to their home countries.

26 - 21

What is the difference between spot rates and forward rates?

- A spot rate is the rate applied to buy currency for immediate delivery.
- A forward rate is the rate applied to buy currency at some agreed-upon future date.
- Forward rates are normally reported as indirect quotations.

26 - 22

When is the forward rate at a premium to the spot rate?

- If the U.S. dollar buys fewer units of a foreign currency in the forward than in the spot market, the foreign currency is selling at a premium.
- For example, suppose the spot rate is 0.7 £/$ and the forward rate is 0.6 £/$.
- The dollar is expected to depreciate, because it will buy fewer pounds.

Continued....

26 - 23

Spot rate = 0.7 £/$ Forward rate = 0.6 £/$.

- The pound is expected to appreciate, since it will buy more dollars in the future.
- So the forward rate for the pound is at a premium.

26 - 24

When is the forward rate at a discount to the spot rate?

- If the U.S. dollar buys more units of a foreign currency in the forward than in the spot market, the foreign currency is selling at a discount.
- The primary determinant of the spot/forward rate relationship is the relationship between domestic and foreign interest rates.

26 - 25

What is interest rate parity?

Interest rate parity implies that investors should expect to earn the same return on similar-risk securities in all countries:

$$\frac{\text{Forward rate}}{\text{Spot rate}} = \frac{1 + r_h}{1 + r_f}.$$

Forward and spot rates are direct quotations.
r_h = periodic interest rate in the home country.
r_f = periodic interest rate in the foreign country.

26 - 26

Assume 1 euro = $0.8100 in the 180-day forward market and and 180-day risk-free rate is 6% in the U.S. and 4% in Spain.

Does interest rate parity hold?

Spot rate = $0.8000.
r_h = 6%/2 = 3%.
r_f = 4%/2 = 2%.

(More...)

26 - 27

$$\frac{\text{Forward rate}}{\text{Spot rate}} = \frac{1 + r_h}{1 + r_f}$$

$$\frac{\text{Forward rate}}{0.8000} = \frac{1.03}{1.02}$$

Forward rate = 0.8078.

If interest rate parity holds, the implied forward rate, 0.8078, would equal the observed forward rate, 0.8100; so parity doesn't hold.

26 - 28

Which 180-day security (U.S. or Spanish) offers the higher return?

- A U.S. investor could directly invest in the U.S. security and earn an annualized rate of 6%.
- Alternatively, the U.S. investor could convert dollars to euros, invest in the Spanish security, and then convert profit back into dollars. If the return on this strategy is higher than 6%, then the Spanish security has the higher rate.

26 - 29

What is the return to a U.S. investor in the Spanish security?

- Buy $1,000 worth of euros in the spot market:

  $1,000(1.25 euros/$) = 1,250 euros.
- Spanish investment return (in euros):

  1,250(1.02)= 1,275 euros.

(More...)

26 - 30

- Buy contract today to exchange 1,275 euros in 180 days at forward rate of 0.8100 dollars/euro.
- At end of 180 days, convert euro investment to dollars:

  €1,275 (0.8100 $/€) = $1,032.75.
- Calculate the rate of return:

  $32.75/$1,000 = 3.275% per 180 days

  = 6.55% per year.

(More...)

26 - 31

The Spanish security has the highest return, even though it has a lower interest rate.

- U.S. rate is 6%, so Spanish securities at 6.55% offer a higher rate of return to U.S. investors.
- But could such a situation exist for very long?

26 - 32

Arbitrage

- Traders could borrow at the U.S. rate, convert to pesetas at the spot rate, and simultaneously lock in the forward rate and invest in Spanish securities.
- This would produce arbitrage: a positive cash flow, with no risk and none of the traders own money invested.

26 - 33

Impact of Arbitrage Activities

- Traders would recognize the arbitrage opportunity and make huge investments.
- Their actions would tend to move interest rates, forward rates, and spot rates to parity.

26 - 34

What is purchasing power parity?

Purchasing power parity implies that the level of exchange rates adjusts so that identical goods cost the same amount in different countries.

$$P_h = P_f(\text{Spot rate}),$$

or

$$\text{Spot rate} = P_h/P_f.$$

26 - 35

If grapefruit juice costs $2.00/liter in the U.S. and purchasing power parity holds, what is price in Spain?

Spot rate = P_h/P_f.
$0.8000= $2.00/$P_f$
P_f = $2.00/$0.8000
= 2.5 euros.

- Do interest rate and purchasing power parity hold exactly at any point in time?

26 - 36

What impact does relative inflation have on interest rates and exchange rates?

- Lower inflation leads to lower interest rates, so borrowing in low-interest countries may appear attractive to multinational firms.
- However, currencies in low-inflation countries tend to appreciate against those in high-inflation rate countries, so the true interest cost increases over the life of the loan.

26 - 37

Describe the international money and capital markets.

- Eurodollar markets
  - Dollars held outside the U.S.
  - Mostly Europe, but also elsewhere
- International bonds
  - Foreign bonds: Sold by foreign borrower, but denominated in the currency of the country of issue.
  - Eurobonds: Sold in country other than the one in whose currency it is denominated.

26 - 38

To what extent do capital structures vary across different countries?

- Early studies suggested that average capital structures varied widely among the large industrial countries.
- However, a recent study, which controlled for differences in accounting practices, suggests that capital structures are more similar across different countries than previously thought.

26 - 39

International Cash Management

- Distances are greater.
- Access to more markets for loans and for temporary investments.
- Cash is often denominated in different currencies.

26 - 40

Multinational Capital Budgeting Decisions

- Foreign operations are taxed locally, and then funds repatriated may be subject to U.S. taxes.
- Foreign projects are subject to political risk.
- Funds repatriated must be converted to U.S. dollars, so exchange rate risk must be taken into account.

26 - 41

Multinational Credit Management

- Credit is more important, because commerce to lesser-developed countries often relies on credit.
- Credit for future payment may be subject to exchange rate risk.

26 - 42

Multinational Inventory Management

- Inventory decisions can be more complex, especially when inventory can be stored in locations in different countries.
- Some factors to consider are shipping times, carrying costs, taxes, import duties, and exchange rates.

27 - 1

CHAPTER 27
Banking Relationships

Receivables management
- Credit policy
- Days sales outstanding (DSO)
- Aging schedules
- Payments pattern approach

■ Cost of bank loans

27 - 2

Elements of Credit Policy

- Cash Discounts: Lowers price. Attracts new customers and reduces DSO.
- Credit Period: How long to pay? Shorter period reduces DSO and average A/R, but it may discourage sales.

(More...)

27 - 3

- Credit Standards: Tighter standards reduce bad debt losses, but may reduce sales. Fewer bad debts reduces DSO.
- Collection Policy: Tougher policy will reduce DSO, but may damage customer relationships.

27 - 4

Receivables Monitoring

Assume the following sales estimates:

January	$100	April	$300
February	200	May	200
March	300	June	100

Terms of sale: Net 30.

27 - 5

Expected Collections

30% pay on Day 10 (month of sale).

50% pay on Day 40 (month after sale).

20% pay on Day 70 (2 months after sale).

Annual sales = 18,000 units @ $100/unit.

365-day year.

27 - 6

What is the firm's expected DSO and average daily sales (ADS)?

DSO = 0.30(10) + 0.50(40) + 0.20(70)
= 37 days.

How does this compare with the firm's credit period?

$$ADS = \frac{18{,}000(\$100)}{365}$$

= $4,931.51 per day.

27 - 7

What is the expected average accounts receivable level? How much of this amount must be financed if the profit margin is 25%?

A/R = (DSO)(ADS) = 37($4,931.51)
= $182,466.

0.75($182,466) = $136,849.

27 - 8

If notes payable are used to finance the A/R investment, what does the firm's balance sheet look like?

A/R	$182,466	Notes payable	$136,849
		Retained earnings	45,617
			$182,466

27 - 9

If bank loans cost 12 percent, what is the annual dollar cost of carrying the receivables?

Cost of carrying receivables = 0.12($136,849)

= $16,422.

In addition, there is an opportunity cost of not having the use of the profit component of the receivables.

27 - 10

What are some factors which influence a firm's receivables level?

- Receivables are a function of average daily sales and days sales outstanding.
- State of the economy, competition within the industry, and the firm's credit policy all influence a firm's receivables level.

27 - 11

What are some factors which influence the dollar cost of carrying receivables?

- The lower the profit margin, the higher the cost of carrying receivables, because a greater portion of each sales dollar must be financed.
- The higher the cost of financing, the higher the dollar cost.

27 - 12

What would the receivables level be at the end of each month?

A/R = 0.7(Sales in that month) + 0.2(Sales in previous month).

Month	Sales	A/R
Jan	$100	$ 70
Feb	200	160
Mar	300	250
April	300	270
May	200	200
June	100	110

27 - 13

What is the firm's forecasted average daily sales (ADS) for the first 3 months? For the entire half-year? (assuming 91-day quarters)

$$\text{Avg. Daily Sales} = \frac{\text{Total sales}}{\text{\# of days}}.$$

1st Qtr: $600/91 = $6.59.
2nd Qtr: $600/91 = $6.59.

27 - 14

What DSO is expected at the end of March? At the end of June?

$$\text{DSO} = \frac{\text{A/R}}{\text{ADS}}.$$

1st Qtr: $250/$6.59 = 37.9 days.
2nd Qtr: $110/$6.59 = 16.7 days.

27 - 15

What does the DSO indicate about customers' payments?

- It appears that customers are paying significantly faster in the second quarter than in the first.
- However, the receivables balances were created assuming a constant payment pattern, so the DSO is giving a false measure of payment performance.
- Underlying cause is seasonal variation.

27 - 16

Construct an aging schedule for the end of March and the end of June.

Age of Account (Days)	March A/R	March %	June A/R	June %
0 - 30	$210	84%	$ 70	64%
31-60	40	16	40	36
61-90	0	0	0	0
	$250	100%	$110	100%

Do aging schedules "tell the truth?"

27 - 17

Construct the uncollected balances schedules for the end of March and June.

Mos.	Sales	Contrib. to A/R	A/R to Sales
Jan	$100	$ 0	0%
Feb	200	40	20
Mar	300	210	70
End of Qtr. A/R		$250	90%

27 - 18

Mos.	Sales	Contrib. to A/R	A/R to Sales
Apr	$300	$ 0	0%
May	200	40	20
June	100	70	70
End of Qtr. A/R		$110	90%

27 - 19

Do the uncollected balances schedules properly measure customers' payment patterns?

- The focal point of the uncollected balances schedule is the receivables -to-sales ratio.
- There is no difference in this ratio between March and June, which tells us that there has been no change in payment pattern. (More...)

27 - 20

- The uncollected balances schedule gives a true picture of customers' payment patterns, even when sales fluctuate.
- Any increase in the A/R to sales ratio from a month in one quarter to the corresponding month in the next quarter indicates a slowdown in payment.
- The "bottom line" gives a summary of the changes in payment patterns.

27 - 21

Assume it is now July and you are developing pro forma financial statements for the following year. Furthermore, sales and collections in the first half-year matched predicted levels. Using Year 2 sales forecasts, what are next year's pro forma receivables levels for the end of March and June?

27 - 22

March 31

Mos.	Predicted Sales	Predicted A/R to Sales Ratio	Predicted Contrib. to A/R
Jan	$150	0%	$ 0
Feb	300	20	60
Mar	500	70	350
Projected March 31 A/R balance			$410

27 - 23

June 30

Mos.	Predicted Sales	Predicted A/R to Sales Ratio	Predicted Contrib. to A/R
Apr	$400	0%	$ 0
May	300	20	60
June	200	70	140
Projected June 30 A/R balance			$200

27 - 24

What four variables make up a firm's credit policy?

- Cash discounts
- Credit period
- Credit standards
- Collection policy

27 - 25

Disregard any previous assumptions.

- Current credit policy:
  - Credit terms = Net 30.
  - Gross sales = $1,000,000.
  - 80% (of paying customers) pay on Day 30.
  - 20% pay on Day 40.
  - Bad debt losses = 2% of gross sales.
- Operating cost ratio = 75%.
- Cost of carrying receivables = 12%.

27 - 26

The firm is considering a change in credit policy.

- New credit policy:
  - Credit terms = 2/10, net 20.
  - Gross sales = $1,100,000.
  - 60% (of paying customers) pay on Day 10.
  - 30% pay on Day 20.
  - 10% pay on Day 30.
  - Bad debt losses = 1% of gross sales.

27 - 27

What is the DSO under the current and the new credit policies?

- Current:
  $DSO_O = 0.8(30) + 0.2(40)$
  $= 32$ days.
- New:
  $DSO_N = 0.6(10) + 0.3(20) + 0.1(30)$
  $= 15$ days.

27 - 28

What are bad debt losses under the current and the new credit policies?

- **Current:**
  $BDL_O = 0.02(\$1,000,000)$
  $= \$20,000.$
- **New:**
  $BDL_N = 0.01(\$1,100,000)$
  $= \$11,000.$

27 - 29

What are the expected dollar costs of discounts under the current and the new policies?

- **$Discount_O = \$0.$**
- **$Discount_N = 0.6(0.02)(0.99)(\$1,100,000)$**
  $= \$13,068.$

27 - 30

What are the dollar costs of carrying receivables under the current and the new policies?

- **Costs of carrying $receivables_O$**
  $=(\$1,000,000/365)(32)(0.75)(0.12)$
  $=\$7,890.$
- **Costs of carrying $receivables_N$**
  $=(\$1,100,000/365)(15)(0.75)(0.12)$
  $=\$4,068.$

27 - 31

What is the incremental after-tax profit associated with the change in credit terms?

	New	Old	Diff.
Gross sales	$1,100,000	$1,000,000	$100,000
Less: Disc.	13,068	0	13,068
Net sales	$1,086,932	$1,000,000	$ 86,932
Prod. costs	825,000	750,000	75,000
Profit before credit costs and taxes	$ 261,932	$ 250,000	$ 11,932

(More...)

27 - 32

	New	Old	Diff.
Profit before credit costs and taxes	$261,932	$250,000	$11,932
Credit-related costs:			
Carrying costs	4,068	7,890	(3,822)
Bad debts	11,000	20,000	(9,000)
Profit before taxes	$246,864	$222,110	$24,754
Taxes (40%)	98,745	88,844	9,902
Net income	$148,118	$133,266	$14,852

Should the company make the change?

27 - 33

Assume the firm makes the policy change, but its competitors react by making similar changes. As a result, gross sales remain at $1,000,000. How does this impact the firm's after-tax profitability?

27 - 34

Gross sales	$1,000,000
Less: discounts	11,880
Net sales	$ 988,120
Production costs	750,000
Profit before credit costs and taxes	$ 238,120
Credit costs:	
Carrying costs	3,699
Bad debt losses	10,000
Profit before taxes	$ 224,421
Taxes	89,769
Net Income	$ 134,653

27 - 35

- Before the new policy change, the firm's net income totaled $133,266.
- The change would result in a slight gain of $134,653 - $133,266 = $1,387.

27 - 36

A bank is willing to lend the brothers $100,000 for 1 year at an 8 percent nominal rate. What is the EAR under the following five loans?

1. Simple annual interest, 1 year.
2. Simple interest, paid monthly.
3. Discount interest.
4. Discount interest with 10 percent compensating balance.
5. Installment loan, add-on, 12 months.

27 - 37

Why must we use Effective Annual Rates (EARs) to evaluate the loans?

- In our examples, the nominal (quoted) rate is 8% in all cases.
- We want to compare loan cost rates and choose the alternative with the lowest cost.
- Because the loans have different terms, we must make the comparison on the basis of EARs.

27 - 38

Simple Annual Interest, 1-Year Loan

"Simple interest" means not discount or add-on.

Interest = 0.08($100,000) = $8,000.

$$r_{Nom} = EAR = \frac{\$8,000}{\$100,000} = 0.08 = 8.0\%.$$

On a simple interest loan of one year, r_{Nom} = EAR.

27 - 39

Simple Interest, Paid Monthly

Monthly interest = (0.08/12)($100,000)
= $666.67.

0	1	...	12
100,000	-666.67		-667.67 -100,000.00

12		100000	-666.67	-100000
N	I/YR	PV	PMT	FV
	0.66667			

(More...)

27 - 40

r_{Nom} = (Monthly rate)(12)
= 0.66667%(12) = 8.00%.

$$EAR = \left(1 + \frac{0.08}{12}\right)^{12} - 1 = 8.30\%.$$

or: 8 ■ NOM%, 12 ■ P/YR, ■ EFF% = 8.30%.

Note: If interest were paid quarterly, then:

$$EAR = \left(1 + \frac{0.08}{4}\right)^{4} - 1 = 8.24\%.$$

Daily, EAR = 8.33%.

27 - 41

8% Discount Interest, 1 Year

Interest deductible = 0.08($100,000)
= $8,000.

Usable funds = $100,000 - $8,000
= $92,000.

0		1
	i = ?	
92,000		-100,000

1		92	0	-100
N	I/YR	PV	PMT	FV
	8.6957% = EAR			

27 - 42

Discount Interest (Continued)

$$\text{Amt. borrowed} = \frac{\text{Amount needed}}{1 - \text{Nominal rate (decimal)}}$$

$$= \frac{\$100,000}{0.92} = \$108,696.$$

27 - 43

Need $100,000. Offered loan with terms of 8% discount interest, 10% compensating balance.

$$\text{Face amount of loan} = \frac{\text{Amount needed}}{1 - \text{Nominal rate} - \text{CB}}$$

$$= \frac{\$100{,}000}{1 - 0.08 - 0.1} = \$121{,}951.$$

(More...)

27 - 44

Interest = 0.08 ($121,951) = $9,756.

$$\text{Cost} = \frac{\text{Interest paid}}{\text{Amount received}}.$$

$$\text{EAR} = \frac{\$9{,}756}{\$100{,}000} = 9.756\%.$$

EAR correct only if amount is borrowed for 1 year.

(More...)

27 - 45

8% Discount Interest with 10% Compensating Balance (Continued)

Time line: 0 to 1, i = ?

Time 0		Time 1
121,951	Loan	-121,951
-9,756	Prepaid interest	+ 12,195
-12,195	CB	-109,756
100,000	Usable funds	

1		100000	0	-109756
N	I/YR	PV	PMT	FV

9.756% = EAR

This procedure can handle variations.

27 - 46

1-Year Installment Loan, 8% "Add-On"

Interest = 0.08($100,000) = $8,000.

Face amount = $100,000 + $8,000 = $108,000.

Monthly payment = $108,000/12 = $9,000.

Average loan outstanding = $100,000/2 = $50,000.

Approximate cost = $8,000/$50,000 = 16.0%.

(More...)

27 - 47

Installment Loan

To find the EAR, recognize that the firm has received $100,000 and must make monthly payments of $9,000. This constitutes an ordinary annuity as shown below:

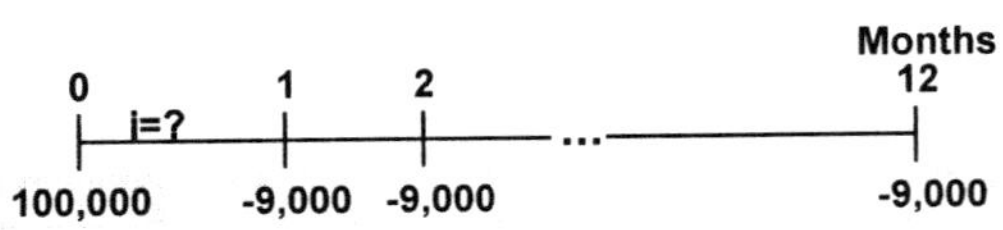

27 - 48

12 [N] [I/YR] 100000 [PV] -9000 [PMT] 0 [FV]

1.2043% = rate per month

r_{Nom} = APR = (1.2043%)(12) = 14.45%.
EAR = $(1.012043)^{12}$ - 1 = 15.45%.

14.45 ■ NOM ⟶ enters nominal rate
12 ■ P/YR ⟶ enters 12 pmts/yr
■ EFF% = 15.4489 = 15.45%.

1 ■ P/YR to reset calculator.

28 - 1

CHAPTER 28
Advanced Issues in Cash Management and Inventory Control

- Setting the target cash balance
- EOQ model
- Baumol Model

28 - 2

Setting the Target Cash Balance

- Theoretical models such as the Baumol model have been developed for use in setting target cash balances. The Baumol model is similar to the EOQ model, which will be discussed later.
- Today, companies strive for zero cash balances and use borrowings or marketable securities as a reserve.
- Monte Carlo simulation can be helpful in setting the target cash balance.

28 - 3

Why is inventory management vital to the financial health of most firms?

- Insufficient inventories can lead to lost sales.
- Excess inventories means higher costs than necessary.
- Large inventories, but wrong items leads to both high costs and lost sales.
- Inventory management is more closely related to operations than to finance.

28 - 4

Assumptions of the EOQ Model

- All values are known with certainty and constant over time.
- Inventory usage is uniform over time.
- Carrying costs change proportionally with changes in inventory levels.
- All ordering costs are fixed.
- These assumptions do not hold in the "real world," so safety stocks are held.

28 - 5

Total Inventory Costs (TIC)

TIC = Total carrying costs + Total ordering costs = CP(Q/2) + F(S/Q).

C = Annual carrying costs (% of inv.).
P = Purchase price per unit.
Q = Number of units per order.
F = Fixed costs per order.
S = Annual usage in units.

28 - 6

Derive the EOQ model from the total cost equation

$$\frac{d(TIC)}{dQ} = \frac{CP}{2} - \frac{FS}{Q^2} = 0$$

$$Q^2 = \frac{2FS}{CP}$$

$$EOQ = Q^* = \sqrt{\frac{2FS}{CP}}.$$

28 - 7

Inventory Model Graph

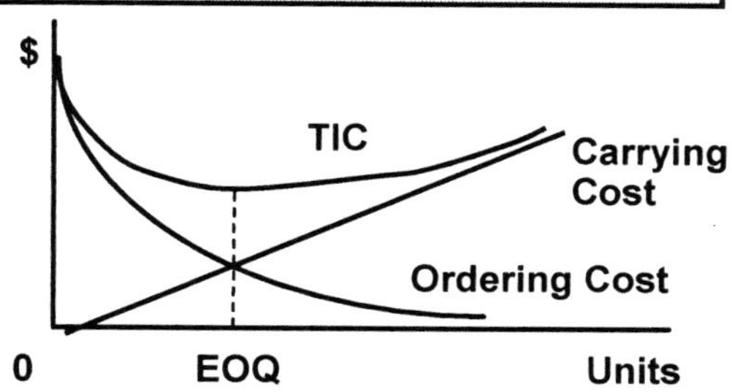

Average inventory = EOQ/2.

28 - 8

Assume the Following Data:

P = \$200.
F = \$1,000.
S = 5,000.
C = 0.2.
Minimum order size = 250.

28 - 9

What is the EOQ?

$$EOQ = \sqrt{\frac{2(\$1,000)(5,000)}{0.2(\$200)}}$$

$$= \sqrt{\frac{\$10,000,000}{40}}$$

$$= \sqrt{250,000} = 500 \text{ units.}$$

28 - 10

What are total inventory costs when the EOQ is ordered?

$$TIC = CP\left(\frac{Q}{2}\right) + F\left(\frac{S}{Q}\right)$$

= (0.2)($200)(500/2) + $1,000(5,000/500)

= $40(250) + $1,000(10)

= $10,000 + $10,000 = $20,000.

28 - 11

Additional Notes

- Average inventory = EOQ/2 = 500/2 = 250 units.
- # of orders per year = S/EOQ = $5,000/500 = 10.
- At EOQ level, total carrying costs = total ordering costs.

28 - 12

What is the added cost if the firm orders 400 units or 600 units at a time rather than the EOQ?

400 units:

TIC = CP(Q/2) + F(S/Q)

= 0.2($200)(400/2) + $1,000(5,000/400)

= $8,000 + $12,500 = $20,500.

Added cost = $20,500 - $20,000 = $500.

28 - 13

600 units:

TIC = CP(Q/2) + F(S/Q)

= 0.2($200)(600/2) + $1,000(5,000/600)

= $12,000 +$8,333 = $20,333.

Added cost = $20,333 - $20,000 = $333.

28 - 14

Notes about EOQ

- At any quantity $\neq$ EOQ, total inventory costs are higher than necessary.
- The added cost of not ordering the EOQ is not large if the quantity ordered is close to EOQ.
- If Q < EOQ, then total carrying costs decrease, but ordering costs increase.
- If Q > EOQ, total carrying costs increase, but ordering costs decrease.

28 - 15

Suppose delivery takes 2 weeks. Assuming certainty in delivery and usage, at what inventory level should the firm reorder?

Weekly usage rate = 5,000/52

= 96 units.

If order lead time = 2 weeks, firm must reorder when:

Inventory level = 2(96) = 192 units.

28 - 16

Assume a 200-unit safety stock is carried. What effect would this have on total inventory costs?

Without safety stocks, the firm's total inventory costs = $20,000.

Cost of carrying additional 200 units

= CP(Safety stock)

= 0.2($200)(200) = $8,000.

Total inventory costs = $20,000 + $8,000

= $28,000.

28 - 17

Alternatively:

Average inventory = (500/2) + 200

= 450 units.

TIC = CP(Avg. Inv.) + F(S/Q)

= 0.2($200)(450) + $1,000(5,000/500)

= $18,000 + $10,000

= $28,000.

28 - 18

What is the new reorder point with the safety stock?

- Reorder point = 200 + 192 = 392 units.
  - The firm's normal 96 unit usage could rise to 392/2 = 196 units per week.
  - Or the firm could operate for 392/96 = 4 weeks while awaiting delivery of an order.

28 - 19

Suppose the firm could receive a discount of 1% on orders of 1,000 or more. Should the firm take the discount?

Discount affects operating inventory only.
Discount price = $200(0.99) = $198.

TIC = CP(Q/2) + F(S/Q)
= 0.2($198)(1,000/2) + $1,000(5,000/1,000)
= $19,800 + $5,000 = $24,800.

(More...)

28 - 20

Savings = 0.01($200)(5,000)	**= $10,000**
Added costs = $24,800 - $20,000	**= $ 4,800**
Net savings = $10,000 - $4,800	**= $ 5,200**

Firm should take the discount.

28 - 21

Can the EOQ be used if there are seasonal variations?

- **Yes, but it must be applied to shorter periods during which usage is approximately constant.**

28 - 22

How would the following factors affect an EOQ analysis?

- Just-in-time system: Eliminates the need for using EOQ.
- Use of air freight for deliveries: Reduces the need for safety stock.
- Computerized inventory control system: Reduces safety stocks.
- Flexibility designed plants: Reduces inventory holdings of final goods.

28 - 23

The Baumol Model

- The EOQ model can be applied to cash management if you view cash as an operating assets, just like inventory.
- In this view, cash has a carrying cost, which is the opportunity cost for investing the funds, and an order cost, which is the cost per transaction of liquidating marketable securities and transferring the money to a checking account.

28 - 24

- C = cash raised each time by selling securities or borrowing
- r = opportunity cost of holding cash—equal to the rate of return on marketable securities or cost of borrowing
- T = total amount of cash needed for transactions during the year
- F = fixed per transaction cost of selling securities or obtaining a loan

28 - 25

Costs of cash—Holding costs

Holding cost
= (average cash balance)
x (opportunity cost rate)
Average cash balance = C/2
Holding cost = C/2 x r = rC/2

28 - 26

Costs of cash—transactions costs

- T = total new cash needed in the year
- T/C = number of transactions
- (T/C)(F) = FT/C = total cost of all of the transactions

28 - 27

Costs of cash

- Total cost of cash
= Holding Costs + Transactions Costs
= rC/2 + FT/C

Just like EOQ, optimal C = $C^* = \sqrt{\frac{2(F)(T)}{r}}$

Baumol Assumptions

Total cash outflows per week = $500,000 per month.

Total cash inflows from operations = $400,000 per month.

Net cash needs = $500,000 - $400,000 = $100,000 per month, or $1,200,000 each year.

Costs:

- Transaction/order costs = $32 per transaction (F)
- r = 7% = rate the firm can earn on its marketable securities

$$C^* = \sqrt{\frac{2(32)(1200000)}{0.07}} = \$33{,}123$$

Optimal cash transfer size

The optimal "order size" is $33,123, so the firm will liquidate marketable securities, or borrow from the bank, in blocks of $33,123. This is approximately $1,200,000/33,123 = 36 times a year, or about every week and a half.

28 - 31

Sensitivity

F, r	C^*
$32, 7%	$33,123
$50, 7%	$41,404
$32, 5%	$39,192

Higher order costs, lower carrying costs increase the optimal order size.

29 - 1

CHAPTER 29
Pension Plan Management

- Pension plan terminology
- Defined benefit versus defined contribution plans
- Pension fund investment tactics
- Retiree health benefits

29 - 2

How important are pension funds?

- They constitute the largest class of investors.
- They hold about 33% of all U. S. stocks.

29 - 3

Pension Plan Terminology

- Defined benefit plan: Employer agrees to give retirees a specific benefit, generally a percentage of final salary.
- Defined contribution plan: Employer agrees to make specific payments into a retirement fund, frequently a mutual fund. Retirees' benefits depend on the investment performance of their own fund. 401(k) is the most common type.

(More...)

29 - 4

- Profit sharing plan: Employer payments vary with the firm's profits. (Defined contribution, but as a percentage of profits).
- Cash balance plan: Employer promises to put a specified percentage of the employee's salary into the plan, and to pay a specified return on the plan's assets.

(More...)

29 - 5

- Vesting: Gives the employee the right to receive pension benefits at retirement even if he/she leaves the company before retirement.
- Deferred vesting: Pension rights are not vested for the first few years.
- Portability: A "portable" pension plan can be moved to another employer if the employee changes jobs.

(More...)

29 - 6

- Fully funded: Value of plan assets equals the present value of expected retirement benefits.
- Underfunded: Plan assets are less than the PV of the benefits. An "unfunded liability" is said to exist.
- Overfunded: The reverse of underfunded.

(More...)

29 - 7

- Actuarial rate of return: The rate of return:
  - used to find the PV of expected benefits (discount rate).
  - at which the fund's assets are assumed to be invested.
- Employee Retirement Income Security Act (ERISA): The federal law governing the administration and structure of corporate pension plans.

(More...)

29 - 8

- Pension Benefit Guarantee Corporation (PBGC):
  - A government agency created by ERISA to ensure that employees of firms which go bankrupt before their defined benefit plans are fully funded will receive some minimum level of benefits.
  - However, for high income employees (i.e., airline pilots), PBGC pension payments are often less than those promised by the company.

29 - 9

Who establishes guidelines for reporting pension fund information on corporate financial statements?

- Financial Accounting Standards Board (FASB), together with the SEC, establishes rules for reporting pension information.
- Pension costs are huge, and assumptions have major effect on reported profits.

29 - 10

How are pension fund data reported in a firm's financial statements?

- Defined Contribution Plan:
  - The annual contribution is shown as a cost on the income statement.
  - A note explains the entry.
- Defined Benefit Plan:
  - The plan's funding status must be reported directly on the balance sheet. (More...)

29 - 11

- The annual pension contribution (expense) is shown on the income statement.
- Details regarding the annual expense, along with the composition of the fund's assets, are reported in the notes section.
- The annual pension contribution is tied to the assumed actuarial rate of return: the greater the assumed return, the smaller the contribution.

29 - 12

Given the following data, how much must the firm contribute annually (at year-end) over the employee's working life to fully fund the plan by retirement age?

- Data/Assumptions:
  - Employee begins work at 25, will work 40 years until 65, and then retire.
  - Employee will live another 15 years, to age 80, and will draw a pension of $20,000 per year.
  - The plan's actuarial rate of return is 10%.

29 - 13

Step 1. Determine the amount the firm must have in the plan at the time the employee retires. It is $152,122.

Input	15	10		20000	0
	N	I	PV	PMT	FV
Output			152,122		

29 - 14

Step 2: Determine the annual contribution during the employment years. With $152,122 to be accumulated, the answer is $343.71.

Input	40	10	0		152122
	N	I	PV	PMT	FV
Output				343.71	

29 - 15

Graph of Pension Fund Assets

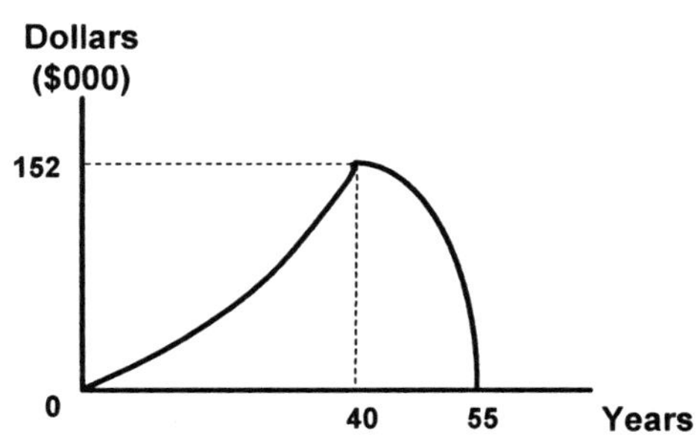

29 - 16

Pension fund management is much more complex than this illustration.

- Don't know how long the employee will work for the firm (the 40 years).
- Don't know what the annual pension payment will be (the $20,000).
- Don't know what rate of return the pension fund will earn (the 10%).
- A large number of employees creates complexities, but it also reduces the aggregate actuarial uncertainty.

29 - 17

What risks are borne by the plan sponsor and plan beneficiaries under the four types of pension plans?

- Defined benefit plan: Most risk falls on the company, because it guarantees to pay a specific retirement benefit regardless of the firm's profitability or the return on the plan's assets.

(More...)

29 - 18

- Defined contribution plan: Places more risk on employees, because benefits depend on the return performance of each employee's chosen investment fund.
- Profit sharing: Most risk to employee, least to employer. Company doesn't pay into fund unless it has earnings, and employees bear investment risk.

(More...)

29 - 19

- Cash balance: "Middle of the road" in terms of risk for both employer and employee. Employer's payment obligations are fixed and known, while employees are guaranteed a specified return.

29 - 20

What type of companies tend to have each type of plan?

- Large, more mature companies (and governments) tend to use defined benefit plans.
- New, start-up companies tend to use profit sharing plans.
- Many older companies are shifting to defined contribution and cash balance plans.

29 - 21

If a company uses either a defined contribution or a profit sharing plan, how are the assets administered?

- Usually set up as a 401(k) plan.
- Employees make tax-deductible contributions into one or more investment vehicles (often mutual funds) established by the company.
- Company may make independent or matching contributions.

29 - 22

Does the type of pension plan influence the possibility of age discrimination?

Defined benefit plans are more costly to firms when older workers are hired. The firm has a shorter time to accumulate the needed funds, hence must make larger annual contributions.

29 - 23

Does the type of pension plan influence the possibility of sex discrimination?

Since women live longer than men, female employees are more costly under defined benefit plans.

29 - 24

How does the type of pension plan influence employee training costs?

- Defined benefit plans encourage employees to stay with a single company, hence they reduce training costs.
- Vesting and portability facilitate job shifts, hence increase training costs.

29 - 25

Does the type of pension plan influence the militancy of unions when a company faces financial adversity?

Benefits paid under defined benefit plans are usually tied to the number of years worked and the final (or last few) year's salary. Therefore, unions are more likely to work with a firm to ensure its survival under a defined benefit plan.

29 - 26

What are the two components of a plan's funding strategy?

- How fast should any unfunded liability be reduced?
- What rate of return should be assumed in the actuarial calculations?

29 - 27

What is the primary goal of a plan's investment strategy?

- To structure the portfolio to minimize the risk of not achieving the assumed actuarial rate of return.
- A low risk portfolio will mean low expected returns, which will mean larger annual contributions, which hurt profits.

29 - 28

How can a company judge the performance of its pension plan managers?

- Alpha analysis: Compare the realized return on the portfolio with the required return on the portfolio.
- Comparative analysis: Compare the manager's historical returns with other managers having the same investment objective (same risk profile).

29 - 29

What's meant by "tapping" pension fund assets?

- This occurs when a company terminates an overfunded defined benefit plan, uses a portion of the funds to purchase annuities which provide the promised pensions to employees, and then recovers the excess for use by the firm.
- First used by corporate raiders after takeovers, with proceeds used to pay down takeover debt.

29 - 30

Why is "tapping" controversial?

- Some people believe that pension fund assets belong to employees, hence tapping "robs" employees. (Excess funds make it easier to bargain for higher benefits.)
- Courts have ruled that defined benefit plan assets belong to the firm, so firms can recover these assets as long as this action does not jeopardize current employees' contractual benefits.

29 - 31

What has happened to the cost of retiree health benefits over the last decade?

Because of the increased number of retirees, longer life expectancies, and the dramatic escalation in health care costs over the last ten years, many firms are forecasting that retiree health care costs will be as high, or higher, than pension costs.

29 - 32

How are retiree health benefits reported to shareholders?

- Before 1990, firms used pay-as-you-go procedures which concealed the true liability.
- Now companies must set up reserves for retiree medical benefits.
- Firms must report current expenses to account for vested future medical benefits.
- The 1990 rule has forced companies to assess their retiree health care liability. Many are now cutting benefits.

30 - 1

CHAPTER 30
Financial Management in Not-for-Profit Businesses

- For-profit (investor-owned) vs. not-for-profit businesses
- Goals of the firm

30 - 2

What are the key features of investor-owned firms?

- Owners (shareholders) are well defined, and they exercise control by voting for the firm's board of directors.
- Firm's residual earnings belong to the owners, so management is responsible to the owners for the firm's profitability.
- Firm is subject to taxation at the federal, state, and local levels.

30 - 3

What is a not-for-profit corporation?

- One that is organized and operated solely for religious, charitable, scientific, public safety, literary, or educational purposes.
- Generally, qualify for tax-exempt status.

30 - 4

What are the major control differences between investor-owned and not-for-profit businesses?

- Not-for-profit corporations have no shareholders, so all residual earnings are retained within the firm.
- Control of not-for-profit firms rests with a board of trustees composed mainly of community leaders who have no economic interests in the firm.

30 - 5

How do goals differ between investor-owned and not-for-profit businesses?

- Because not-for-profit firms have no shareholders, they are not concerned with the goal of maximizing shareholder wealth.
- Goals of not-for-profit firms are outlined in the firm's mission statement. They generally relate to providing some socially valuable service in a financially sound manner.

30 - 6

Is the WACC relevant to not-for-profit businesses?

Yes. The WACC estimation for not-for-profit firms parallels that for investor-owned firms.

30 - 7

Is there any difference between the WACC formula for investor-owned firms and that for not-for-profit businesses?

- Because not-for-profit firms pay no taxes, there are no tax effects associated with debt financing.
- A not-for-profit firm's cost of equity, or cost of fund capital, is much more controversial than for an investor-owned firm.

30 - 8

What is fund capital?

Not-for-profit firms raise the equivalent of equity capital, called fund capital, by retaining profits, receiving government grants, and receiving private contributions.

30 - 9

How is the cost of fund capital estimated?

- The cost of fund capital is an opportunity cost to the not-for-profit firm.
- It is the return the firm could realize by investing the capital in securities of similar risk.

30 - 10

Is the trade-off theory of capital structure applicable to not-for-profit businesses?

- Not-for-profit firms' optimal capital structures should be based on the tradeoffs between the benefits and costs of debt financing.
- Not-for-profit firms have about the same effective costs of debt and equity as investor-owned firms of similar risk.

(More...)

30 - 11

- The firm's opportunity cost of fund capital should rise as more and more debt is used, and the firm should be subject to the same financial distress and agency costs from using debt as encountered by investor-owned firms.

30 - 12

Is the asymmetric information theory applicable to not-for-profit businesses?

The asymmetric information theory is not applicable to not-for-profit firms, since they do not issue common stock.

30 - 13

What problems do not-for-profit businesses encounter when they attempt to implement the trade-off theory?

- The major problem is their lack of flexibility in raising equity capital.
- Not-for-profit firms do not have access to the typical equity markets. It's harder for them to raise fund capital.
- It is often necessary for not-for-profit firms to delay worthy projects because of insufficient funding, or to use more than the theoretically optimal amount of debt.

30 - 14

Why is capital budgeting important to not-for-profit businesses?

- The financial impact of each capital investment should be fully understood in order to ensure the firm's long-term financial health.
- Substantial investment in unprofitable projects could lead to bankruptcy and closure, which obviously would eliminate the social value provided by the firm to the community.

30 - 15

What is social value?

Social value are those benefits realized from capital investment in addition to cash flow returns, such as charity care and other community services.

30 - 16

How can the net present value method be modified to include the social value of proposed projects?

- When the social value of a project is considered, the total net present value of the project equals the standard net present value of the project's expected cash flow stream plus the net present social value of the project.
- This requires the social value of the project provided over its life to be quantified and discounted back to Year 0.

30 - 17

Which of the three project risk measures--stand-alone, corporate, and market--is relevant to not-for-profit businesses?

- *Corporate risk*, or the additional risk a project adds to the overall riskiness of the firm's portfolio of projects, is the *most relevant risk* for a not-for-profit firm, since most not-for-profit firms offer a wide variety of products and services. (More...)

30 - 18

- *Stand-alone risk* would be relevant only if the project were the only one the firm would be involved with.
- *Market risk* is not relevant at all, since not-for-profit firms do not have stockholders.

30 - 19

What is a corporate beta?

- A quantitative measure of corporate risk.
- Measures the volatility of returns on the project relative to the firm as a whole.

30 - 20

How does a corporate beta differ from a market beta?

A project's market beta is a similar quantitative measure of a project's market risk, but it measures the volatility of project returns relative to market returns.

30 - 21

How is project risk actually measured within not-for-profit businesses?

- Not-for-profit firms often use the project's stand-alone risk, along with a *subjective notion* of how the project fits into the firm's other operations, as an estimate of corporate risk.
- *Corporate risk and stand-alone risk tend to be highly correlated*, since most projects under consideration tend to be in the same line of business as the firm's other operations.

30 - 22

What are municipal bonds?

- Bonds issued by state and local governments.
- Municipal bonds are exempt from federal income taxes and state income taxes in the state of issue.

30 - 23

How do not-for-profit health care businesses access the municipal bond market?

- Not-for-profit firms *cannot issue* municipal bonds *directly* to investors. The bonds are issued through some municipal health facilities authority.
- The authority acts only as a *conduit* for the issuing corporation.

30 - 24

What is credit enhancement, and what effect does it have on debt costs?

- Credit enhancement is, simply, bond insurance that *guarantees* the *repayment* of a municipal bond's principal and interest.
- When issuers purchase credit enhancement, the bond is rated on the basis of the insurer's financial strength rather than the issuer's. (More...)

30 - 25

- Because credit enhancement raises the bond rating, *interest costs are reduced.* However, the issuer must bear the added cost of the bond insurance.

30 - 26

What are a not-for-profit business's sources of fund capital?

- Excess of revenues over expenses
- Charitable contributions
- Government grants

30 - 27

What impact does the inability to issue common stock have on a not-for-profit business's capital structure and capital budgeting decisions?

- The lack of access to equity capital effectively *imposes capital rationing*, so the firm may not be able to undertake all projects deemed worthwhile.
- In order to invest in projects considered necessary, the firm may have to take on more than the optimal amount of debt capital.

30 - 28

What unique problems do not-for-profit businesses encounter in financial analysis and planning and short-term financial management?

- In general these tasks are the same regardless of the type of ownership.
- However, the unique features of not-for-profit organizations--especially the lack of financial flexibility--creates some minor differences in implementation.